Red Pedagogy

Red Pedagogy

Native American Social and Political Thought

Sandy Grande

ROWMAN & LITTLEFIELD PUBLISHERS, INC.
Lanham • Boulder • New York • Toronto • Oxford

ROWMAN & LITTLEFIELD PUBLISHERS, INC.

Published in the United States of America
by Rowman & Littlefield Publishers, Inc.
A wholly owned subsidiary of The Rowman & Littlefield Publishing Group, Inc.
4501 Forbes Boulevard, Suite 200, Lanham, Maryland 20706
www.rowmanlittlefield.com

PO Box 317
Oxford
OX2 9RU, UK

British Library Cataloguing in Publication Information Available

Library of Congress Cataloging-in-Publication Data

Grande, Sandy, 1964–
    Red Pedagogy : Native American social and political thought / Sandy Grande.
    p. cm.
    Includes bibliographical references.
    ISBN 0-7425-1828-0 (cloth : alk. paper) — ISBN 0-7425-1829-9 (pbk. : alk.
paper)
    1. Indians of North America—Politics and government. 2. Indians of North
America—Education. 3. Indian philosophy—United States. 4. Self-
determination, National—United States. 5. Multicultural education—United
States. 6. United States—Race relations. 7. United States—Social policy. 8.
United States—Politics and government. I. Title.

    E98.T77G73 2004
    305.897—dc22   2004003446

Printed in the United States of America

∞™ The paper used in this publication meets the minimum requirements of American
National Standard for Information Sciences—Permanence of Paper for Printed Library
Materials, ANSI/NISO Z39.48-1992.

Contents

Foreword

Contrary to popular belief, education as it has been applied to the Native American people in the United States is not "Indian education." While the concept of education from the Native American perspective has always been present in the form of traditional education, the "history of Indian education" as it is widely written tends to be a chronology of federal policies experimenting with reinventing Native American people in the likeness of white people. In fact, the history of Indian education often neglects discourse about colonization and genocide and acculturation and instead focuses on the survival of identity, community, and culture. However, in recent times, Native American people have increasingly begun to empower themselves with the very tools of colonization that have been used against them. They are exercising their sovereignty, revitalizing language and culture, and becoming legitimate contenders in the political arena. At the same they continue to sustain, maintain, and form their identity. In this book, Sandy Grande, offers a discussion around a boldly worded terminology of critical theory as it is applied to Native American people, which, until now, has been absent in discourse on Native American education.

"Indian education" or a colonized form of education has been practiced by educators for the past century in federally operated schools under the false assumption that the goal of "education" is to mold all students to become part of the mainstream. In this book, as Native American educators, we are given a wakeup call to analyze critically education as we know it and to reflect and recognize the intersection of traditional knowledge systems' controversial intersection with the mainstream Western knowledge system. We need to look no further than among our own people and in our communities and recognize the value of the knowledge and ways of knowing that have been in place long before the current mainstream concept of education as we know it. The Native American classroom existed in the natural environment and in contexts wherever children could be found. They learned through experience—by testing, exploring, learning, and trial and error. The Native American child did not have one teacher but many, and each was responsible for a particular lesson or discipline. So, by the time the child reached adulthood, he or she was learned in ways taught by family and clan members—a diverse education. Teaching and learning naturally happened in a contextual environment and across all disciplines. Native American people have long practiced the expression that it takes a village to raise a child.

The utilization of the traditional and Western knowledge systems collided with the arrival of Europeans and Spaniards. Yet the value of being educated remained a high priority. The collision shifted the two systems of learning as one was quashed by the other because of the lack of understanding of local knowledge systems. More important, the Western form of education completely eliminated the other through all means of dominance; a central strategy of colonization. Even though the two forms of education competed and eventually evolved to its present form today, scholars such as Sandy Grande have only begun to analyze this conflicting history of education systems through the frame of critical theory and now critical pedagogy. In this book, Grande challenges scholars and educators to take a closer view of Native American people and their hegemonic relationship with the federal government that is riddled with broken promises, domination, and forced adaptation. Critical pedagogy arms educators while challenging them to think differently about the impact of Western education on Native American people. In the twenty-first century, it is time to take the discourse to the next level where one can feel invigorated and empowered. This book is the beginning. Enjoy.

Timothy Begaye
Assistant Professor
Educational Leadership and Policy Studies
College of Education, Arizona State University

Preface

I am a Quechua woman. This is not only who I am but also, in these "postcolonial" times, an identity I feel increasingly obligated to claim. At the time of Spanish invasion, the indigenous population of Peru was approximately twelve million but after the first one hundred years of conquest, numbers dwindled to 150,000—a decimation of nearly 80 percent. Despite centuries of genocide, Peru today retains a majority indigenous population,[1] a statistic that speaks more to the fortitude and resilience of the Quechua and Aymara peoples than to the virtues of colonialist regimes. This is evident in the fact that although indigenous peoples continue to comprise the majority, the historical–material spoils of imperialism (economic and political power) belong to the white and mestizo minority.

In Peru colonialist regimes have taken many forms. At different moments in history, Marxist, capitalist, socialist, and even "democratic" regimes participated in the ethnic cleansing of Peru's indigenous peoples. Among the most destructive actions undertaken were those by General Juan Velasco and his Marxist-inspired *Special Statute of Peasant Communities* (1970). As part of a broader platform on agrarian reform, the statute legally declassified indigenous peoples as *indios* and reclassified them as *campesinos* (peasants). This act of rhetorical genocide not only aimed to erase indigenous peoples as a distinctive population defined by history, language, and culture, but also to absorb them into a social class framework—"modernizing" them into "compatibility" with Western notions of "progressive economic development and organization" (Yashar, forthcoming). Over time, the terms *indio* and *indígena* began to disappear from Peru's official discourse and historical memory. Eventually, indigenous peoples themselves began to reason it was better to be classified "poor" (*campesino*) and hope for a better future than to be viewed as an anachronism (*indio*)—a conquered people earmarked for extinction. Despite centuries of such genocidal and assimilationist tactics, the Quechua and Aymara peoples persist in their efforts to maintain, recover, and reclaim *indigenismo* as their rightful identity.

Unfortunately, Peru's history is not unlike that of other colonizing nations. While the rules of engagement have changed, the world's indigenous peoples continue to struggle against the forces of imperialism. Despite the pressures in Peru and across the Americas they continue to persevere. In recognition of these struggles, in honor of my ancestors, and in recognition of my own family's journey through, with, and against the tides of history, I once again and with moral indignation, assert: I am a Quechua woman.

NOTE

1. According to statistics reported on the University of Louisville Ekstrom Library Government Publications website on "Peru: Census and Demographics," 47.1 percent of Peru's population is Quechua and 5.4 percent Aymara peoples. At library. louisville.edu/government/international/peru/perucensus.html, March 2, 2004.

Acknowledgments

The first note of thanks goes to Pachamama and all she sustains. The sun, the sky, the earth, and the moon have surely guided my way, illuminating the footsteps of my ancestors so that I may attempt to follow the same path. I also owe a debt of gratitude and thanksgiving to all my relations. I am especially grateful to the indigenous peoples of Peru and to those communities that welcomed me as one of their own—Passamaquoddy, Penobscot, Diné, and the peoples of the Eastern Woodlands—your lands and peoples are beautiful.

This project has been an odyssey. The original draft of this manuscript was lost, stolen one autumn night along with my laptop computer. While the loss was devastating, the journey of recovery has unfolded in a most heartwarming and poignant manner. The love and support I received from my family and friends was overwhelming and humbling, sustaining me through my darkest days and bleary-eyed nights. Indeed, this project would not have been possible without my dad Raul, mom Rosa, sister Anne-Marie, brother-in-law Dave, nephew Craig, sister Suzanne, brother-in-law Billy, nieces Kelsey and Taylor, and the rest of the tribe: Priscilla, Jay, Lucia, Marcy, Lucille, Trent, Lana, Naya, and Kirsten. I am also especially indebted to the Untenured Faculty of Color (UFOC) for providing the inspiration to carry on, to Chuck who graciously read and edited numerous drafts, to Geoffrey who offered his company and office space, to Mab and Aida who offered their labor in the final hours, to Catherine for her support and enouragement, to Nicky for never letting me give up, to Gail and Kendra for being the ground under my feet and to Leslie who stood by me throughout it all, helping me to keep my sanity and soul. I love you all so much. My dear friends and colleagues at Connecticut College, Colby College, Syracuse University, Kent State University and John Marshall High School also played a critical role.

I have also had the honor and privilege of having many mentors in my life. First and foremost, I wish to thank Peter McLaren. From those early days at Colby where you sustained and sparked our little revolution to the present time you have served as an unwavering voice of support. I am so grateful to you and Jenny for opening your home, your hearts and lives to me. Also, Donna Deyhle who read the early draft of this manuscript and the rest of the Utah gang who have served as warm inspiration. I am thankful to Bernardo Gallegos and George Noblitt for not only mentoring me but also legions of young scholars. We all owe you more than we could ever return.

I also greatly appreciate the material support of the Ford Foundation and everyone at the American Indian Leadership Program at Pennsylvania State University for allowing me the privilege of time to write. I am especially grateful to John Tippeconnic and Francis Rains who served as my Penn State sponsors and to Scott, Barbara, Estevan, Angela, and the rest of the Ford Foundation gang for your friendship and support. Also the work of Taiaiake Alfred, Joann Archibald, Duane Champagne, Mike Charleston, Vine Deloria, Donna Deyhle, Donald Fixico, Bernardo Gallegos, Joe Kalt, Tasianna Lomawaiima, Devon Mihesuah, Grayson Noley, Michael Pavel, Joel Spring, Karen Swisher, Huanani Kay Trask, Linda Thuwai Smith, John Tippeconnic, Sofia Villenas, Robert Allen Warrior among many other notables have all inspired my work.

Finally, I would not be who I am today without believing and surrendering to the love, hope, and wisdom of the Creator, the strength and power of the sun and the integrity of the mountains. Thank you, gracias, yuspagrasunki.

Introduction

This book examines the tensions and intersections between dominant modes of critical educational theory and issues relative to American Indian[1] education. Though at the forefront of educational struggles for equity and social justice, critical theorists have failed to recognize and, more importantly, to theorize the relationship between American Indian tribes and the larger democratic imaginary. This failure has severely limited their ability to produce political strategies and educational interventions that account for the rights and needs of American Indian students. To compound the issue, American Indian scholars have largely resisted engagement with critical educational theory, concentrating instead on the production of historical monographs, ethnographic studies, tribally centered curriculums, and site-based research.[2] The combined effect of external neglect by critical scholars and internal resistance among indigenous scholars has kept matters of American Indian education on the margins of educational discourse.

This lack of interchange has additionally raised a series of important questions: How has the marginalization of critical analyses within American Indian education contributed to the "culturalization" of American Indian issues and concerns? How has the focus on "cultural" representations of Indian-ness contributed to a preoccupation with parochial questions of identity and authenticity? And, finally, how has this preoccupation obscured the social–political and economic realities facing indigenous communities, substituting a politics of representation for one of radical social transformation?[3]

Before responding to these questions, it is important to acknowledge that the lack of engagement with the broader educational discourse on the part of American Indian scholars derives from real pressures to address the social and political urgencies of their own communities. The impulse to concentrate time, energy, and resources on recovering, developing, and refining tribally

1

centered forms of schooling is, after all, an effect of the severe loss of tribal knowledge suffered through centuries of colonization. Indeed, centuries of "rhetorical imperialism" committed by "mainstream" scholars pressures indigenous scholars to concentrate their research efforts on their own communities.[4] In this context, restorative projects that affirm and sustain the value of indigenous languages, cultural knowledge, and intellectual history are a first priority. Against such immediate needs, engagement in abstract theory seems indulgent—a luxury and privilege of the academic elite. Further, theory itself is viewed as definitively Eurocentric—inherently contradictory to the aims of indigenous education.

Though perhaps justified, it is important to consider how the "Native theory of antitheory" ultimately limits possibilities for broad-based coalition and political solidarity. Particularly at a time when indigenous communities are under siege from the forces of global encroachment, such a limitation has serious implications. Communities either unable or unwilling to extend borders of coalition and enact *transcendent* theories of decolonization will only compound their vulnerability to the whims and demands of the "new global order." These realities indicate that the time is ripe for indigenous scholars to engage in critique-al[5] studies. In addition, the current explosion in American Indian scholarship renders the once small and insular field of American Indian education both broad and deep enough to sustain internal reflection as well as external engagement. Further still, the burgeoning diversity among peoples who identify themselves as Native American increasingly transforms "the Native American experience" into a multifarious, polyvocal space.

In Peru, roads and airports have brought people and tourism to communities previously inaccessible to all but well-funded anthropologists and wealthy individuals. In the United States, reservation communities experience an even greater influx of tour buses, social service agencies, religious organizations, and corporate prospectors. The effect has transformed once pastoral communities like Chinle, Arizona, and Ayacucho, Peru, into quasi-urban landscapes and, cities like Lima, Peru, and Los Angeles, California, into virtual denizens for a vast array of dislocated and relocated Indian peoples. Indeed, over the centuries, the forces of conquest, genocide, removal, colonization, imperialism, detribalization, urbanization, and relocation have deeply altered indigenous communities worldwide.

As indigenous communities continue to be transformed by movement, access, border crossing, and transgression, it becomes even more pertinent for American Indian scholars to abandon what Robert Allen Warrior (1995) refers to as the "death dance of dependence"—the vacillation between wholesale adoption of Anglo-Western theories and the declaration by American Indian scholars that they need nothing outside of themselves to understand their world or place within it. In other words, as the sociocultural geography of Indian Country expands, so too must the intellectual borders of indigenous intellectualism. While there is nothing inherently healing, liberatory, or revolutionary about theory, it is one of our primary responsibilities as educators to link the lived experience of theorizing to the processes of self-recovery and social transformation.

That being said, this is not a call for American Indian scholars to simply join the conversation of critical theorists. Rather, I aim to initiate an indigenous conversation that can, in turn, engage in dialogical contestation with critical and revolutionary theories. Such analyses may be viewed by some as a dangerous discourse, equally threatening to the fields of critical theory and American Indian education. Similar to black feminism (which forced white feminists and black male intellectuals to examine how they remained blind to the continued exploitation of black women) my hope is that American Indian critique-al studies will compel critical theorists and American Indian scholars to examine how their lack of interchange has hindered the struggle for spiritually vibrant, intellectually challenging, and politically operative schools for both Indian and non-Indian students.

To begin, the predominantly white, middle-class advocates of critical theory will need to examine how their language and epistemic frames act as homogenizing agents when interfaced with the conceptual and analytical categories persistent within American Indian educational theory and praxis. They will especially need to examine the degree to which critical pedagogies retain the deep structures of Western thought—that is, the belief in progress as change, in the universe as impersonal, in reason as the preferred mode of inquiry, and in human beings as separate from and superior to the rest of nature.

American Indian scholars will similarly need to challenge their own propensity to privilege local knowledge and personal experience over the macroframes of social and political theory. As valuable as the production of public confessionals, historical narratives, "collected wisdoms," and autobiographies is, there is much more to the Indian story. Thus, while the whitestream market may crave "the Native informant," it is up to indigenous scholars to resist the notion that experience is self-explanatory and work instead to theorize the inherent complexity of Indian-ness. Indeed, the relatively recent emergence of the doubly marginalized voices of urban, detribalized, and gay and lesbian Indians compels a rethinking of the public voice of Indian-ness. Such perspectives not only deserve sincere engagement and analysis but also command us to confront the internalized racism, sexism, and homophobia within indigenous communities.

The above aims render this book somewhat of an insurgent text. Its limited use of narrative and autobiography, its theoretical focus, its integral use of non-Indian scholars to assist in the explanation of American Indian experience, and its refusal to engage and replay the micropolitics of tribal-centric discourses all transgress prevailing codes of "mainstream" indigenous writing. This transgression is intended to not only call attention to the fact that such forms no longer adequately theorize the indigenous diaspora but also to their rootedness in the desires of the whitestream[6] marketplace. While some indigenous scholars, pressured by a variety of colonialist forces, often fall complicit to such demands, the desire to preserve the images and fantasies of the white man's Indian—as stoic, silent, tragic, apolitical, "traditional," close to nature—is ultimately perpetuated by whitestream appetites.

In contrast to such work, I write in the tradition of indigenous intellectuals and educators who have continuously and tirelessly worked to push disciplinary boundaries and transgress intellectual borders, both strengthening and broadening the field of indigenous education. Specifically, the work of Taiaiake Alfred, Duane Champagne, Mike Charleston, Vine Deloria, Donna Dehyle, Donald Fixico, Bernardo Gallegos, Tsianna Lomawaiima, Devon Mihesuah, Grayson Noley, Michael Pavel, Joel Spring, Karen Swisher, Haunani Kay-Trask, Linda Thuwai-Smith, John Tippeconnic, Sofia Villenas, and Robert Allen Warrior, among others, have been deeply inspiring.

Though greatly motivated by such scholars, my own desire to engage "transgression" emanates from the experience of what it means to be an indigenous student and scholar. I was born, raised, and schooled in the United States—a quintessential first generation child. From the Andean highlands to the urban landscapes of Lima, Peru, to New York City, and to Hartford, Connecticut, my family traversed the geographies of land, identity, and social capital. Through it all (despite my parent's concerted efforts to blend), I was acutely aware of *the presence of difference,* especially in school. While I lacked the vocabulary to name the injustices I endured as "institutional racism," I found school to be dull, spiritless, and deeply irreverent to the life experiences of indigenous peoples. Eventually I came to embody that irreverence, and with each successive year, my struggles against dropping out became increasingly acute.

As such, this book is a long-time-coming rejoinder to those feelings of anger and alienation. It is the testimony of a journey of consciousness, a coming to know *through* transgression. More specifically, I came to know through transgressing the illicit borders of race, class, and gender, typically off-limits to a brown-skinned girl whose family dared to move from the ghettos to an all-white suburb. I came to know by transgressing the disciplinary boundaries and ossified borders of academia—between fact and fiction, teacher and activist, spirit and reason, theory and practice—highly guarded by the sentinels of the ivory tower. Finally, I came to know by transgressing the borders between the traditional, modern, and postmodern worlds, and through rejecting the temporality of Western space and insisting upon the fluidity of traditional time.

From all of this, I learned that experience is far from self-explanatory; that language and the ability to name one's experience are precursors to emancipation; that teachers, schools, and Western frames of intelligibility still desire to "kill the Indian and save the man"; and that Native America is not only a place but also a social, political, cultural, and economic space. Ultimately, however, I learned that transgression is the root of emancipatory knowledge, and emancipatory knowledge is the basis of revolutionary pedagogy.

These experiences have all contributed to my desire to extend the spaces of indigenous intellectualism and to appeal to American Indian youth caught at the crossroads of tradition and contemporary globalization. In the liminal spaces of everyday life they are the ones on the front lines, forced to navigate the ongoing and dilatory effects of colonization at the same time the continued saliency of the colonialist project is denied. As Arif Dirlik (1999) notes, "Today Native Americans struggle not only with colonial histories but also with postmodern and cultural critics who take for granted that nations are 'imagined,' traditions are 'invented,' subjectivities are 'slippery' (if they exist at all), and cultural identities are myths." While such theories rightfully call attention to the myriad "collisions" between the once discrete worlds of the "colonizer" and the "colonized," their facile reasoning ultimately serves to occlude the brut reality that twenty-first-century America fosters internal colonies.

The trauma of struggling against colonialism in a postcolonial zeitgeist manifests most acutely in American Indian students. They exhibit the highest dropout rates, the lowest academic performance rates, and the lowest college admission and retention rates in the nation (American Council on Education 2002). In addition, Robin Butterfield (1994) reports that Native students frequently get categorized and treated as remedial students, are often subjected to racial slurs, endure low teacher expectations, and experience extreme alienation. In response to the persistence of such issues, the vanguard of Indian education recently levied a powerful entreaty calling for school reform strategies that "recognize and address the linguistic and socio-cultural uniqueness of American Indian and Alaska Native learners" (Trujillo 2000, 2). They call attention to the high correlation between school success and the centrality of indigenous knowledge and language programs to underscore their mandate.

While the dire need to provide American Indian students with culturally relevant and affirming educational experiences is well noted, it is not sufficient. At a time when 90 percent of American Indian students attend non-Indian schools (Gallagher 2000), it is not only imperative for Indian educators to insist on the incorporation of indigenous knowledge and praxis in schools but also to transform the institutional structures of schools themselves. In other words, in addition to the development of Native curricula, indigenous educators need to develop systems of analysis that help theorize the ways in which power and domination inform the processes and procedures of schooling. They need pedagogies that work to disrupt the structures of inequality. Consequently, such are the aims of critical pedagogy.

As it has evolved, "critical pedagogy" operates in the educational landscape as both a rhetoric and a social movement. Specifically, critical theorists extend critiques of the social, economic, and political barriers to social justice as well as advocate for the transformation of schools along the imperatives of democracy. In so doing, they position schools as "sites of struggle" where the broader relations of power, domination, and authority are played out. In addition to their analyses of schools, critical educators theorize the intersections of race, class, gender, and sexuality as the fault lines of inequality. Within these analyses they include the naming and examination of "whiteness" as a significant marker of racial, class, and gender privilege. Finally, and perhaps most relevant to the concerns of American Indian education, "revolutionary" forms of critical pedagogy are centrally committed to the transformation of capitalist social relations, recognizing that the attainment of real equity is impossible within the current imperialist system of economic exploitation. In other words, they take seriously the claims and struggles of colonized peoples, recognizing that movements against imperialism begin with dismantling a "Eurocentric system of cultural valuation that rationalizes globalization as 'development' and 'progress'" (Rizvi 2002).

Such pedagogies offer an entryway for American Indian scholars and educators to engage the broader, public discourse on schooling and education. They also provide potential tools for American Indian students struggling to make sense of their experiences with institutional racism, labor exploitation, class struggle, and other encounters with whiteness. It warrants repeating here that I am not advocating the wholesale adoption of critical pedagogy or, for that matter, any theory not initially conceived as part of an indigenous educational project. Rather, I see the task ahead as defining the common ground between American Indian intellectuals and other critical scholars engaged in anti-imperialist and anticapitalist struggles (i.e., decolonization).

Though they may arrive by different roads and aspire to different destinations, critical theorists and indigenous scholars are committed to defining schools and societies that are free from oppression and subordination and stand for justice and emancipation. This book builds upon this common ground as well as seeks to reveal additional pathways of intersection. I begin

the search for such pathways in the first chapter with a review of the historical relationship between schooling and American Indians. Next, the deep constructs and salient issues within critical educational theory are examined,
defining points of tension and intersection within the discipline. In the final
section, the beginning frameworks of a new Red pedagogy are outlined.
Within this and subsequent analyses, it is important to note that the constructs, theories, and pedagogies of indigenous education (not critical theory)
are foregrounded and privileged as the intellectual space from which the proposed new Red pedagogy will emerge.

The second chapter examines the struggles for democracy and indigenous
sovereignty as competing moral visions within U.S. society. The chapter begins with a review of the history of democracy and the ways in which it has
been imposed upon American Indians. This review is followed by a critical
analysis of the implications of nationalism and globalization on indigenous
communities. In the end, despite the seeming disjuncture, I maintain that once
sufficiently troubled and divested from its Western, capitalist desires, democracy can be reimagined as a viable concept for both critical and indigenous
forms of education.

The third chapter examines conceptions of land and nature within critical
theory and American Indian education. I submit that while critical theorists
account for the state of the environment as an extension of social justice issues, the Western human–nature dichotomy is ultimately retained. In contrast,
indigenous pedagogies tend to dispense of the human–nature dichotomy and
construct nature as a sovereign entity in symbiotic relationship with human
subjectivity. Consequently, I argue that as long as the political project of critical education fails to theorize the interrelationship between human consumption, capitalist exploitation, and the struggle for "democracy," it will fail
to provide emancipatory pedagogies that are sustainable and pertinent for the
global age.

Chapter four surveys the ever-shifting landscape of American Indian identity. It is ascertained that current modes of identity theory fail to consider the
unique location of indigenous peoples and therefore erase the distinctiveness
of tribal identity. In contrast to dominant modes of identity theory, American
Indian subjectivity is discussed in terms of an "identity paradox"—that is, at
the same time American Indian communities face internal pressures (racism,
sexism, homophobia, detribalization, urbanization) to mediate more fluid
constructions of Indian-ness, they are also compelled by external threats (encroachment, ethnic fraud, corporate commodification. and culture loss) to
maintain more restrictive definitions of Indian-ness. Implications for education are discussed as they intersect with students' notions of identity, agency,
and collectivity.

Chapter five examines the tensions and intersections between dominant modes of feminist theory and the existing lives of American Indian women. Unlike dominant modes of feminist critique that situate women's oppression in the structures of patriarchy and capitalist exploitation, the collective oppression of indigenous women is discussed as an effect of colonialism—a multidimensional force underwritten by Christianity, defined by racism, and fueled by global capitalism. Issues of gender and indigenous education are discussed within this framework.

Finally, chapter six provides a synthesis of the preceding chapters and proposes the need for continual engagement between indigenous scholars, educators, and advocates of critical theory. The foundation of a new Red pedagogy is defined as that which emerges from a collectivity of critique and solidarity between and among indigenous peoples, other marginalized groups, and peoples of conscience.

In the end, I ask that as we examine our own communities, policies, and practices, we take seriously the notion that to know ourselves as revolutionary agents is more than an act of understanding who we are. It is the act of reinventing ourselves, of validating our overlapping cultural identifications and relating them to the materiality of social life and power relations (McLaren 1997). This book is, thus, a bold but humble first step toward building transcultural and transnational solidarity among indigenous peoples and others committed to reimagining a democratic space free of imperialist, colonialist, and capitalist exploitation. Together I hope we can build an insurgent but poetic vision for education, one that is dedicated to the principles of sovereignty, emancipation, and equity—for all human beings and the rest of nature.

NOTES

Though Marxist-feminist Teresa Ebert uses (I'm not sure if she "coined" the term) the term Red Pedagogy to signify her own project of revitalizing the Marxist critique of feminist discourse, I employ the term as a historical referent to such empowering metaphors as "Red Power" and "The Great Red Road," reappropriating the signifier "Red" as a contemporary metaphor for the ongoing struggles of indigenous peoples to retain sovereignty and establish self-determination.

1. In recognition of the diversity of terminology currently in use, the terms Native American, indigenous, and American Indian are used interchangeably. However, when referencing issues specific to the tribal peoples in the United States who hold treaty rights and sovereign status, the term American Indian is used.

2. The comprehensive literature reviews of Robert Allen Warrior (1995) and of Donna Dehyle and Karen Swisher (1997) provide adequate evidence of the lack of intersection between American Indian scholarship on education and the broader field of critical studies.

3. See Teresa Ebert's *Lucid Feminism and After: Postmodernism, Desire, and Labor in Late Capitalism* (1999, 3).

4. As a result of myriad injustices committed by whitestream scholars using and abusing indigenous communities as a means to further careers, profits, and/or racist anti-Indian agendas, there is a movement underfoot to restrict scholarship on Indians to Indian researchers only. Scholars that have expressed this viewpoint include Elizabeth Cook-Lyn, Donald Fixico, Devon Mihesuah, Grayson Noley, and Karen Swisher, among others. Though the impulse to restrict access is valid, when interfaced with the question of who is Indian enough, it becomes problematic.

5. Marxist-feminist scholar Teresa Ebert distinguishes critical from critique-al studies as a means of re-centering the importance of critique as opposed to criticism in discourse.

6. Adapting from the feminist notion of "malestream," Claude Denis (1997) defines "whitestream" as the idea that while American society is not "white" in sociodemographic terms, it remains principally and fundamentally structured on the basis of the Anglo-European, "white" experience.

Chapter One

Mapping the Terrain of Struggle: From Genocide, Colonization, and Resistance to Red Power and Red Pedagogy

The War for Indian Children will be won in the classroom.

—Wilma Mankiller

The right to be indigenous is an essential prerequisite to developing and maintaining culturally appropriate and sustainable education for indigenous peoples.

—The Coolangatta Statement on Indigenous
Peoples' Rights in Education (1.5)

The miseducation of American Indians precedes the "birth" of this nation. From the time of invasion to the present day, the church and state have acted as coconspirators in the theft of Native America, robbing indigenous peoples of their very right to be indigenous.[1] In terms of education, the thievery began in 1611 when French Jesuits opened the first mission schools expressly aimed at educating Indian children "in the French manner"[2] (Noriega 1992, 371). Not to be outdone, Spanish and British missionaries soon followed, developing full-service educational systems intent on "de-Indianizing" Native children. By the mid-eighteenth century Harvard University (1636), the College of William and Mary (1693), and Dartmouth College (1769) had all been established with the charge of "civilizing" and "Christianizing" Indians as an inherent part of their institutional missions. The American school was therefore a well-established weapon in the arsenal of American imperialism long before the first shots of the Revolutionary War were ever fired.

While it falls outside the bounds of this book to provide a thorough history of American Indian education, its importance is duly noted.[3] The following brief review of some significant moments in American Indian education is meant only to provide a rudimentary template from which to theorize the contemporary landscape. We begin with an examination of the historical relationship between American Indians and schooling, followed by a brief review of the literature on critical pedagogy. The reviews of the history of American Indian education and critical pedagogy are then interfaced, mapping the tensions and intersections between these analyses as a means of developing the framework for a Red pedagogy.

THE HISTORICAL RELATIONSHIP BETWEEN SCHOOLING AND AMERICAN INDIANS

Though the history of Indian education is mapped in a variety of ways (e.g., chronologically, thematically) it is delineated here in terms of eras that reflect the prevailing systems of power: (1) the period of missionary domination, from the sixteenth to the nineteenth centuries; (2) the period of federal government domination from the late nineteenth to the mid-twentieth centuries; and, (3) the period of self-determination from the mid-twentieth century to the present (Thompson 1978; Szasz 1999).

Perhaps at no other time in U.S. history did the church and state work so hand in hand to advance the common project of white supremacy as it did during the period of missionary domination. During this era, missionary groups acted as the primary developers and administrators of schools while the federal government served as the not-so-silent partner, providing economic and political capital through policies such as the Civilization Fund.[4] In 1819 Secretary of War John Calhoun declared it was the duty of all employees in government-funded missions, particularly teachers, to promote U.S. policies aimed at "civilizing" Indians. In Calhoun's words, it was their job to "[i]mpress on the minds of the Indians the friendly and benevolent views of the government . . . and the advantages to . . . yielding to the policy of the government and cooperating with it in such measures as it may deem necessary for their civilization and happiness" (Layman 1942, 123, cited in Reyhner and Eder in Reyhner, ed., 1992, 40). Indeed, the work of teachers, church leaders, and missionaries were hardly distinguishable during this era; saving souls and colonizing minds became part and parcel of the same colonialist project.

While missions retained control well into the late nineteenth century, the period of federal government domination ideologically commenced with the passage of the Indian Removal Act in 1830.[5] The fallout from removal necessitated the appointment of a commissioner of Indian affairs, tellingly positioned in the U.S. Department of War. The collateral damage levied by removal, namely, the decimation of Indian economies via displacement, required a systematic effort to "reeducate" Indians to live "domesticated" lives. Thus, in addition to dealing with the removed tribes, the commissioner was charged with overseeing a retooled system of Indian education, one which emphasized vocational training as the new panacea for assimilating Indians to industrial society.

In the following decades, the church and state conspired in the development of a variety of "manual labor schools." In addition to providing vocational training, such schools introduced the concept of forced labor as part of Indian education, transforming the ostensibly "moral" project of civilizing Indians into a for-profit enterprise. Under this experiment, churches were endowed with hundreds of acres of land for Indian children to plow, maintain, and harvest. Many dioceses yielded high profits from the "free" labor, creating a windfall that ignited increased competition for federal funding. Ironically, the ensuing friction and discord among rival churches contributed to the repeal of the Civilization Fund (1873), bringing their reign of power to an end. The federal government stepped in to fill the void, ushering in a new era of federal control over Indian schools (Reyhner and Eder 1992).

Building on the models established by manual labor and earlier boarding schools (e.g., Dartmouth and the Choctaw Academy), the government looked to define its own system of Indian education. Federal planners were weary of the established day school model, which "afforded Indian students too much proximity to their families and communities." Such access was deemed detrimental to the overall project of deculturalization (Noriega 1992, 380), making the manual labor boarding school the model of choice. The infamous Carlisle Indian School (1879–1918) was the first of its kind in this new era of federal control.

By the turn of the century, the Bureau of Indian Affairs (BIA) was operating twenty-five such boarding schools in fifteen states. Administering the entire apparatus was the newly created education division of the BIA (Reyhner and Eder 1989). Like earlier models, the "new" boarding schools were designed, first and foremost, to serve the purposes of the federal government and only secondarily the needs of American Indian students. Such imperialistic purposes were reflected in curriculums that included teaching allegiance to the U.S. government, exterminating the use of Native languages, and destroying Indian customs, particularly Native religions (Spring 2001).

Though the above aims for Indian education were all integral components of the colonialist curriculum, perhaps the most important feature of boarding schools was the inculcation of the industrial or "Protestant" work ethic. In his annual report in 1881, Commissioner of Indian Affairs Hiram Price argued that previous attempts to civilize Indians failed because they did not teach "the necessity of labor" (Spring 1997, 173). He maintained that this ethic could only be taught by making Indians responsible for their own economic welfare, achievable through the cultivation of a proper appreciation for private property. Price specifically advocated for an allotment program that conferred Indians "a certain number of acres of land which they may call their own."[6] Richard Pratt, founder of the Carlisle Indian School, echoed the sentiments of the commissioner, attacking the tribal way of life as socialistic and contrary to the values of civilization. Indeed, Pratt laid the "failure" of Indian assimilation at the feet of missionary groups and their failure to "advocate the disintegration of tribes." In a letter to the commissioner of Indian affairs, he wrote: "Pandering to the tribe and its socialism as most of our Government and mission plans do is the principal reason why the Indians have not advanced more and are not advancing as rapidly as they ought to."[7] As such, Pratt made indoctrination to capitalist logic an explicit aim of Indian education.

The era of Indian boarding schools reigned from the nineteenth century through the early twentieth century. Such schools worked explicitly with the U.S. government to implement federal policies (i.e., allotment) servicing the campaign to "kill the Indian and save the man." The process began with the (often forcible) removal of young children from their homes and communities and transporting them to a geographically and ideologically foreign place. Upon arrival children were subjected to English-only and Anglocentric curricula and to a cocurriculum that incorporated paramilitary structures of forced labor and "patriotic" propaganda. In addition, children were often undernourished and subjected to overcrowded living spaces that encouraged "the spread of tuberculosis and trachoma." Moreover, compulsory attendance laws made it virtually impossible for children to escape, exposing a hidden curriculum that not only advocated the termination of Indian-ness but also of Indians (Spring 1997, 175).

By the turn of the century, the combined effects of rapidly increasing enrollments (due to compulsory attendance laws), a decrease in federal funding, a changing political tide, and a growing resistance among tribes began to encumber the boarding school experiment, rendering it too unwieldy for federal officials to maintain. Not only did the schools become political and economic liabilities, but also proved to be an ineffective means of achieving the government's aim of complete assimilation. As Noriega (1992, 383) reports, "despite the efforts of BIA officials, missionaries, and teachers to stamp them out, indigenous languages, spiritual practices, and sociopolitical forms were not only continued by tribal elders, but transmitted from generation to generation." The century thus ended with a pervasive sense of futility and failure regarding Indian education and with the government continuing to search for the next best solution to the "Indian problem." Despite the growing litany of failed experiments, belief in the virtue of forced assimilation persisted, continually compelling new strategies and tactics.

In 1906, Commissioner of Indian Affairs Francis Leupp initiated the next grand plan—the wholesale transfer of Indian students into public schools. In addition to saving the government from the ever-increasing cost of Indian education, the immersion of Indian children into public and predominantly white schools was seen as a strategic means of propelling the process of "Americanization." By 1912 there were more Indian children in public schools than government (BIA) schools, and by 1924 the "Committee of One Hundred Citizens" officially sanctioned Leupp's assessment of public education as the most efficient means by which to train Indians to "think white."[8]

The transition from boarding schools to public education was mounted in the wake of the Meriam Report in 1928, which not only dealt the final blow to the boarding school experiment but also levied the decisive political spark that launched the next era of "reform." Among other things, the report not only harshly criticized the existing educational policies of removing Indian children from their homes and communities, but criticized the institutional practices of forced manual labor and severe discipline as well. The report summarily states that the most fundamental need in Indian education was a "change in government attitude" (Spring 1997, 176). In 1933, leading reformer and advocate of Indian "rights" John Collier became the commissioner of Indian affairs. He oversaw the implementation of many recommendations iterated in the Meriam Report, including the end of allotment, increased Indian religious freedom, and greater tribal self-government[9] (Reyhner and Eder 1992). Also passed during Collier's tenure was the Johnson-O'Malley Act, which authorized payments to states or territories for the education of Indians in public institutions. Such reforms were prominent features of Collier's "Indian New Deal," the net impact of which significantly increased the number of Indian children being served by both federal (BIA) and public educational institutions.

Over time, the notion of reform popularized by Collier's "New Deal" fueled liberal sentiments to "free" the Indian from government control, particularly from the reservation system. During the so-called termination period (1945–1968),[10] the government sought to relocate Indians to urban areas, turning the responsibility for Indian education over to individual states (Reyhner and Eder 1992). Despite its "liberatory" rhetoric, however, Margaret Connell Szasz (1999, 137) contends that the aim of termination was to support "any action that would assimilate the Indian into urban society."

Along with other aspects of termination, the educational implications of relocation were devastating. Hildegard Thompson, director of the branch of education, criticized the lack of foresight in educational planning. For instance, in reference to the "termination" of the Paiutes, she stated, "We all recognize that the [termination of the Paiute] was enacted without too much preplanning with the Tribe" and that in the future "such programs and contracts should come in the preparation stage with the Tribe instead of at the termination time" (Szasz 1994, 138). The experience of the Paiutes was not an isolated one, as the vast majority of tribes were ill-informed and unprepared for the myriad and pervasive effects of termination. Therefore, it was not long before this program was added to the pile of failed government experiments, brought down by its own inherent deficiencies and a growing tide of Indian resistance.

While resistance took many forms, Indians implicitly expressed their antipathy toward termination by refusing to enroll in the associated ill-conceived vocational training programs ostensibly designed for their benefit (read: ready labor exploitation). By the dawn of the civil rights movement, American Indians were more directly voicing their opposition to termination and other oppressive government policies. Such displays of resistance psychologically marked the beginning of the era of self-determination.

By the 1960s, tribes had developed a core leadership capable of articulating Indian rights and concerns (Reyhner and Eder 1992, 54). In addition to their protests of existing federal policies, the new Indian leadership advocated an agenda of self-determination or the idea of "letting Indian people . . . determine their own destiny." The spirit of self-determination gave rise to a number of Indian organizations, including the National Indian Education Association in 1967, the Coalition of Indian Controlled School Boards in 1971, and the American Indian Movement in 1972. The political energy of such organizations helped galvanize efforts to establish tribally controlled schools such as the Rough Rock Demonstration School and Navajo Community College, founded in 1966 and 1968, respectively.

The efforts of Indian educators and leaders also prompted the publication of two major studies in Indian education: "Indian Education: A National Tragedy—A National Challenge" (U.S. Senate, 1969), commonly known as "The Kennedy Report" and, "The National Study of American Indian Education" (Havighurst 1970). These reports helped secure passage of the Indian Self-Determination and Education Act in 1975, which provided American Indians increased control over their children's education. Among other measures, the act authorized special funding for programs in reservation schools and, for the first time, off-reservation, urban schools. It also advocated for parent involvement in program planning, for the establishment of community-run schools, and for culturally relevant and bilingual curriculum materials (Reyhner and Eder 1992, chapter 3; Szasz 1999).

A number of seminal political documents were also published during the era of self-determination, including the "Indian Nations at Risk" report in 1991, the "White House Conference on Indian Education" report in 1992, the "Comprehensive Federal Indian Education Policy Statement" in 1997, and the "Executive Order on American Indian and Alaska Native Education" in 1998. In general these reports indicate that while the past thirty years witnessed much progress in Indian education, the road ahead was replete with challenges, providing a litany of statistics that portend a grim picture for Indian education. Specifically, in addition to exhibiting the highest dropout and lowest achievement rates, American Indian and Alaska Native students were reported to endure Euro-centric curriculums, high faculty and staff turnover rates, underprepared teachers, limited access to relevant cultural library and learning resources, limited access to computers and other technologies, and overt and subtle forms of racism in schools. Such conditions were exacerbated by a general decline in federal spending, particularly for BIA schools and tribal colleges.

Above all, however, the reports testify to the fact that centuries of genocidal and assimilationist polices cannot be undone in a matter of years. The voices of prominent American Indian scholars, educators, and leaders are registered throughout, collectively asserting that systematic oppression, levied at the hands of the federal government, requires an equally systematic federal plan of affirmative action. In other words, an education for decolonization. The "Comprehensive Federal Indian Education Policy Statement" (CFIEPS), in particular, reflects the virtual consensus among leaders that school reform must be systematic and inclusive of all aspects of tribal life. The relationship between educational reform and the struggles to "preserve tribal homelands, governments, languages, cultures, economies, and social structures" is made explicit (National Indian Education Association and National Congress of American Indians 1996, 3).

Ironically, though the CFIEPS is often referred to as a revolutionary document in the history of American Indian education, it ultimately states little that is either new or revolutionary. Rather, it merely rearticulates the scope of federal responsibility as defined in existing laws, treaties, and policies. Beginning with a directive for the "recognition and support of tribal sovereignty," the report details the responsibilities of various federal agencies to assist tribes in assuming "control of education programs and governance of Indian education" (NIEA/NCAI 1996, 4). It covers everything from the "support of native languages and cultures" to provisions for "Indian education outside of Indian country," and is contextualized in language that makes it definitively clear that the federal government must act in consultation with, and in service to, the tribes. Furthermore, it stipulates that this "government-to-government" relationship should be heeded as an inherent aspect of tribal sovereignty and not as a delegated privilege.

Due to its comprehensive nature, the CFIEPS served as the model for "The Executive Order on American Indian and Native Alaskan Education" issued in 1998 by the Clinton administration. Much of its original, somewhat strident, language was, however, lost in the translation from political statement to federal policy. In particular, the importance placed on the need for broad-based educational reform, institutionalized recognition of Indian sovereignty, and accountability of federal agencies to uphold their moral, legal, and fiscal responsibility to support Indian education was noticeably diminished. Nevertheless, the issuance of this executive order was a historic moment, symbolizing the efforts of contemporary American Indian leaders to not only insist on self-determination but also on the government's acknowledgment of this inherent right.

Indian Education in the Twenty-First Century

While at the beginning of the twenty-first century it is important to recognize that progress has been made, Indian students, in comparison to all others, are still the most disproportionately affected by poverty, low educational attainment, and limited access to educational opportunities (Beaulieu 2000, 33). Their severely marginalized status is perhaps most evident in the overrepresentation of Native youth engaging in high-risk behaviors. A study conducted by the U.S. Department of Health and Human Services in 2001 (cited in Clarke 2002) reported the following data regarding American Indian/Alaska Native (AI/AN) youth aged twelve to seventeen:

- Illicit drug use is more than twice (22.2%) the national average (9.7%).
- Binge alcohol use is higher (13.8%) than the national average (10.3%).
- Heavy alcohol use is higher (3.8%) that the national average (2.5%).
- Motor vehicle and other accidents are the leading cause of death among AI/AN persons aged fifteen to twenty-four, whose death rate due to accidents is higher than the rate for the total U.S. population.
- Suicide is the second leading cause of death for AI/AN youth aged fifteen to twenty-four, and the overall suicide rate is 2.5 times higher than the combined rate for all races in the United States.

In recognition of the seeming sociocultural nature of these behaviors, some educators have advocated multicultural education for American Indian students (Butterfield 1994; Hamme 1996; Reyhner 1992; St. Germaine 1995; Wilson 1991). According to Nieto (1995), multicultural education can be defined as "a process of comprehensive school reform and basic education for all students."

> It challenges and rejects racism and other forms of discrimination in schools and society and accepts and affirms the pluralism (ethnic, racial, linguistic, religious, and gender, among others) that students, their communities, and teachers represent. Multicultural education permeates the curriculum and instructional strategies used in schools, as well as the interactions among teachers, students, and parents, and the very way that schools conceptualize the nature of teaching and learning.

While acknowledgment of the relationship between education and culture is important, unless the relationship between culture and the socioeconomic conditions within which it is produced is recognized, the so-called at-risk conditions common to peoples living under siege will persist. With regard to American Indians, this means understanding that "the Indian problem" is not a problem of children and families but rather, first and foremost, a problem that has been consciously and historically produced by and through the systems of colonization: a multidimensional force underwritten by Western Christianity, defined by white supremacy, and fueled by global capitalism.

Indian education was never simply about the desire to "civilize" or even deculturalize a people, but rather, from its very inception, it was a project designed to colonize Indian minds as a means of gaining access to Indian labor, land, and resources. Therefore, unless educational reform happens concurrently with analyses of the forces of colonialism, it can only serve as a deeply insufficient (if not negligent) Band-Aid over the incessant wounds of imperialism. The call to engage Indian education reform from a macroperspective — one that emanates from a historical–material analysis of the relationship between U.S. society and Native communities — is not new. One of the more eloquent and passionate entreaties issued on behalf of the need for comprehensive reform was delivered by Mike Charleston (1994, 15) in the draft report of the Indian Nations at Risk task force entitled, "Toward True Native Education: A Treaty of 1992."[11] He begins:

> It is time for a new treaty, a Treaty of 1992, to end a shameful, secret war. For five hundred years, our tribal people have been resisting the siege of the non-Native societies that have developed in our native land. The war is over the continued existence of tribal societies of American Indians and Alaska Natives. We inherited the conflict from our ancestors. Our children face the consequences of this war today. Every tribal member has felt the bitter pangs of this relentless siege. It dominates our lives. It is killing our children. It is destroying our Native communities.

Charleston's piercing language, particularly the use of such metaphors as "war" and "siege" to describe the imperialistic relationship between the United States and tribal societies, indicates his understanding of the systemic and unrelenting nature of colonialism. In addition, while he rightfully places liability in the hands of the U.S. government, Charleston also acknowledges that change will only occur when Native and nonnative societies make the commitment to work together; referencing the importance of political solidarity and coalition-building.

Though the final published report of the task force is an obviously tempered version of Charleston's impassioned plea, it still manages to identify colonization as the central culprit in creating and maintaining the marginalized "at-risk" status of Native nations. Specifically, it begins from the standpoint that Native nations are at risk because:

- Schools have failed to nurture the intellectual development and academic performance of Native children.
- Schools have discouraged the use of Native languages in the classroom.
- Indian lands and resources are constantly besieged by outside forces interested in further reducing their original holdings.
- Political relationships between tribes and the federal government fluctuate with the will of the U.S. Congress and decisions by the courts.

Though the relationship between schools and colonialist forces is only implied, the tacit correlation remains both pointed and powerful. In the end, both documents generated by the task force deliver the resounding message that school reform is merely one battleground in the "war" against colonialism. The central implication is that the struggle for self-determined schools must be engaged alongside other revolutionary struggles, specifically those that seek to end economic exploitation, political domination, and cultural dependency. Consequently, such are the aims of critical pedagogy.

CRITICAL PEDAGOGY AND ITS DISCONTENTS

Simply stated, critical pedagogy is that discourse that emerged when "critical theory encountered education" (Kincheloe and Steinberg 1997). Typically envisioned as leftist or *beyond* multicultural education, the "theoretical genesis" of North American critical pedagogy is traced back to the work of Paulo Freire, John Dewey, and other social reconstructionists writing in the post-Depression years (McLaren 2003). According to Peter McLaren, leading exponents have always "cross-fertilized critical pedagogy with just about every transdisciplinary tradition imaginable, including theoretical forays into the Frankfurt School . . . [with] the work of Richard Rorty, Jacques Lacan, Jacques Derrida, and Michael Foucault" (2003, 66). With such transdisciplinary beginnings, it is not surprising that critical pedagogy has emerged, in more recent years, as a kind of umbrella for a variety of educators and scholars working toward social justice and greater equity (Lather 1998). As such, postmodern, post-structuralist, feminist, postcolonial, Marxist, and critical race theorists have all developed their own forms of critical pedagogy. Even so, there is a core of unifying principles and salient features that constitute the heart of the discipline.

According to McLaren (2003), critical pedagogy is first and foremost an approach to schooling—teaching, policymaking, curriculum production—that emphasizes the political nature of education. "The antagonistic terrain of conflicting and competing discourses, oppositional and hegemonic cultural formations, and social relations linked to the larger capitalist social totality" forms the foundation of schooling (McLaren 2003, 66). As such, critical pedagogy aims to understand, reveal, and disrupt the mechanisms of oppression imposed by the established order, suturing the processes and aims of education to emancipatory goals.

Leading critical scholar Henry Giroux (2001, 3) emphasizes the emancipatory nature of critical pedagogy, asserting that, at base, critical pedagogy must be envisioned as "part of a broader ethical and political project wedded to furthering social and economic justice and making multicultural democracy operational." In terms of the pedagogical implications of such a project Giroux (2001, 20) writes:

> Critical pedagogy must address the challenge of providing students with the competencies they need to cultivate the capacity for critical judgment, to thoughtfully connect politics to social responsibility and expand their own sense of agency in order to curb the excesses of dominant power, to revitalize a sense of public commitment, and to expand democratic relations. Animated by a spirit of critique and possibility, critical pedagogy at its best attempts to provoke students to deliberate, resist, and cultivate a range of capacities that enable them to move beyond the world they already know without insisting on a fixed set of meanings.

Though such aims are often dismissed as idealistic, critical scholar Glenda Moss (2001, 11) found that "real" teachers, in "real" classrooms, are able to employ critical pedagogy. Specifically, she found that such teachers used "reflective-reflexive" skills to institute "changed practices that work for authentic participation of all members of the broader society." Buttressed by the work of others, Moss (2001) identified the following pedagogical practices to be common among critical educators: (1) they question whose beliefs, values, and interests are served by classroom content and practices, challenging the hidden curriculum that socializes students into the dominant culture; (2) they address social oppression as tied to race, gender, and class and, (3) they challenge the "banking" or transmission style of teaching as a learning ritual that maintains the status quo.

Though a modicum of consensus has been achieved among critical practitioners, the multifarious nature of critical pedagogy's theoretical foundation has bred intellectual tensions among critical scholars. Indeed, Patti Lather (1998, 487) maintains that "an ensemble of practices and discourses with competing claims of truth, typicality, and credibility" among critical scholars have always been present, especially between (postmodern/post-structuralist) feminist and (Marxist) critical scholars. Though at times petty and unproductive, the publicly aired differences and ongoing interchanges between such scholars—commenced by Elizabeth Ellsworth's critique (1989) of critical pedagogy as a white, male discourse—has helped to articulate one of the central fissures in the field. That is, whether the struggle for educational equity is primarily cultural or economic. The fulcrum upon which the conflict turns is Marxist theory.

Advocates of liberal forms of critical pedagogy—postmodernists, post-structuralists, and (liberal/postmodern) feminists—are suspicious of marxism and indeed of any "grand narrative" that invokes the "masculinist voice" of abstraction and universalization (Lather 1998, 488). They reject the extension of what they view as positivistic macrotheories or "grand narratives of legitimation" in favor of a microtheory and politics that deals with the nature of "difference" (Lyotard 1984). The general cadence of such theories signals a movement away from the certainty and totalizing effects of grand narratives toward what Lather (1998, 488) refers to as "Jacques Derrida's 'ordeal of the undecidable' and its obligations to openness, passage and non-mastery." In such a theoretical space, writes Lather (1998, 495) "questions are constantly moving and one cannot define, finish, or close. . . . [It] is a praxis of not being so sure" (1998, 488). The aim of such postmodern/post-structural theories is to trouble and disrupt the masculinist or patriarchal presumptions of modernist theories and their universalizing projects, embracing instead a "praxis that moves away from the Marxist dream of 'cure, salvation, and redemption'" (Lather 1998, 495).

Insofar as they theorize against "certainty," postmodernists tend to advocate a negative pedagogy, one more identifiable by what it stands against than what it stands for. The discomfort with asserting any one affirmative and universal claim stems from a (postmodern) sense of the world as being "too complex, the range of views too wide, and the diversity of concerns too differentiated to imagine that there can, any more, be some simple unanimity of goals or interests that unites [us all]" (Shapiro 1995, 20). The implications of such a world for critical educators, according to Svi Shapiro, is to struggle "for a public discourse that privileges no one group of people; one that tries to speak to and include the experience, needs and hopes of a broad spectrum of people in our society" (1995, 32). In other words, postmodernists argue that the multiplicity of the millennial world necessitates a political imaginary that is as reflexive and indeterminate as the social imaginary.

As such it isn't that postmodernists reject the validity of grand narratives (e.g., the anticapitalist agenda of Marxist theories), but rather that they perceive them as too narrow and therefore insufficient for imagining a new social reality. As Shapiro writes: "[T]he politics that emerge from the fluidity and complexities of identity in contemporary America do not, it must be emphasized, negate those historically important struggles. . . . [O]ur goal is however, to offer an educational language—and later an agenda—that can be as inclusive as possible, to recognize the fullest possible range of human struggles and concerns" (1995, 29–30). In other words, postmodernists presume a "praxis of undecidability." That is, one that resists modernist impulses to privilege "containment over excess, thought over affect, structure over speed, linear causality over complexity, and intention over aggregate capacities" (Lather 1998, 497). In so doing, they seek to replace the "one right story" of universalist discourses with a "nonreductive praxis that calls out a promise of a practice on shifting ground" (Lather 1998, 497).

Despite the potential allure of theories that valorize difference and heterogeneity—particularly for peoples marginalized by the modernist project of white supremacy—not all critical scholars embrace the marriage of critical pedagogy to postmodern and post-structural theories. Marxist scholars have been especially critical of what they perceive as the abandonment of emancipatory agendas, in general, and of the struggle against capitalist exploitation, in particular. As McLaren (2003, 67) notes, in their effort to try to be everything to everyone, postmodern theorists have (re)cast the net of critical pedagogy so wide and so cavalierly that it has come to be associated with everything from "classroom furniture organized in a 'dialogue friendly' circle to 'feel-good' curricula designed to increase students' self-image." Moreover, insofar as postmodern and other progressive scholars have distanced themselves from the labor/capital problematic, they are construed by radical educators as advocating pro-capitalist forms of schooling. The central argument is that while post-al theories of education have undoubtedly advanced knowledge of the hidden trajectories of power, particularly within processes of representation and identity, they have been "woefully remiss in addressing the constitution of class formations and the machinations of capitalist social organization"

(Scatamburlo-D'Annibale and McLaren 2002, 4). In short, revolutionary theorists argue that postmodernism has been used to substitute the project of radical, social transformation with a politics of representation.

In the wake of the relentless march of capitalism, Marxist and other radical scholars view such a stance as grossly insufficient, if not negligent. They contend that to ignore the "totalizing effects" of capitalism and to reduce class to just another form of "difference" is to act as an accomplice to capitalist imperatives and desires. In other words, to remain "enamored with the 'cultural' and seemingly blind to the 'economic'" in this moment of late capitalism is not simply an act of ignoring, but one of complicity (Scatamburlo-D'Annibale and McLaren 2002, 4–5). It requires turning a blind eye to the roughly 2.8 billion people (nearly half the world's population) living on less than two dollars a day (McQuaig 2001, 27) and the 100 million people in the industrial world living below the poverty level (Scatamburlo-D'Annibale and McLaren 2002).[12] Radical educators view such statistics as clear indicators that the inherent contradictions of capitalism are "taking us further away from democratic accountability" and closer toward what "Rosa Luxemborg referred to as an age of 'barbarism'" (McLaren and Farahmandpur 2001, 277). Thus, from the vantage point of revolutionary critical scholars we do not simply need an education for equity and social justice, but rather an anticapitalist education for economic democracy.

Advocates of radical forms of critical pedagogy thus insist on a theory and praxis of schooling with an unabashed emancipatory intent, one that is future-centered and forward looking to a time when "wage labor disappears with class society itself" (McLaren 2003, 80). In accordance with these aims critical scholars have developed a "revolutionary critical pedagogy" (Allman 2001)—the synthesis of contemporary Marxist scholarship with a rematerialized critical pedagogy. Leading advocates of revolutionary critical pedagogy include Paula Allman (who penned the term), Peter McLaren, as well as Mike Cole, Terry Eagleton, Ramin Farahmandpur, Dave Hill, Jane Kenway, Helen Raduntz, Glen Rikowski, and Valerie Scatamburlo-D'Annibale. Others whose work has greatly influenced the formation of revolutionary critical pedagogy include Teresa Ebert, Paulo Friere, Martha Gimenez, Antonio Gramsci, Henry Giroux, Rosemary Hennessy, Chrys Ingraham, Karl Marx, and Ellen Meskins Wood.

While each of these scholars emphasizes different aspects of the discourse, they all remain committed to a core of abiding principles that formulate the foundation of revolutionary critical pedagogy: (1) to recognize that capitalism, despite its power, is a "historically produced social relation that can be challenged (most forcefully by those exploited by it)" (McLaren and Farahmandpur 2001, 272); (2) to foreground historical–materialist analysis that "provides critical pedagogy with a theory of the material basis of social life rooted in historical social relations" and assigns primacy to uncovering the structures of class conflict and the effects produced by the social division of labor (McLaren 2002, 26);[13] and, (3) to reimagine Marxist theory in the interests of the critical educational project. As McLaren and Farahmandpur write, "Marxist revolutionary theory must be flexible enough to reinvent itself . . . [and] is not set forth here as a universal truth but as a weapon of interpretation" (2001, 301–302).

Beyond the theoretical commitments of revolutionary critical pedagogy, some practical implications have also been established. In order to prepare students "to glimpse humanity's possible future beyond the horizon of capital" (Allman 2001, 219), McLaren and Farahmandpur (2001, 299) submit that revolutionary students and educators must "question how knowledge is related historically, culturally, (and) institutionally to the process of production and consumption," and ask: How is knowledge produced? Who produces it? How is it appropriated? Who consumes it? How is it consumed? With such questions formulating the base, McLaren (2003, xvii) defines the following foundational principles of revolutionary critical pedagogy that parallels Deborah Brandt's (1991) five pillars of popular education.[14]

1. A revolutionary critical pedagogy must be a *collective process*, that involves utilizing a Frierian dialogical learning approach.
2. A revolutionary critical pedagogy must be *critical*; that is, by locating the underlying causes of class exploitation and economic oppression within the social, political, and economic infrastructure of capitalist social relations of production.
3. A revolutionary critical pedagogy is profoundly *systematic* in the sense that it is guided by Marx's dialectical method of inquiry, which begins with the "real concrete" circumstances of the oppressed masses and moves toward a classification, conceptualization, analysis, and breaking down of the concrete social world into units of abstractions to get at the essence of social phenomena. It then reconstructs and makes the social world intelligible by transforming and translating theory into concrete social and political action.
4. A revolutionary critical pedagogy is *participatory*, involving building coalitions among community members, grassroots movements, church organizations, and labor unions.
5. A revolutionary critical pedagogy is a *creative process* incorporating elements of popular culture (i.e., drama, music, oral history, narratives) as educational tools to politicize and revolutionize working-class consciousness.

Whereas McLaren (2003) outlines the academic principles of revolutionary critical pedagogy, Allman (2001, 177–186) defines the more visceral, motivating principles or "vital powers" necessary in the struggle for social justice. McLaren (2002, 31) recounts these principles as those of:

mutual respect, humility, openness, trust and co-operation; a commitment to learn to "read the world" critically and expending the effort necessary to bring about social transformation; vigilance with regard to one's own process of self-transformation and adherence to the principles and aims of the group; adopting an "ethics of authenticity" as a guiding principle; internalizing social justice as passion; acquiring critical, creative, and hopeful thinking; transforming the self through transforming the social relations of learning and teaching; establishing democracy as a fundamental way of life; developing critical curiosity; and deepening one's solidarity and commitment to self and social transformation and the project of humanization.

Such principles are clearly relevant to American Indian students and educators and their need for pedagogies of disruption, intervention, affirmative action, hope, and possibility.

Insofar as the project for colonialist education has been imbricated with the social, economic, and political policies of U.S. imperialism, an education for decolonization must also make no claim to political neutrality, and engage a method of analysis and social inquiry that troubles the capitalist, imperialist aims of unfettered competition, accumulation, and exploitation. Beyond an approach to schooling that underscores the political nature of education, American Indian students and educators also require a praxis that enables the dismantling of colonialist forces. They need a pedagogy that cultivates a sense of collective agency, both to curb the excesses of dominant power and to revitalize indigenous communities.

These aims and imperatives of American Indian education not only illuminate the deep deficiencies of off-the-shelf brands of multiculturalism, which espouse the empty rhetoric of "respecting differences" and market synthetic pedagogies that reduce culture to the "celebration" of food, fad, and festivals, but also point to the relevance and necessity of critical pedagogies of indigenous education. Indeed, revolutionary critical pedagogy's conception of culture as conditioned by material forces and of schooling as a site of struggle offers great potential for indigenous peoples working toward pedagogies for self-determination.

AMERICAN INDIAN EDUCATION AND REVOLUTIONARY CRITICAL PEDAGOGY: TOWARD A NEW RED PEDAGOGY

In the end, though the history of American Indian education and, more broadly, the history of the relationship between the U.S. government and American Indian nations is often characterized as being one of cultural domination, a critical examination reveals the principal relationship as one of exploitation—that is, the imposed extraction of labor and natural resources for capital gain. For example, while the Indian Removal, Dawes, and Termination Acts can all be viewed as legislated attempts to destroy Indian *culture,* in the end they all provided greater access to Indian lands and resources and, as such, proffered the federal government a windfall in capital gains. Similarly, while manual labor and boarding schools attempted to extinguish Indian-ness by imposing culturally imperialistic curriculums, they also profited from child labor as well as helped to establish a permanent Indian proletariat.

Though the federal government is no longer as explicitly connected to schooling as it once was, exploitative relations between the U.S. government and American Indian nations persist. As such, the unambiguous anticapitalist aims of revolutionary critical pedagogy make it more applicable to the imperatives of American Indian education than liberal/progressive forms. That being said, there are significant points of tension between the structures of revolutionary theory and the concerns of American Indian schools and communities.

The central tension is that revolutionary theorists, like other Western scholars, often fail to consider, and thus, theorize, the fundamental "difference" of American Indians and their dual status as U.S. citizens and members of sovereign "domestic dependent nations." Indeed, the myriad implications of this basic failure form the foundation of each subsequent chapter in this book. For instance, in chapter 2, this tension is discussed in terms of the implications of Marxist pedagogies (still contingent on Western notions of democracy) for indigenous schools and communities. The question is, do Marxist pedagogies of emancipation sustain a geopolitical landscape any more receptive to the notion of indigenous sovereignty than capitalist pedagogies? In chapter 3, the failure of radical scholars to consider that even in the socialist-democratic imaginary, the end game remains human liberation: a profoundly anthropocentric notion, rooted in a humanist tradition that presumes the superiority of human beings over the rest of nature. In other words, both Marxists and capitalists view land and natural resources as commodities to be exploited, in the first instance, by capitalists for personal gain, and in the second by Marxists for the good of all.

In chapter 4, the tension is discussed in terms of its implications for the construction of American Indian subjectivity. Specifically, while the theorizations of feminist, postmodern, and post-structural scholars are essential to understanding the complex layers of American Indian subjectivity, their displacement of a "politics grounded in the mobilization of forces against the material sources of political and economic marginalization" is deeply problematic (Scatamburlo-D'Annibale and McLaren 2002, 7). Indeed, the historical–material realities of American Indian schools and communities require emancipatory pedagogies that retain clear and explicit emancipatory agendas. Finally, in chapter 5 the failure of "mainstream" feminists to recognize that most American Indian women view their lives as shaped, first and foremost, by the historical–material conditions of colonization and not some "universal" patriarchy is discussed. By insisting on gender as the primary conceptual framework from which to interpret inequality, such theorists not only blur the actual structures of power but also obfuscate feminism's implication in the projects of colonization and global capitalism. Thus, as previously stated, it is critical to question how the experiences and historical–material realities of indigenous peoples are reshaped and transformed when articulated through the epistemic frames of Western theory, whether liberal or revolutionary. As American Indian scholar and educator Greg Cajete (1994, 3) notes, Indian people must question the effects of contemporary educational theories on the collective cultural, psychological, and ecological viability of indigenous communities.

Further examination of the tensions and intersections between American Indian education and revolutionary forms of critical pedagogy unfolds in the subsequent chapters. This analysis takes seriously the assertions of McLaren and Farahmandpur who note, "no theory can fully anticipate or account for the consequences of its application but remains a living aperture through which specific histories are made visible and intelligible" (2001, 301). The quest for a new Red pedagogy is, thus, at base, a search for the ways in which American Indian education can be deepened by its engagement with critical educational theory and for critical theory to be deepened by Indian education. While a Red pedagogy privileges "revolutionary critical pedagogy" as a mode of inquiry, it does not simply appropriate or absorb its language and epistemic frames, but rather employs its vision as one of many starting points for rethinking indigenous praxis. The aim is "to diversify the theoretical itineraries" of both indigenous and critical educators so that new questions and perspectives can be generated (McLaren 2002, 29).

Finally, what distinguishes Red pedagogy is its basis in hope. Not the future-centered hope of the Western imagination, but rather, a hope that lives in contingency with the past—one that trusts the beliefs and understandings of our ancestors as well as the power of traditional knowledge. A Red pedagogy is, thus, as much about belief and acquiescence as it is about questioning and empowerment, about respecting the space of tradition as it intersects with the linear time frames of the (post)modern world. Most of all, it is a hope that believes in the strength and resiliency of indigenous peoples and communities, recognizing that their struggles are not about inclusion and enfranchisement to the "new world order" but, rather, are part of the indigenous project of sovereignty and indigenization. It reminds us that indigenous peoples have always been peoples of resistance, standing in defiance of the vapid emptiness of the bourgeois life.

This is the spirit that guides the ensuing engagement between critical theory and American Indian education. The hope is for a Red pedagogy that not only helps sustain the lifeways of indigenous peoples but also provides an explanatory framework that helps us understand the complex and intersecting vectors of power shaping the historical–material conditions of indigenous schools and communities. A logical place to begin this journey of understanding is at the point of "encounter," examining the various dimensions of conflict and contradiction between the sovereign peoples of the Americas and the colonizers, asking the question: Can democracy be built upon the bloody soils of genocide?

NOTES

1. I use the phrase "right to be indigenous" with the same intent and manner as it is used in the "Coolangatta Statement on Indigenous Peoples' Rights in Education." That is a right that embraces indigenous peoples' language, culture, traditions, and spirituality, including the right to self-determination.

2. Specifically, the Jesuits provided academic instruction in French language and customs, and vocational training in the areas of animal husbandry, carpentry, and handicrafts.

3. Perhaps as a reflection of the relegated role of Native Americans, the literature is replete with histories of Indian education. For example, see Szasz (1998; 1999), Reyhner and Eder (1989), and Fuchs and Havighurst (1972) among numerous other seminal articles.

4. According to Szasz (1999, 270), in 1819, the first year in which Congress voted for a fund for "civilization" of the Indian, total expenditures did not exceed $10,000; by 1880 congressional appropriations reached $130,000 and continued to rise exponentially through the following decade. Also, in addition to congressional funding, many treaties incorporated "provisions" for such educational and civilization purposes, with some incorporated at the request of tribes who began to associate survival with access to Anglo education (Reyhner and Eder 1992).

5. The Indian Removal Act (ch. 48, 4 *Stat.* 411), passed May 26, 1830, by the Twenty-first Congress, provided for "an exchange of lands with any of the Indians residing in any of the states and territories, and for their removal west of the river Mississippi." Passage of this act set in motion the mass forced relocations of the Creek, Cherokee, Choctaw, Chickasaw, and Seminole, among other Eastern nations. In the words of Churchill and Morris (1992), "the idea was to 'clear' the native population from the entire region east of the Mississippi, opening it up for the exclusive use and occupancy of Euroamericans and their Black slaves."

6. "Indian Commissioner Price on Civilizing Indians, October 24, 1881," in *Documents of United States Indian Policy*, as quoted in Spring (2001, 173).

7. Quoted in Joel Spring's *The American School: 1642–2000* (1997, 173).

8. U.S. House of Representatives, Committee of One Hundred, *The Indian Problem: Resolution of the Committee of One Hundred Appointed by the Secretary of the Interior and Review of the Indian Problem*, as cited in Noriega (1992).

9. Such reforms were implemented as part of the Indian Reorganization Act, commonly known as the Wheeler-Howard Act.

10. The termination policy was embodied in House Concurrent Resolution (HCR) No. 108, passed August 1, 1953. It reads:

> Whereas it is the policy of Congress, as rapidly as possible, to make Indians within the territorial limits of the United States subject to the same laws and entitled to the same privileges and responsibilities as are applicable to other citizens of the United States, and to grant them all of the rights and prerogatives pertaining to American citizenship; and Whereas the Indians within the territorial limits of the United States should assume their full responsibilities as American citizens; Now, therefore, be it Resolved by the House of Representatives (the Senate concurring), That it is declared to be the sense of Congress that, at the earliest possible time, all of the Indian tribes and the individual members thereof located within the States of California, Florida, New York and Texas, and all of the following named Indian tribes and individual members thereof, should be freed from Federal supervision and control and from all disabilities and limitations specially applicable to Indians. (U.S. Congress, 1953, 67 Stat. B132)

11. According to deputy project director of the task force Gaye Leia King, Dr. Charleston's version was not submitted as the final report as "the majority of the (task force) members believed that Mike's preliminary draft was too harsh and would offend most people." Moreover, she notes that the political climate of the times determined the "need to critically strategize on the content of the report" in order to ensure its release to the public (King 1994).

12. Even more problematic is the fact that casualties continue to mount. For example, in 2001 there were 1.3 million more poor people in the United States than in 2000.

13. Unlike other contemporary narratives that focus on one form of oppression or another, Scatamburlo-D'Annibale and McLaren (2002, 14) note that the power of historical materialism resides in "its ability to reveal (a) how forms of oppression based on categories of difference do not possess relative autonomy from class relations but rather constitute the ways in which oppression is lived/experienced within a class based system and (b) how all forms of social oppression function within an overlapping capitalist system."

14. These principles are articulated by Farahmandpur (2003, xvii) in the foreword of McLaren's seminal text *Life in Schools*.

Chapter Two

Competing Moral Visions: At the Crossroads of Democracy and Sovereignty

There is certainly a link between sovereignty and how Indian people have fared over the last two hundred years. As sovereignty has been infringed, Indian people have been harmed; as sovereignty has been reaffirmed they have recovered.

—Thurman Lee Hester

Our claims to sovereignty entail much more than arguments for tax-exempt status or the right to build and operate casinos; they are nothing less than our attempt to survive and flourish as a people.

—Scott Richard Lyons

The United States is a nation defined by its original sin: the genocide of American Indians. Everything afterward is just another chapter in the fall from grace. And, just as in the Christian creation story, there is no going back. No reparation, no penance, no atonement can ever erase the eternity of genocide. Life ever after will be forever stained by the attainment of this "carnal knowledge." Such an inauspicious beginning raises significant questions about the viability of this so-called democratic experiment: Is it possible for democracy to grow from the seeds of tyranny? Can the "good life" be built upon the deaths of thousands?

Indeed, from the time of "discovery" to the present day, the United States has continually and opportunistically defined and redefined the political status of Indian nations. This ephemeral approach has left in its wake a legislative quagmire that charts the fickle but deliberate path of American imperialism. This history not only maps the legacy of oppression but also stands as a testimony of fear. Specifically, American Indian tribes are viewed as an inherent threat to the nation, poised to expose the great lies of U.S. democracy: that we are a nation of laws and not random power; that we are guided by reason and not faith; that we are governed by representation and not executive order; and, finally, that we stand as a self-determined citizenry and not a kingdom of blood or aristocracy.

At virtually every turn in this country's development, its treatment of American Indians belies these democratic aims, revealing the tensions between indigenous struggles for tribal sovereignty and whitestream struggles for democracy. From the vantage point of the federal government, the very notion of tribes as internal sovereigns or "domestic dependent nations" is destabilizing to democracy, defying the principle of America as one people, one nation. Yet, from the perspective of American Indians, "democracy" has been wielded with impunity as the first and most virulent weapon of mass destruction.

Resisting the tides of history, this chapter begins from the premise that indigenous sovereignty does not oppose democracy. On the contrary, I maintain that sovereignty is democracy's only lifeline and ask the question: What is more destabilizing for the United States—full recognition of American Indian nations as internal sovereigns or the continued denial of this status? The playing field for this discussion is the terrain of American education, where "the production of democracy, the practice of education, and the constitution of the nation-state" have been interminably bound together (Mitchell 2001, 51).

Historically, schools arose amidst tensions instigated by "universal" (white, male) suffrage, the threat of cultural pluralism, and the increasing demand for an efficient and compliant workforce, irrevocably fusing the project of public education to the formation of the nation-state (Spring 2001). Specifically, schools were envisioned as ameliorative sites, as places where such tensions could be reduced through the broad dissemination of a "common culture." The "common culture" was, of course, a Eurocentric culture that further legitimated the ambitions of the nation-state—that is, the naturalization of white superiority, the maintenance of class domination, and propagation of Protestant morality (Spring 2000; Kaestle 1983; Katz 1968).

It wasn't until the early nineteenth century and the onset of mass immigration and industrialization that the heavy-handed assimilationist model of schools was broadly questioned. During this period, educational philosopher John Dewey worked to articulate and emphasize the relationship between schooling and the "centrality of the nation-building project" (Mitchell 2001). He believed that as democracy expanded the nation, so too should the nation expand democracy. As such, Dewey is typically revered as the grandfather of progressive education, working tirelessly to democratize schooling and align it with the pragmatic goals of a developing nation.

Like other whitestream thinkers, however, Dewey's vision for an educational system presumed the colonization of indigenous peoples. Indeed, as Katharyne Mitchell (2001, 53) reports, Dewey employed the term "frontier" as a "metonym" for the expansion of democracy. She maintains that once the literal spaces of the frontier were "closed," Dewey advocated the logical substitute: "the extension of democracy through the spaces of the body politic." He wrote: "At the present time, the frontier is moral, not physical. The period of free lands that seemed boundless in extent has vanished. Unused resources are now human rather than material" (Mitchell 2001, 53). Dewey's theories of democracy and nation-building were, thus, built upon the notion of ever-expanding possibility—the idea of the "frontier" as a "free space awaiting settlement and inviting possession and use" (Boydston 1987, 168).[1] As many critical scholars note, it is of great consequence that one of the premier philosopher's of American education advanced a decidedly Eurocentric view of democracy.

Indeed, it wasn't until after World War II that whitestream educators felt the need to address the growing discrepancy between democratic ideals and practice, particularly as they related to race. By the 1950s, liberal educators were championing the notion of cultural pluralism as the pathway to democracy, imbricating the constructs of national unity, multicultural harmony, and inclusion as the guiding principles of American education. Within this rhetoric, schools were to become an extension of the public sphere, a place where citizens could participate in the democratic project by coming together and transcending their racial, class, and gender differences to engage in "rational discourse."

Though an improvement on "traditional" models of schooling, progressive education retained an assimilationist agenda: to absorb cultural difference by "including" marginalized groups in the universality of the nation-state, advocating a kind of multicultural nationalism. Liberal scholars of this era reasoned "democracy could not 'live up to its faith in the potentialities of human beings' if all Americans were not allowed the opportunity to participate" and "by the same token, American bodies" could not represent or "operate as the new carriers of the national narrative of expandable democracy if they were segregated spatially and, disenfranchised legally, economically, and culturally" (Mitchell 2001, 54). Thus, in the postwar years, "the philosophy of American pluralism was framed as an extension of equality of opportunity to all members of the national body, particularly those disenfranchised by racism" (Mitchell 2001, 55). As it evolved, this general spirit informed educational theory and practice in the Progressive education movement of the 1930s and 1940s, the intergroup education movement of the 1950s, and the liberal multicultural movement from the 1960s to the present day.

Contemporary revolutionary scholars critique liberal models of democracy and education, naming their "politics of inclusion" as an accomplice to the broader project of assimilation. Specifically, they argue that such models ignore the historic, economic, and material conditions of "difference," conspicuously averting the whitestream gaze away from issues of power. Critical scholars therefore maintain that while liberal theorists may invest in the "theoretical idealism" of democracy, they remain "amnesiatic toward the continued lived realities of democratically induced oppression" (Richardson and Villenas 2000, 260).

In contradistinction to liberal models of democratic education, revolutionary scholars call attention to the "democratically induced" subjugation and oppression experienced by colonized and marginalized groups. Building upon this understanding, such scholars work to reenvision American education as a project "rooted in a radical and liberatory politics," replacing liberal conceptions of democracy with Marxist formulations of a *socialist* democracy (Richardson and Villenas 2000, 261). In so doing, they reconstitute democracy as a perpetually unfinished process, explicitly linked to an anticapitalist agenda. As such, the discourse on education and democracy is re-centered around issues of power, dominance, subordination, and stratification.

Within this context, "democratic pedagogies" are defined as those that motivate teachers, students, schools, and communities to make choices with "the overarching purpose of contributing to increased social justice, equality, and improvement in the quality of life for all constituencies within the larger society" (Fischman and McLaren 2000, 168). Henry Giroux (2001, 21) maintains that such democratic pedagogies contest the dominant views of democracy propagated by "neoliberal gurus"—where profit-making and material accumulation are defined as the essence of the good life. With these directives in mind, Peter McLaren and Ramin Farahmandpur (2001) articulate two fundamental principles of a revolutionary critical pedagogy: (1) to recognize the "class character" of education in capitalist schooling, and (2) to advocate a "socialist reorganization of capitalist society." Ultimately, they argue that education can never be "free" or "equal" as long as social classes exist (McLaren and Farahmandpur, 2001, 298).

While revolutionary theorists help articulate a more genuine democracy, they still theorize within a Western, linear political framework that essentially moves from Right to Left. For this reason José Barreiro (1995) notes that "in the context of jurisdiction and political autonomy, traditional Indigenous political processes are characterized by the struggle to stay independent of both left and right wing ideologies, political parties and their often sanguine hostilities."[2] Indeed, one would be hard pressed to convince the Miskitus, Sumus, Ramas, Quechua, and Aymara Indians of Central and South America that leftist or specifically Marxist-inspired regimes held any more promise for indigenous peoples than other Western governments (Richardson and Villenas 2001). Thus, while the Marxist, leftist, and socialist politics of revolutionary theorists expose important linkages between colonialist forces and capitalist greed, they do not, in and of themselves, represent emancipatory politics.

That is not to say, however, that revolutionary critical pedagogy cannot inform indigenous struggles for self-determination. On the contrary, its incisive critique of global capitalism raises important questions about sovereignty, the future of the nation-state, and the scope and purpose of American education. What effect do global forces impose on conceptions of sovereignty and citizenship? What is the relationship between education and democracy in the age of *trans*nationalism? And, how do we educate students for democracy in a nonnationalist (global) framework?

Such questions inform the analysis of this chapter, framing the discussion of tribal sovereignty in terms of how it has been challenged and impeded by this nation's rise to power. The first section examines the early tensions between American Indian tribes and the developing nation-state, charting the historical path of U.S. imperialism as it unfolds in three distinct eras: denial and dispossession, imposed democracy, and self-determination. It more specifically demonstrates how the early Christian myths of unity and hierarchy continue to deeply inform contemporary federal Indian law. The second section is an examination of how revolutionary critical pedagogy has successfully troubled dominant definitions of democracy, pluralism, and the nation-state by infusing the discourse with a cogent critique of global capitalism. It also asks whether the revolutionary construct of "democratization" carries any greater recognition of indigenous sovereignty. The chapter concludes in the third section with an analysis of the deep structures of democracy (i.e., sovereignty, self-determination, emancipation) and their embeddedness in Western political thought. More specifically, while a Red pedagogy agrees with revolutionary theorists that "democracy" (once sufficiently troubled and divested from its Western capitalist desires) can be reimagined as a viable concept for education, it de-centers it as the primary struggle concept. This repositioning distinguishes the aim of indigenization (sovereignty) from the aim of democratization (enfranchisement). In accordance with this distinction, a Red pedagogy is historically grounded in local and tribal narratives, intellectually informed by ancestral ways of knowing, politically centered in issues of sovereignty, and morally inspired by the deep connections among the Earth, its beings, and the spirit world.

THE HISTORY OF DEMOCRATICALLY
INDUCED OPPRESSION

Particularly with respect to a colonized people, the conqueror's law and legal doctrine permit him to peacefully and in good conscience pursue the
same goals that he formerly accomplished by the sword with imperialistic
fury.

—Robert A. Williams Jr.

But the "tides of history" did not wash away native tradition, the tides of
Europeans did.

—Thurman Lee Hester

The questions posed at the beginning of this chapter haunt the collective consciousness of America, forcing it to continually "reconcile its right to exist
with its own recognition of the injustices that gave it birth and nurtured it"
(Hester 2001, 210). Such dark family secrets compel denial and other manipulations of the truth. Indeed, whitestream articulations of the birth of a nation
begin by denying the existence of Native peoples, weaving a tale of "discovery" and "democracy." Indigenous articulations of the same history chronicle
a harrowing saga of conquest and dispossession. These narrations of seemingly parallel universes ultimately tell the same story—a people's struggle for
identity and power.

Denial and Dispossession: 1492–1830

Critical race theorist and American Indian legal scholar Robert A. Williams
maintains that the seeds of conquest were sown long before Columbus ever
stumbled upon these shores (1986, 224). He writes:

> The white man's theoretical engine of colonialism had built a five-hundred-year
> head of steam prior to reaching the station of its destiny in the virgin forest of
> America. Long-held notions of the rightness of subjugating non-Christian peo-
> ples for purposes of their remediation provided a firm roadbed upon which Eu-
> ropean colonial theory might claim its right-of-way in lands occupied by the
> "heathen" and "infidel" savages of the New World.

Under this doctrine the pope was virtually obligated to wage war against the
infidels, and divinely ordered to commence the Christian Crusades[3]
(Williams 1986, 239). As a matter of fact, Columbus, one of the church's
premier conquistadores, bore a cross on his breast as he ventured forth, con-
scripting "new" lands and new soldiers for Christ.

Whitestream history suggests that as democracy progressed and the state replaced the church as the central political structure, the idea of a crusade grew increasingly archaic. Williams (1986), however, argues that this "progression" is a myth and that "the universalized hierarchical structures of medieval thought" continue to define Western legal and political theory and therefore democratic praxis. Though effectively "de-sacralized," he maintains that the laws of our land retain the basic belief in Christian supremacy. Williams writes:

> Even with the passage of nearly half a millennium . . . European Christian laws remain as mediating universal precepts in judging normatively divergent cultures. Radical difference from the European justifies subjugation and remediation. All that has changed in this somewhat more secularized form of legal consciousness is that the secular king has assumed the hierarchical function formerly held by the Pope to license the spread of the Christian message into an infidel world of darkness and ignorance at perpetual war with Christianity. (1986, 246)

Williams cites the Second Charter of Virginia, written in 1606, as evidence of the saliency of Christian law. The charter reads:

> We, greatly commending, and graciously accepting of, their Desires for the Furtherance of so noble a Work, which may, by the Providence of Almighty God, hereafter tend to the Glory of his Divine Majesty, in propagating of Christian Religion to such People, as yet live in Darkness and miserable Ignorance of the true Knowledge and Worship of God, and may in time bring the Infidels and Savages, living in those Parts, to human Civility, and to a settled and quiet Government; Do, by these our Letters Patents, graciously accept of, and agree to, their humble and well-intentioned Desires. (cited in Williams 1986, 246)

Indeed, written hundreds of years after the Crusades, the charter retains the language of ordained supremacy.

In particular, the Christian "organizing myths" of unity and hierarchy[4] remain central to the discourse of Euro-American law wherein "assimilation" replaces "unity" and "appropriative conquest" replaces hierarchy (Williams 1986). Together such constructs form a totalizing ideology that presupposes the absorption of Indian nations within the "overriding superior sovereignty of the 'conqueror,' the United States" (Williams 1986, 256). This presupposition is evident throughout the early doctrines of federal Indian law, perhaps most obviously in the trifecta of Supreme Court decisions commonly known as the Marshall trilogy—a set of cases that established the legal template for virtually all future deliberations of tribal status.

The first case, *Johnson v. McIntosh,*[5] is viewed as the one most responsible for infusing the discourse and consciousness of American legal theory with intimations of white-Christian supremacy. The question before the Court in this decision was whether "a land title, given by the Indians under British supervision at an open public sale, was superior to a title derived from the United States through a sale by designated land officers" (Deloria 1992, 299).[6] The case was decided with Justice John Marshall citing the "Doctrine of Discovery" as the precedent by which the United States could levy the claim of "absolute dominion" over Indian territories. The infamous rhetoric of Marshall's opinion is worth quoting at length. He wrote:

> On the discovery of this immense continent, the great nations of Europe were eager to appropriate to themselves so much of it as they could respectively acquire. Its vast extent offered an ample field to the ambition and enterprise of all; and the character and religion of its inhabitants afforded an apology for considering them as a people over whom the superior genius of Europe might claim ascendancy. The potentates of the old world found no difficulty in convincing themselves that they made ample compensation to the inhabitants of the new, by bestowing on them civilization and Christianity. . . . But, as they were all in pursuit of nearly the same object, it was necessary, in order to avoid conflicting settlements, and consequent war with each other, to establish a principle, which all should acknowledge as the law by which right of acquisition, which they all asserted, should be regulated as between themselves. This principle was, that discovery gave title to the government by whose subjects, or by whose authority, it was made, against all other European governments, which title might be consummated by possession.[7]

Thus, through the invocation of the language and logic of medieval papal bulls, Marshall argued that "discovery" bestowed title, reducing the legal claim of tribes to their own lands to a mere "right of occupancy." This "finding" established the enduring "landlord–tenant relationship" that persists today between the federal government and Indian tribes.[8]

Given that the so-called Doctrine of Discovery became the primary basis for all U.S. claims to indigenous lands, the most remarkable aspect of the Marshall opinion is perhaps the unremarkable manner in which it was both unfurled and accepted. One would expect, even by the standards of nineteenth-century democracy, that the invocation of fifteenth-century doctrines of Christian supremacy by a Supreme Court justice would be viewed as an act of sedition, especially since the nation was concurrently struggling to maintain the "wall of separation" between church and state.

Even more telling was that while the United States invoked Old-World logic and Europe's Law of Nations, the Old World itself was moving away from the kind of imperialism where "discovery" ordained exclusive title. Specifically, Europe was grappling with the aftereffects of the French Revolution and the raising of class consciousness. At minimum the revolution portended the demise of the Old World, ruled by tradition, blood-right, and fixed social status. Hence, the irony; as Europe democratized, the United States was busy creating a legal foundation by which "future acts of genocide" could "proceed upon a rationalized basis" (Williams 1986, 256). Specifically, the Johnson decision set the stage, if not opened the floodgates, for future, unremitting attempts to dispossess Indians of their land. Indeed, five years after *Johnson v. McIntosh*, Andrew Jackson was elected president after running on a platform of Western expansion. Less than a month after the presidential election, the Georgia state legislature passed an act to add Cherokee territory to a number of Georgia counties (Deloria and Lytle 1983). Within the first two years of Jackson's term in office the Indian Removal Act was passed, providing the impetus for the second case in the Marshall trilogy.

In the *Cherokee Nation v. Georgia*[9] the tribe filed a petition with the Supreme Court asking for protection against the vulgar transgressions enacted by the state of Georgia. The question before the Court was whether the Cherokee Nation had the right to sue the state of Georgia in federal court (a right typically reserved for "foreign states"). In his opinion, Justice Marshall determined that the Cherokee did not have the right to sue a state because the status of Indian tribes was neither the same as "a state nor a foreign nation within the meaning of the Constitution" (Deloria and Lytle 1983, 29). They were, rather, "domestic dependent nations" existing "in a state of pupilage" to the United States, their relationship resembling "that of a ward to his guardian." Prygoski (1998, 3) maintains that the Court's characterization of the tribes as "domestic dependent nations" not only established the basis for the "trust" relationship between the United States and Indian tribes but embedded the implication that tribes, as "wards," were "incompetent to handle their own affairs."

One year later, in the last case of the Marshall trilogy, the Court addressed the question of whether the state of Georgia could impose criminal penalties on non-Indians. In *Worcester v. Georgia*,[10] the Court ruled in favor of the white petitioner, determining that the state had no authority over persons and actions within the boundaries of the Cherokee Nation and that state laws did not extend into Indian Country. While on one level the decision affirmed indigenous sovereignty, it also reaffirmed that tribes fell under the "protection" of the federal government, institutionalizing the plenary power[11] of Congress over Indian nations.

Nevertheless, Jackson—the consummate Confederate—was incensed by the Worcester decision and its apparent intrusion into states' rights. Upon hearing the decision, he is reported to have exclaimed, "John Marshall made his decision: now let him enforce it" (Deloria and Lytle 1983, 33). Shortly afterward, in an unprecedented display of executive power, Jackson refused to comply with the Court's ruling and ordered the removal of Eastern Indians to Western reservations, sending thousands of Cherokees to their death on the Trail of Tears. If there existed any doubt, this single act of executive defiance confirmed the imperialist power of the presidency, exiling tribes to their eternal status as *colonies* of the United States and reinforcing the notion of "democracy" as a white man's game. Indeed, the aggregate effect of centuries of subjugation and Marshall's own assertions of white supremacy through the Doctrine of Discovery created a climate wherein state and federal officials felt free to overlook and deny indigenous rights without any fear of retribution. This basic asymmetry of power has ensured the interminability of the battle for indigenous sovereignty against the forces of democracy.

Imposed Democracy: 1871–1968

In 1871, shortly after the Civil War, the war-weary nation formed the Indian Peace Commission to resolve lasting hostilities with the Plains Indians. Despite the commission's efforts, however, members of the House of Representatives objected to some of the terms of peace and in a display of surreptitious power, attached a rider to an appropriations bill that brought an end to treaty making (Deloria 1992, 293).[12] Thus, with the ostensible "democratic" power of the vote, Congress terminated Indians' rights to negotiate treaties as well as extinguished their only direct means of federal representation. Though the United States continued to negotiate with tribes up through the 1950s, the end of treaty making signified a marked decline in the sovereignty of Indian nations, placing them in a state of political limbo—no longer recognized as capable of formally treating with the federal government, yet remaining separate nonconstitutional political entities (Wilkins and Lomawaima 2001).

More significantly, the end of treaty making ushered in the era of imposed democracy where the difference of American Indian nations as "distinct, independent, political communities"[13] was slowly erased through the "democratic" processes of incorporation and enfranchisement. In other words, for American Indians "democratization" was a homogenizing force. At times it was imposed with reckless abandon, as in the Major Crimes Act (1885),[14] the General Allotment Act (1887), and the Termination Act (1953).[15] At other times, it was dressed up in the language and spirit of "enfranchisement," as in the Indian Citizenship Act (1924), the Indian Reorganization Act (1934),[16] and the Indian Civil Rights Act (1968).[17] The net effect of such legislation was a severe attenuation of tribal sovereignty, with allotment levying the most devastating strike.

Like other policies in federal Indian law, the groundwork for allotment was laid in the seventeenth and eighteenth centuries when "the narrative tradition of tribalism's incompatibility with white civilization generated a rich corpus of texts and legal arguments for dispossessing the Indian" (Williams 2000, 103). It was during this era when John Locke penned his theory of property, essentially arguing that uncultivated land, by definition, was not "owned" and therefore free for individual appropriation. He more specifically argued that it was "individual labor upon the commons" that removed land "out of the state of nature," beginning private property. This difference of "labor" is what Locke used to establish "the cultivator society's" privilege "to deny the wasteful claims of tribalism to the underutilized 'common' of America" (Williams 2000, 103). He wrote:

> There cannot be a clearer demonstration of any thing, than several Nations of the Americans are of this (the value added to land by labor) who are rich in Land, and poor in all Comforts of Life; whom nature having furnished as liberally as any other people, with the materials of Plenty, i.e. fruitful soil, apt to produce in abundance, what might serve as food, rayment, and delight; yet for want of improving it by labor, have not one hundredth part of the Conveniences we enjoy; and the king of a large fruitful territory there feeds, lodges, and is clad worse than a day labourer in the England. (cited in Williams 2000, 103–104)

Nearly two hundred years later, U.S. senator and self-proclaimed "friend of the Indians" Henry Dawes advocated for the reallocation of tribal lands based on Locke's theory of property, by then a firmly established marker of civilized peoples and democratic organization. In short, he argued that the normative "deficiency" of tribalism constituted proper grounds for the dissolution of tribal lands. In a speech to the Senate, Senator Dawes articulated the essential differences between "tribal" and "civilized" societies:

> The head chief told us that there was not a family in the nation that had not a home of its own. There is not a pauper in that nation, and that nation does not owe a dollar. It built its own capitol, in which we had this examination, and built its schools and hospitals. Yet the defect of the system was apparent. They have got as far as they can go, because they hold their land in common. It is (the socialist writer) Henry George's system, and under that there is no enterprise to make your home better than that of your neighbors. There is no selfishness, which is at the bottom of civilization. Till these people will consent to give up their lands, and divide them among their citizens so that each can own the land he cultivates, they will not make much progress. (cited in Hendrix 1983, 32)

Based on this reasoning Dawes and his counterparts convinced Congress that Indian "civilization" could be achieved only through teaching Indians the

virtues of private property.[18] In 1887 the General Allotment Act was inaugu-
rated, "authorizing the President, at his discretion, to survey and break up the
communal land holdings of tribes" into individual allotments (Wilkins and
Lomawaima 2001, 108).

Depending upon various criteria[19] established by the Dawes Commission
and the BIA, individual (male) tribal members received 160-, 80-, or 40-acre
land parcels.[20] Allotments were held in trust by the government for a period
of twenty-five years, during which time "the Indian owner was expected to
learn proper business methods" (Deloria and Lytle 1983, 8). At the end of the
trust period,[21] the allottee received free and clear title to their land and was
"awarded" U.S. citizenship, which placed him under state jurisdiction. Finally, after all allotments were dispensed, the balance of reserve territory was
declared "surplus" and opened to non-Indian homesteading, corporate utilization, and/or incorporation into national parks and forests (Churchill and
Morris 1992). As a result of the Dawes Act, the aggregate Indian land base
was legally reduced from approximately 138 million to 48 million acres or by
nearly two-thirds[22]; tribes were divested of their right to determine their own
membership; specious identification procedures created various "classes" of
Indians, commencing enduring divisions between "full-bloods," "mixed-
bloods," "traditional," and "assimilated" Indians; and, the trust doctrine was
severely violated.

Arguably more devastating than the direct implications of allotment was
the ensuing conflation of dispossession with citizenship. The decimation of
collective land holdings and renouncement of tribal membership were explicit preconditions for citizenship. Indeed, at the zenith of allotment, naturalization ceremonies involving the explicit repudiation of tribal ways and ac-
ceptance of the "civilized" life were commonplace. For example, some
ceremonies required the Indian-citizen-to-be to take a final symbolic shot of
his bow and arrow and to then place his hands on a farmer's plow.[23]

Such ceremonies clearly linked the act of becoming a citizen to the performance of cultural suicide, requiring Indians to demonstrate proper submission to the superior norms of patriarchy, husbandry, private property, and
the nuclear family.[24] Rather than improving status, citizenship merely conscripted Indians to (whitestream) civil, criminal, and inheritance laws, without extending the same civil rights of other citizens. The process of imposed
democracy was thus manifold with the denigration and dismantling of both
Indian cultural *and* economic systems. Specifically, it was believed that only
after the cultural difference of tribalism was erased could the economic project of assimilation succeed. In other words, after assimilated Indians were effectively placed under the jurisdiction of the state, so too could their lands and
resources.

Ironically, the sweeping intentions of the Dawes Act contributed as much to its own downfall as it did to that of tribal rights. As Vine Deloria Jr. and Clifford M. Lytle (1983, 10) observe, "difficulties in interpretation arose . . . so that by the first decade of the [twentieth] century it no longer resembled a national policy but an ad hoc arrangement [due to] the numerous exceptions and exemptions that had been attached to it." The incoherent method of implementation weakened the overall impact and, as a result, the Dawes Act never became the panacea or final solution to the "Indian problem" that the government anticipated. In 1924, the Indian Citizenship Act was passed as a "clean-up measure" to the Dawes Act, imposing U.S. citizenship on all American Indians not previously naturalized. The unilateral imposition of citizenship (re)incited both collective and individual resistance among Native peoples. For instance, the entire Grand Council of the Six Nations (Iroquois Confederacy) declined U.S. citizenship, stating in a letter to the president that "they were not then, had never been, and did not intend to become American citizens"(Deloria 1985, 18). Though Indians gained some measure of protection from citizenship status, it ultimately forced greater incorporation, providing the rationale for even more pernicious attacks on tribalism such as the Indian Reorganization and Termination Acts. While the Indian Reorganization Act (IRA) put an end to allotment policies (providing for the purchase of new lands and the restoration of some unallotted lands), virtually all provisions were contingent upon a tribe's pledge to "reorganize"—to adopt Western-style constitutions, to form and elect tribal councils, and to implement a variety of economic development plans (e.g., Western conservation measures, community and educational loan programs).

Thus, the net effect of the IRA was that it dramatically increased federal supervision over Indian nations. As Hauptman (1992, 328–329) notes, "even when the majority of an Indian nation valued the opportunity to rebuild . . . many viewed the increased federal supervision as . . . [an] unpleasant trade-off." Indeed, there is ample evidence that reorganization was primarily fueled by the growing desire to gain credible access to tribal resources. Specifically, the establishment of puppet governments provided federal officials and their corporate accessory's increased access to Indian resources, paving the way for the future control and appropriation of Indian lands.[25]

The next marked rise in state power over Indian Country came in the 1950s, otherwise known as the "termination era" after the official federal policy of that time (Wilkins and Lomawaima 2001, 208). As previously discussed, "termination" referred to the U.S. government's decision to officially sever (terminate) federal benefits and support services to certain tribes, bands, and California rancherias, forcing the dissolution of their reservations (Wilkins and Lomawaima 2001, 209). The act effectively abrogated all federal government to tribal government relations, passing authority over to the states and violating the federal government's own constitutionally mandated trust responsibilities.[26]

Despite the numerous violations of their rights, Indians did not immediately involve themselves in civil rights issues as they arose in the early 1960s. On the contrary, they worked hard to distinguish themselves from other minorities so as to prevent further conflation of their issues and status with that of other marginalized groups. Nevertheless, when the Indian Civil Rights Act (ICRA) was surreptitiously attached to the Fair Housing Act (1968), Indians suddenly found themselves deeply enmeshed in civil rights rhetoric and law. Though the ICRA fettered state jurisdiction over Indian affairs (enhancing sovereignty), it represented an overall diminishment in tribes' abilities to self-govern.

Specifically, it greatly restricted the power of tribal court judges by re-making the entire judicial system "in the White man's image" (Deloria 1983, 213). Even more damaging than the direct assault on the powers of tribal judges was the collateral damage of the ICRA. Deloria (1983, 213) writes:

[Before the ICRA] [t]raditional Indian society understood itself as a complex of responsibilities and duties. The ICRA merely transposed this belief into a society based on rights against government and eliminated any sense of responsibility that the people might have felt for one another. Granted, many of the customs that made duties and responsibilities a serious matter of individual action had eroded badly in the decades since the tribes had agreed to move onto the reservations, the impact of the ICRA was to make these responsibilities impossible to perform because the act inserted the tribal court as an institution between the people and their responsibilities. People did not have to confront one another before their community and resolve their problems; they had only to file suit in tribal court. [Thus while] the Indian Civil Rights Act [is] understood by most people as a major step in the fulfillment of Indian self government . . . was it what Indians really wanted?

As articulated by Deloria, the ICRA merely exacerbated the existing "class" divisions among Indians (i.e., traditional versus assimilated) initially enacted by the Dawes Act. These divisions took on greater significance as traditional Indians fought to retain what was left of tribal governance structures while assimilated Indians sought the power and protection of "democracy." These growing tensions played out in the national spotlight in the infamous siege at Wounded Knee. While the siege was depicted as a "civil war" among the Oglala, it was clearly a battle between traditional peoples (representing seventy-five different nations) and whitestream forces embodied in agents of the FBI and BIA.

Though the occupation of Wounded Knee is an extreme manifestation of intratribal divisions, Deloria contends that it symbolizes the conflict that rages in all Indian communities—one typically characterized as Indian versus Indian but is ultimately about the psychosocial, economic, and political effects of colonization (a.k.a. "democratization").

On the other hand, while the ICRA policies of imposed democracy significantly depreciated Indian sovereignty, they continued to deal with Indians on a federal level, de facto conceding their status as tribal peoples and "domestic dependent nations." This de facto concession of sovereignty kept alive the possibility of self-determination. Indeed, the decade came to a close with the publication of "Indian Education: A National Tragedy—A National Challenge" (the Kennedy report), a comprehensive report that addressed the multitude of issues facing Indian Country. Among other things, the Kennedy report finally brought a strong congressional voice to Indian concerns, bolstering hope for the coming era.

Self-Determination: 1970–Present

In 1970, in an address to Congress, President Nixon promised "self-determination without termination," stating more specifically that "every Indian community wishing to do so should be able to control its own Indian schools" (AIPRC 1976, 111). Later that same year, promises were also made to transform the BIA "from a management to a service organization" (AIPRC 1976, 117). Such professions intimated that 1970 would be a "turning point in Indian affairs" (AIPRC 1976; Fuchs and Havighurst 1972; Lomawaima and McCarty 2002; Szasz 1999). Indeed, the post–civil rights ethos, given voice in the Kennedy report, led to the passage of the Indian Education Act in 1972 and the Indian Self-Determination and Education Assistance Act in 1975, two of the most significant pieces of legislation aimed at establishing indigenous control.

Among other things, the Indian Education Act of 1972 aimed to increase Indian participation and control over Indian education by allowing more direct access to operating funds (Deloria and Lytle 1984). Unfortunately, since the act was based on hearings conducted a decade prior (for the Kennedy report), several of its provisions assumed conditions that no longer existed while others "solved" problems already being addressed by the Office of Economic Opportunity and other agencies (Deloria and Lytle 1983). Furthermore, while the act defined a national policy for Indian education, it evidenced "the same basic flaws as previous poverty legislation" (Deloria and Lytle 1983, 219). That is, instead of offering a new and comprehensive organization of Indian educational programs, it simply amended existing structures to include "an Indian component."

Still, the legislation put Indian educational concerns on the congressional radar screen, laying the groundwork for passage of the Indian Self-Determination and Education Assistance Act three years later. This legislation authorized tribes not only to initiate *new* educational programs but also to determine the level of tribal participation in existing programs. At long last, it appeared that American Indians had the freedom and legislative support to exercise educational self-determination.

The promise of Indian-controlled education was, however, mixed. First, years of colonization left tribes with little experience and knowledge of how to construct a Native educational system. As such, few of the "new" programs significantly deviated from the established whitestream norm. The other major challenge to innovation was funding. Specifically, promises of self-determination did little to change the fact that responsibility for funding remained divided among the Department of Education, Congress, and the BIA.

Despite the stumbling blocks, however, there were, by 1978, thirty-four indigenous community-controlled schools (Lomawaima and McCarty 2002, 291). The shining example among them was the Rough Rock Demonstration School, uniquely created through a contract between the Office of Economic Opportunity, the BIA, a tribal trustee board, and a locally elected school board (Lomawaima and McCarty 2002, 290). Regardless of their success, however, community schools became just another option on the growing menu of Indian education. So while Indians theoretically controlled education through their own tribal schools, Indian students (and resources) remained dispersed among BIA, mission, and public schools, greatly limiting the possibility of a truly self-determined, Indian-controlled educational system.

While tribes were the beneficiaries of many programs instituted under the new policy of "self-determination,"[27] Deloria and Lytle (1984, 216) maintain that, "When the dust finally clears . . . [people] will realize that the progress of the sixties and seventies was purchased at an enormous price." That price, according to the authors, is the fact that Indians were forced "to pose as another American domestic minority" in order to benefit from national social welfare legislation. This observation captures the quintessential dilemma of Indian peoples, that is, to "pose" as domestic minorities and secure civic benefits at the price of absorption, or to claim their distinction as sovereign peoples and "domestic dependent nations," risking continued subjugation for cultural integrity.[28]

Summary

As delineated thus far in this chapter, the deep structures of American democracy and its attendant institutions, including schools, have been designed for the express purpose of extinguishing tribalism. As argued by Williams, the Christian myths of unity and hierarchy have been transposed to federal Indian law. Specifically, unity under God has been replaced by unity under the nation-state, and the hierarchy of the church by that of the federal government. As a result, tribal peoples have been significantly divested of the traditional organizational structures and knowledge necessary to create and sustain truly self-determined, indigenous systems of governance and education. Such a history leaves significant questions at the turn of the twenty-first century. First and foremost, how can schools—which are deeply embedded in the exhaustive history of colonization—be reimagined as sites of indigenous sovereignty and self-determination?

It is evident from this discussion that liberal models of democracy, "founded upon discourses and practices of structural exclusion," have given rise to liberal models of education that are deeply inadequate to the need of American Indian students (McLaren 1997, 294). They have been especially failed by the liberal project to tie "multiculturalism" to democracy. Though advocated as a "democratic" model premised on the incorporation of all peoples and values, "multiculturalism" operated in a homogenizing way, centered on unifying all peoples in the nation-state. Within this model, "diversity" could be expressed only within the preexisting, hegemonic frames of the nation-state, reading democracy as "inclusion." As Mitchell explains, "Historically, liberal practitioners have 'generously' attempted to include members of the nation who have been disenfranchised legally and culturally. . . . Yet this inclusion springs from the premise that Western liberalism is not only a superior philosophical foundation but also that its institutional application in realms such as education is good for everyone" (2001, 69).

Such logic fails to account for those who represent the "constitutive outside."[29] That is, peoples who can "never participate fully or unproblematically as democratic citizens of the nation because they are always already located outside of it" (Mitchell, 2001, 70). Moreover, in the "generous" rhetoric of inclusion it is patently unacceptable for groups to "step outside the discourse and argue for separateness" as a *more advantageous* location for their own cultural survival and the good of the nation (Mitchell, 2001, 70). The history of indigenous peoples clearly illustrates this limitation of liberal democracy. Indeed, the tragedies of American Indian history epitomize the degree to which "separateness"—expressed as a desire to step outside the "multicultural" project and sustain a different notion of the "good life"—is viewed as antithetical to the precepts of democracy.

In contrast, revolutionary critical theorists recognize the political importance of struggling over the meaning and definition of democracy, creating a much-needed space for examining the tensions between the political projects of sovereignty and democracy. In addition, they push the boundaries of democracy even further, raising questions about the relevancy of nationhood in this age of transnationalism and global capitalism. Critical theorists maintain that the forces of global imperialism are paving the way for a world "increasingly divided between those who enjoy opulent affluence and those who live in dehumanizing servitude and economic misery" (Scatamburlo-D'Annibale and McLaren, 2003, 148).

According to the Human Development Report (1998), 100 million people worldwide live below the poverty line (16.5 percent of which are Americans), 37 million are unemployed, 100 million are homeless, and nearly 200 million have a life expectancy of less than sixty years—and, these statistics refer to the world's richest nations. For revolutionary theorists, such data not only "charts the perilous course of history" but is also a retreat from democracy (McLaren 2003, 31). As such, Native scholars perceive their central task as challenging the rule of capital and engaging the process of "democratization"—a term that stresses the idea that democracy is an unfinished process (McLaren and Farahmandpur 2001, 295, 307). By defining such goals, revolutionary educators represent a significant departure from the liberal projects of democracy and education.

SOVEREIGNTY AND NATIONALISM IN A TIME OF GLOBALIZATION: REVOLUTIONARY CRITICAL PEDAGOGY AND INDIGENOUS SELF-DETERMINATION

As distilled by history, the quest for sovereignty is as indissolubly tied to issues of land as whitestream conceptions of democracy are tied to issues of property.[30] Indeed, ever since *Johnson v. McIntosh* imposed the Western concept of "title" on Native common land, the struggle for Indian sovereignty has centrally entailed the reassertion of indigenous concepts of land over whitestream claims of property. For American Indians, the process of "democratization" therefore necessitates the unpacking of established assumptions regarding the relationship between (individual) labor, property, citizenship, and nationhood; what Troy Richardson and Sofia Villenas (2000, 268) identify as a critique of "assumed democracy."

Moreover, given the inexorable ties between land and sovereignty, sovereignty and citizenship, and citizenship and the nation-state, one of the most glaring questions for tribes in the twenty-first century is how the acceleration of *trans*national forces (i.e., globalization) impact these relations.[31] From the perspective of indigenous peoples, globalization, or the so-called new imperialism (when did the "old" imperialism desist?), simply imposes upon a broader sector of the whitestream world what it has imposed on indigenous peoples since the time of invasion (i.e., the buying and selling of human lives as commodities). The second key question, then, is whether a revolutionary socialist politics also envisages the "new" social order as unfolding upon occupied land?

Land versus Property

While revolutionary theorists advocate a "socialist commitment to (the) egalitarian distribution of economic power and exchange and a mutually beneficial division of labor" (McLaren and Farahmandpur 2001, 306), I question: How does the "egalitarian distribution" of colonized lands constitute greater justice for Indigenous peoples? In other words, if the emancipatory project begins with the assumption of the "finished" project of indigenous colonization, how is that liberatory for American Indians? Thus, while revolutionary scholars rightly challenge the inherent inequalities of capitalist society, the metaphors of power, exchange, and labor remain tied to whitestream notions of property.

The failure to problematize the issue of (colonized) land is perhaps the major deficiency of Marxist and other Western-centric politics—traditional or revolutionary. Indeed, Karl Marx premised the very formation of human subjectivity on the rational regulation of the relationship with nature (land). In his words, "Freedom . . . can only consist in socialized men . . . rationally regulating their interchange with Nature, bringing it under their common control, instead of being ruled by it as by the blind forces of Nature" (Marx 1977, 820).

In this context, Indians can be seen only as primitive deviants from the whitestream norm, and tribes as immature precursors to the nation-state. Engels writes: "However impressive the people of this epoch appear to us, they are completely undifferentiated from one another; as Marx says, they are still attached to the navel string of the primitive community. The power of this primitive community had to be broken, and it was broken" (Engels 1972, 8). Indeed both Marx and Engels perceived the fate of tribes as essentially "doomed," destined to be absorbed by the more powerful organization of class-based societies.

In contradistinction, contemporary Marxist and revolutionary theorists readily acknowledge the aporias of early marxism. As such, they do not advocate the use of Marxist theory as a "universal truth" but as a "weapon of interpretation" (McLaren and Farahmandpur 2001, 302). They also lament the dogmatism that has often accompanied socialist regimes, striving instead for a socialism that rethinks and re-creates democracy through the development of a collective or communal concept of rights and responsibilities (McLaren 2000, 192). In the end, revolutionary critical educators insist on a praxis that operates beyond politics and is committed to the transformation of all social practices that lay at the root of human exploitation and misery. Clearly, this leaves room for a reconceptualization of the relationship between land (property) and democracy.

McLaren, in particular, seems to demonstrate a clear understanding of the unique positionality of indigenous peoples:

> Indigenous peoples have the right to speak their own truth without seeking permission to narrate from those who would continue to oppress them. Not only must voices of Indigenous agents be sounded, but also they must be granted opportunity to be heard without their voices being bent into the decibels most harmonious to Western ears by imperializing systems of regulation and the gross postulates of the colonial attitude. In creating the "new agent" of socialism, the preferential option is to listen to the voices that are sounded from the standpoint of the oppressed. (2000, 200–201)

McLaren's desires for a "new agent" of socialism rejects the fundamentalist Marxist notion that "all societies naturally lead to state formation or that state formation is even a social desire" (d'Errico 1997). He also clearly rejects the profoundly racist and Eurocentric notion that tribal or non-state societies have only two choices: (1) to assimilate to the state system, giving up self-definition; or, (2) maintain self-definition and be denied a place in the world's legal and political order (d'Errico 1997). On the contrary, he seems to recognize that the self-determination of indigenous peoples will be attained "through means other than those provided by a conqueror's rule of law and its discourses of conquest" (Williams 1986).

On the Question of Globalization

While revolutionary theorists recognize that indigenous societies have endured centuries of violence in the name of state sovereignty (bringing into question the validity of the nation-state itself), they do not succumb to the neoliberal logic that the state itself has given way to the forces of globalization.[32] Rather, they argue that such a position is an "ideological façade," camouflaging the purposeful exaggeration of global capitalism "as an indefatigable power that apparently no nation-state has the means to resist or oppose" (Mclaren and Farahmandpur 2001, 284). Revolutionary theorists suggest that this deceitfully and erroneously purports that "capitalism no longer needs the protection of the nation-state" (McLaren and Farahmandpur 2001, 284).

Indeed, the neoliberal notion that the state has become irrelevant or rendered impotent by the politics of globalization is absurd when interfaced with the current political realities faced by indigenous peoples. Consider, for example, one of the most recent assertions of the power and aggression of the state. On July 14, 2003, the governor of Rhode Island ordered a police raid on the Narragansett Indian reservation for selling tax-free cigarettes. State police and government officials descended upon the Narragansett Indians with dogs, bully-whips, and guns, assaulting a pregnant woman and cuffing Chief Sachem Matthew Thomas as they invaded sovereign territory. Since such transgressions are nearly daily occurrences in Indian Country, there can be no denying the power, oppression, and "absolute dominion" of the state over indigenous nations.

Though the precepts of a revolutionary critical pedagogy and Red pedagogy agree on the enduring relevancy of the nation-state and its role as an agent of capital, they diverge in their ideas of how these relations should reconceptualize democracy. Revolutionary theorists insist that the only way to manage diversity is through the practice of "genuine democracy," which is only possible in a socialist economy (McLaren and Farahmandpur 2001, 295)—that is, by foregrounding class struggle. For example, McLaren and Farahmandpur (2001, 20) write: "Following Samir Amin, we believe that it is important to resist attempts to devalue the term 'democracy' by vulgarizing it and domesticating it as synonymous with community development that 'negates the unity of the human race in favor of races, communities, cultural groups and the like.'" In this context "democracy" remains a universalist construct that not only is reconceptualized along class lines but also is indivisible along the lines of race, gender, and sexuality. Indeed they explicitly argue against "dividing up democracy" into such "isolated communities" (McLaren and Farahmandpur 2001, 295).

The history of federal Indian law clearly demonstrates that it was not indigenous peoples who "divided up democracy" but rather democracy that divided them. Indigenous peoples and their political organizations predate both capitalism and (whitestream) democracy's advent on this continent. Thus, contrary to the assertions of revolutionary theorists, capitalist (exploitative) modes of production are not predicated on the exploitation of free (slave) labor but rather, first and foremost, premised on the annihilation of tribalism. The privileging and distinguishing of "class struggle" and concomitant assertion of capitalism as *the* totality underestimates the overarching nature of decolonization—a totality that places capitalism, patriarchy, white supremacy, and Western Christianity in radical contingency. This tension alone necessitates an indigenous reenvisioning of the precepts of revolutionary theory, bringing them into alignment with the realities of indigenous struggle.

INDIGENIZATION: TOWARD A POLITICS OF ENSOULMENT

Just as the imperialist project of imperialism was political, intellectual, and spiritual, so too must be the project of indigenous self-determination. Politically, indigenous peoples need to question whether sovereignty and the quest for nationhood are indeed useful constructs for their respective communities: Why should indigenous peoples choose models of thinking, organization, and development that were used to destroy non-state societies? Intellectually, the question becomes whether a system of education initially designed to serve the needs and interests of the nation-state can be reconstituted to meet the needs and desires of tribal peoples. Spiritually, as noted by d'Errico, "the most pressing problem for Indigenous self-determination is 'the problem' of "the people" (d'Errico 1997). In other words, centuries of colonization have left indigenous peoples with a profound crisis of meaning, compelling us all to ask the question: What does it mean to be a people, a tribe, a community? What does it mean to be indigenous?

To Be or Not to Be Sovereign

Several scholars have questioned the appropriateness of the concept and aim of "sovereignty" for indigenous peoples (Alfred 1999; Deloria and Lytle 1984; d'Errico 1997; Lyons 2000; Richardson and Villenas 2000; Cheyfitz 2003). Deloria and Lytle (1984, 15), for example, dismiss "self-government" as an idea that "originates in the minds of non-Indians" who have reduced traditional ways to dust, or at least believe they have, and "now, wish to give, as a gift, a limited measure of local control and responsibility." Taiaiake Alfred (1999, 57) similarly maintains that even though the discourse has served as an "effective vehicle for indigenous critiques of the state's imposition of control," sovereignty is an inappropriate goal because it implies a set of values and objectives that are "in direct opposition to those found in traditional indigenous philosophies" (i.e., respect, harmony, autonomy, and peaceful coexistence). Specifically, Alfred argues that traditional indigenous nations, which had "no absolute authority, no coercive enforcement of decisions, no hierarchy, and no separate ruling entity," stand in sharp contrast to the dominant understanding of the state (Alfred 1999, 2). Therefore, some indigenous scholars argue that the retention of sovereignty as the goal of indigenous politics signifies the ultimate concession to the forces of assimilation.

In other words, by accepting the "fiction of state sovereignty," Native communities negate their own power, determining that they will forever and only remain in a dependent and reactionary position to the state (Alfred, 1999, 59). And, within this hegemonic framework, progress toward social justice can only be inadequate and marginal. "In fact," writes Alfred (1999, 57), "progress] will only be tolerated by the state to the extent that it serves, or at least does not oppose" its own interests. He asks us to consider the issue of land claims as a case in point. While the pursuit of land claims is viewed in liberal–progressive circles as "a step in the right direction," unless the colonialist structures undergirding such claims are simultaneously dismantled, the resolution of such claims can be defined only by relations of domination. For instance:

> In Canada . . . the ongoing definition of . . . "Aboriginal rights" by the Supreme Court . . . is widely seen as progress. Yet even with the legal recognition of collective rights to certain subsistence activities within certain territories, indigenous people are still subject to state control . . . [and] must . . . meet state-defined criteria for Aboriginal identity . . . to gain access to these legal rights. . . . [So] to what extent does the state-regulated "right" to food-fish represent justice for people who have been fishing on their rivers and seas since time began? (Alfred, 1999, 58)

As such, Alfred insists, "to argue on behalf of indigenous nationhood within the dominant Western paradigm is self-defeating" (Alfred, 1999, 58).

On the contrary, the task is to detach and *dethink* the notion of sovereignty from its connection to Western understandings of power and relationships and base it on indigenous notions of power.[33] Building upon Deloria's expressed need for Native communities to "blend the inherent power of tradition with the skills required to manage the institutions of modern society," Alfred suggests altering indigenous patterns of governance to achieve four basic goals (Alfred, 1999, 136):

1. Structural reform: Legitimating Native governments by rejecting electoral politics and restructuring to accommodate traditional decision making, consultation, and dispute resolution. This requires minimizing dependency on non-Indian advisors by educating and training community members, enhancing capacities of self-management.
2. Reintegration of Native languages: Insofar as language serves as a symbol and source of nationhood, Native languages should be made the official language of their communities—"the one in which leaders speak, the processes of government are conducted, and the official versions of all documentation are written." In order to achieve this objective, communities must make teaching the Native language "a top priority."
3. Economic self-sufficiency: Movement toward this goal requires the expansion of Native land bases and increased control over the "economic activities" within Indian country. Additionally, communities must focus on

"business and technical education" as a means of enhancing human resources.

3. Nation-to-nation relations with the state: "A political space must be created for the exercise of self-determination. Native communities must reject the claimed authority of the state, assert their right to govern their own
   territories and people, and act on that right as much as their capacity to do
   so allows.

Data collected by the Harvard Project on American Indian Economic Development[34] seems to support the validity of Alfred's rubric. Contrary to whitestream
models of economic development, the Harvard studies indicate that "resources"—natural, human, educational, or capital—do not ensure success.
Rather, successful tribes are those that adopt a broad "nation-building" approach. That is, they recognize "development" as primarily "a political problem," focusing attention on building institutional foundations, strategic thinking, and informed action. Indeed, the most successful tribes tend to be those that
first assert sovereignty and then "back up their assertions of self-governance
with the ability to govern effectively" (Cornell and Kalt 1998, 195).

Like Alfred, Stephen Cornell and Joseph P. Kalt (1998) find that meaningful sovereignty is dependent upon the development of effective governing institutions, that is, governments with stable institutions and policies, fair and
effective processes of dispute resolution, effective separation of politics from
business management, a competent bureaucracy, and cultural match.[35]
Among these criteria, the notion of "cultural match" is perhaps the most intriguing. It suggests that one of the most important factors in Native governments' establishment of legitimacy and power is the degree to which they
match the people's ideas of authority and leadership—whether those ideas are
"traditional or not."

Above all, Cornell and Kalt argue that successful nation-building is dependent upon the "federal acknowledgment of tribal sovereignty as not only a legal but practical matter" (1998, 208). In other words, beyond the typical legal
and historical arguments for sovereignty, Cornell and Kalt insist that the most
powerful argument for tribal sovereignty is "the simple fact that it works"
(1998, 209). They write: "Nothing else has provided as promising a set of political conditions for reservation economic development. Nothing else has produced the success stories and broken the cycles of dependence on the federal
system the way sovereignty, backed by capable tribal institutions, has done"
(Cornell and Kalt 1998, 209). Of course, fear of Native empowerment and autonomy is likely the very reason the federal government continues to question
and fetter sovereignty. From the vantage point of the whitestream, empowered
"domestic dependent nations" still equal a threat to democracy.

From the vantage point of indigenous nations, however, "sovereignty" remains a central lifeline.[36] Sovereignty is critical if for no other reason than because, simply stated, "people who believe they have little or no control over their destiny as a people" will despair (Wunder 1996, 14). Building upon this notion, Thurman Lee Hester (2001) discusses sovereignty in terms of the psychological construct of "locus of control." As a theory pertaining to individuals, the notion of "locus of control" refers to one's perception of life's turns and events. Specifically, individuals with an "internal locus of control" feel that they command outcomes in their lives (i.e., success and failure is a function of one's ability and effort) and, as a result, demonstrate higher levels of self-esteem, self-efficacy, and general satisfaction (Seligman 1990). Contrarily, those with an "external locus of control" do not feel that they determine outcomes in their lives and, as a result, evidence low levels of self-esteem, self-efficacy, and life satisfaction. Additionally, "some research suggests that what underlies the internal locus of control is the concept of 'self as agent,'"[37] that is, the degree to which is self-determining is an effect of one's ability to realize themselves as a source of agency (McCombs 1991)

Hester employs the notion of locus of control to help explain the psychological state of Indian nations. He argues that the cycles of despair and poverty impacting many nations are, in part, a function of their perceived lack of agency. This perception is fed by the actuality that the sovereignty of Indian nations is indeed externally controlled. As Hester notes, "the specter of federal control" always looms with the threat of "plenary power," hanging like a perpetual cloud over all Indian nations. It is highly plausible that the constancy of this threat has the same impact on a nation that it does on an individual, inviting despair, hopelessness, and self-destruction.

As such, John Wunder (1997) implores that our examinations of U.S. Indian policy should be guided by a vigilance for laws and policies that take control of Indian life out of their hands and, furthermore, that "directly harmful policies should . . . be examined not only for their harm, but as further [cause] for an external locus of control among Native Americans" (Wunder 2001, 14). The argument for sovereignty as a measure of insuring an internal locus of (tribal) control is among the most persuasive. Especially for students and educators who must first believe in the future stability of their nations, if they are to exercise agency on an individual level.

Intellectual and Pedagogical Sovereignty

However the question of sovereignty is resolved politically, there will be significant implications on the intellectual lives of indigenous peoples, particularly in terms of education. Lyons (2000, 452) views the history of colonization, in part, as the manifestation of "rhetorical imperialism," that is, "the ability of dominant powers to assert control of others by setting the terms of debate." He cites, for example, Marshall's use of "rhetorical imperialism" in the *Worcester v. Georgia* opinion: "'[T]reaty' and 'nation' are words of our own language, selected in our diplomatic and legislative proceedings . . . having each a definite and well-understood meaning. We have applied them to Indians, as we have applied them to other nations of the earth. They are applied to all in the same sense" (Lyons 2000, 452). Indeed, throughout the history of federal Indian law terms and definitions have continually changed over time. Indians have gone from "sovereigns" to "wards" and from "nations" to "tribes," while the practice of treaty making has given way to one of agreements (Lyons 2000, 453). As each change served the needs of the nation-state, Lyons argues that "the erosion of Indian national sovereignty can be credited in part to a rhetorically imperialist use of language by white powers" (2000, 453).

Thus, just as language was central to the colonialist project, it must be central to the project of decolonization. Indigenous scholar Haunani-Kay Trask writes, "Thinking in one's own cultural referents leads to conceptualizing in one's own world view which, in turn, leads to disagreement with and eventual opposition to the dominant ideology" (1993, 54). Thus, where a revolutionary critical pedagogy compels students and educators to question how "knowledge is related historically, culturally and institutionally to the processes of production and consumption," a Red pedagogy compels students to question how (whitestream) knowledge is related to the processes of colonization. Furthermore, it asks how traditional indigenous knowledges can inform the project of decolonization. In short, this implies a threefold process for education. Specifically, a Red pedagogy necessitates: (1) the subjection of the processes of whitestream schooling to critical pedagogical analyses; (2) the decoupling and dethinking of education from its Western, colonialist contexts; and, (3) the institution of indigenous efforts to reground students and educators in traditional knowledge and teachings. In short, a Red pedagogy aims to create awareness of what Trask terms "disagreements," helping to foster discontent about the "inconsistencies between the world as it is and as it should be" (Alfred 1999, 132).

Though this process might state the obvious, it is important to recognize the value and significance of each separate component. I wish to underscore that the project of decolonization demands students to acquire not only the knowledge of "the oppressor" but also the skills to dismantle and negotiate the implications of such knowledge. Concurrently, traditional perspectives on power, justice, and relationships are essential, both to defend against further co-optation and to build intellectual solidarity—a collectivity of indigenous knowledge. In short, "the time has come for people who are from someplace Indian to take back the discourse on Indians" (Alfred 1999, 143).

Spiritual Sovereignty

Finally, it needs to be understood that sovereignty is not a separatist discourse. On the contrary, it is a restorative process. As Warrior suggests, indigenous peoples must learn to "withdraw without becoming separatists"; we must be "willing to reach out for the contradictions within our experience" and open ourselves to "the pain and the joy of others" (Warrior 1995,124). This sentiment renders sovereignty a profoundly spiritual project involving questions about who we are as a people. Indeed Deloria and Lytle (1984, 266) suggest that indigenous sovereignty will not be possible until "Indians resolve for themselves a comfortable modern identity."

This resolution will require indigenous peoples to engage the difficult process of self-definition; to come to consensus on a set of criteria that defines what behaviors and beliefs constitute acceptable expressions of their tribal heritage (Deloria and Lytle 1984, 254). While this process is necessarily deliberative it is not (as in revolutionary pedagogies) limited to the processes of "conscientizacão."[38] Rather, it will remain an inward- and outward-looking process, a process of reenchantment, of ensoulment, that is both deeply spiritual and sincerely mindful.

The guiding force in this process must be the tribe, the people, the community; the perseverance of these entities and their connection to indigenous lands and sacred places is what inherits "spirituality" and, in turn, the "sovereignty" of Native peoples. As Lyons notes, "rather than representing an enclave, sovereignty . . . is the ability to assert oneself renewed—in the presence of others. It is a people's right to rebuild its demand to exist and present its gifts to the world . . . an adamant refusal to dissociate culture, identity, and power from the *land*" (Lyons 2000, 457). In other words, the vision of tribal stability—of community stability—rests in the desire and ability of indigenous peoples not only to listen to each other but also to listen to the land. The question remains whether the ability to exercise spiritual sovereignty will continue to be fettered, if not usurped, by the desires of a capitalist state intent on devouring the land.

NOTES

1. It is also worth noting that Dewey made this rhetorical shift at the same time Germany and Japan were engaging in their own "imperialist land grabs," compelling the United States to differentiate its own hegemonic and genocidal practices (Mitchell 2001, 54). Spring (2001, 231), moreover, notes that Dewey's pontifications on the need for democratic education came at a time when "racist laws and court rulings were supporting segregation and cultural genocide," yet set up his laboratory school without any consideration of these pressing issues. While Dewey was not a

segregationist, Spring (2001, 231) maintains that his noteworthy "lack of participation in fighting educational deculturalization" was another "form of racism."

2. Barreiro cites the recent massacres of indigenous peoples in Brazil and Peru (by right- and left-wing elements, respectively) as evidence for the ongoing relevance of this struggle.

3. According to the *Catholic Encyclopedia* (www.new.advent.org, June 29, 2003), "since the Middle Ages, the meaning of the word 'crusade' has been extended to include all wars undertaken in presence of a vow, and directed against infidels (i.e., Mohammadeans, pagans, heretics) or those under the ban of excommunication." By this definition, most historians identify the age of the Crusades as expanding from approximately 1095–1270, with some including the fourteenth-century crusade and the Ottoman invasion.

4. Of central importance in the Christian narrative is the belief that all men are *united* in Christ and *hierarchically* ordered under God and his representatives.

5. *Johnson v. McIntosh*, 21 U.S. (8 Wheat) 543 (1823).

6. Given its significant impact on federal Indian law, it is ironic that no tribe or individual Indian was a party in the case. Rather, the plaintiff and defendant were two white males, both of whom laid claim to the same tract of land; one purchased directly from the Piankeshaw and Illinois Indian nations and the other from the U.S. government (Williams 1986).

7. *Johnson v. McIntosh*, 572–573.

8. As "the ultimate landlord," the United States not only established its power to terminate the "tenancy" of its Indian occupants and control and regulate land use, but also institutionalized the notion of *federal responsibility* (Deloria and Lytle 1983, 26–27).

9. *Cherokee Nation v. Georgia*, 30 U.S. (5 Pet.) 1 (1831).

10. *Worcester v. Georgia*, 31 U.S. (6 Pet.) 515 (1832).

11. Wilkins and Lomawaima (2001, 14) provide a cogent critique and explanation of plenary power. They write, "Plenary power as an *exclusive* power of Congress (not a power of the executive or judicial branches of the federal government, nor a power of the states) is a constitutionally based and appropriate understanding of the term. *Preemptive* plenary power, when Congress preempts the action of states toward tribes, is also constitutionally based and appropriate. *Unlimited and absolute* plenary power over tribes is insupportable, however."

12. The bill declared: "[H]ereafter, no Indian nation or tribe within the territory of the United States shall be acknowledged or recognized as an independent nation, tribe or power with whom the United States may contract by treaty: Provided further, That nothing herein contained shall be construed to invalidate or impair the obligation of any treaty heretofore lawfully made and ratified with any such Indian nation or tribe" (Ch. 120, 16 *Stat.* 544, 566, now codified as House Resolution 25 U.S.C. 71).

13. *Worcester v. Georgia*, 31 U.S. (6 Pet.), 515, 559–560 (1832).

14. The Major Crimes Act, passed by Congress in 1885, granted the federal government criminal jurisdiction over major felonies committed in Indian Country — crimes that previously fell under tribal jurisdiction. Congress reasoned that criminal

jurisdiction was too important to leave to Indians' "primitive" sense of justice (Deloria and Lytle 1983, 11).

15. The economic impact of World War II required the federal government to get spending under control, not only by reducing expenditures but also by reducing the overall size of government. Within this ethos, social and economic forces brought together a "strange coalition of forces," calling for the unilateral termination of federal assistance to Indians. Conservatives lobbied for a traditional "small government" approach, arguing that once Indians were "freed from government" they would experience "a more profound reawakening"; and liberals, anxious to "release America's racial minorities from the onerous burden of discriminatory legislation," became self-proclaimed advocates for Indian "freedom" (Deloria and Lytle 1983, 17). Such lobbying led to the passage of House Concurrent Resolution 108 (67 Stat. B 132) or the Termination Act (1953). As a result of the act, the federal government was able to sever its trust responsibilities for 109 Indian nations or, elements thereof, all of which were "terminated," losing federal assistance, federal recognition, and, ultimately, their status sovereign nations (Churchill and Morris 1992). As such the impact of termination was profound and indeed "terminal" for many of the nations involved.

16. The ostensible aim of "reorganization" was to "minimize the enormous discretion and power exercised by the Department of Interior and the Office of Indian Affairs" and to decentralize by moving the source of power from Washington to the reservations (Deloria and Lytle 1983, 14). Though the move to recognize tribal governance was a step forward in the overall project of Indian sovereignty, the structures of Indian governance had been so decimated by centuries of oppression that much of what could have been restored under "the IRA climate of cultural concern" was never realized (Deloria and Lytle 1983, 15). Instead, the erosion of traditional forms of governance created a void that the federal government was more than happy to fill with the structures and modes of democracy. As a result of reorganization, "familiar cultural groups and methods of choosing leadership" gave way to "elected" tribal councils and new "constitutions" that utilized "standardized by-laws" and other methods of American democracy that "viewed people as interchangeable and communities as geographical marks on a map" (Deloria and Lytle 1983, 15). The IRA ultimately proved to be another vehicle for whitestream ways to infiltrate Indian communities.

17. It was not until the passage of the Indian Civil Rights Act (1968) that the particular concerns of American Indians were addressed by legislation. While the act prohibited states from assuming jurisdiction over Indian Country without first securing tribal consent, Churchill and Morris (1992) argue that the act did more to further bind Native governments to the federal system. They argue that, "in effect, it made native governments a functional part of the federal system . . . affording Indian people only constraints upon their sovereignty rather than any of the constitutional protection of basic rights and other benefits" (Churchill and Morris 1992, 16).

18. Wilkins and Lomawaima (2001, 108) write, "policymakers had such abiding faith in the deeply transformative powers of America's Protestant mercantile culture that they believed the mere prospect of private property ownership would magically transform tribal Indians into ruggedly individualistic, Christian, self-supporting yeoman farmers."

19. The Dawes Commission, together with the BIA, determined tribal membership based on the specious notion of blood-quantum, recording results in official "tribal rolls." This process was, at best, racist, and, at worst, a gross violation of the sovereign right of each nation to define its own citizenry. Further implications of this process, particularly on issues of identity and membership, are discussed in chapter 3.

20. More specifically, land was allotted according to the following formula: (1) To each head of family, one-quarter of a section; (2) To each single person over eighteen years of age, one-eighth of a section; (3) To each orphan child under eighteen years of age, one-eighth of a section; and, (4) To each single person under eighteen now living, or who may be born prior to the date of the order of the president directing an allotment of the lands embraced in any reservation, one-sixteenth of a section (U.S. 24 Stat: 388–391).

21. The secretary of the interior also had full discretion to either shorten or extend the trust period, dependent upon his determination of any individual Indian's "competency" to manage his or her own affairs. Graduation from an Indian school, possession of a sufficient degree of white blood, and/or demonstration of "self-sufficiency" were all considered legitimate grounds for determining "competency" (Wilkins and Lomawaima 2001, 283, note 20).

22. Though the motivation for Dawes is typically understood as being predominantly *cultural*, the economic incentives were equally compelling. Specifically, federal policymakers were under significant pressure from corporate elites and state politicians hungry for Indian land and resources.

23. For the full text of such a ceremony and "oath of allegiance" see Deloria (1971, 141–143).

24. In some instances citizenship required the adoption of other "civilized habits" such as English literacy and proof that the family was "self-supporting" (Witkin 1995, 367).

25. For instance, the American Indian Policy Review Commission (the Abourezk Commission) found that while 595, 157 acres of land were restored under the IRA, that government agencies condemned 1,811,010 acres of Indian land during this same period (American Indian Policy Review Commission, *Final Report,* vol. 1 [Washington, D.C.: U.S. Government Printing Office, 1977], 309–310).

26. In response to whether termination abrogated treaties between the United States and Indian nations, Senator Arthur V. Watkins (R-UT), one of the leading proponents of termination, argued: "[I]t is doubtful now, from here on, that treaties are going to be recognized where the Indians themselves have gone to the point where they have accepted citizenship in the United States and have taken advantage of its opportunities. So that question of treaties, I think, is going to largely disappear" (Senate Comm. on Labor and Public Welfare, 91st Cong., 1st Sess., 4).

27. Deloria and Lytle (1984) report that millions of dollars were invested in reservation communities during this time period, establishing, among other things, industrial parks, resort motels, recreation areas, new homes, tribal courts, and Indian-controlled schools.

28. The most glaring example of how "minority status" served to oppress Indians is termination. Proponents of this legislation argued that "tribes should have no standing at all, as governments, and that Indian individuals should be distinguished by nothing more than a particular 'ethnicity,' rather than a treaty-based political relationship with the United States" (Wilkins and Lomawaima 2001, 219).

29. The idea of a "constitutive outside" refers to the fact that in order for a nation's territorial borders and narratives to "work" as containing devices for a given population, there must be another population that is forever located outside and in opposition to it. In other words, in order to constitute a 'we' there must be a 'they'" (Mitchell, 2001, 74, note 40).

30. Cheyfitz defines the indigenous conception of land as "the inalienable foundation for the processes of kinship," distinguishing it from "property" which is defined by relations of alienability (2003, 224).

31. *Globalization* can be defined succinctly as "the unfolding of capitalism's central contradiction: the separation of the worker from the product of her labor" and more elaborately as the "recent acceleration in the international flow of goods, information, capital, culture, and people," further characterized by "a shifting mode of capitalist organization to one of greater flexibility and by the structural reorganization (on a global scale) of systems of production, consumption, and exchange" (Mitchell 2001, 59). By extension, Ebert determines that the politics of globalization is ultimately about "[t]he continuous privatization of the means of production; the creation of expanding markets for capital and the creation of a limitless market of highly skilled and very cheap labor in order for capitalists to maintain their competitive rate of profit" (cited in McLaren and Farahmandpur 2001, 284). This rapid "internationalization of capitalist relations of exploitation" moves revolutionary educators to "decouple" democracy from capitalist development, insisting instead on a pedagogical practice that is tied to a larger socialist political project (McLaren and Farahmandpur 2001, 284, 296).

32. In effect, theories of globalization continue Marx's thesis on the natural evolution of civilization: that clan gives way to tribe, tribe to gens, gens to nation-state, and nation-state to transnational entity.

33. Indigenous notions of power are defined as being rooted in concepts of respect, balance, reciprocity, and peaceful coexistence.

34. The Harvard Project on American Indian Economic Development is a research project operated under the auspices of the Kennedy School of Government at Harvard University and the Udall Center for Studies in Public Policy at the University of Arizona. At the time of this writing, the project was being directed by Dr. Manley Begay (Harvard), Professor Stephen Cornell (Arizona), and Professor Joseph P. Kalt (Harvard).

35. "Cultural match refers to the match between governing institutions and the prevailing ideas in the community about how authority should be organized and exercised" (Cornell and Kalt 1998, 201).

36. I use the term "sovereignty" here not in reference to whitestream definitions of self-government but to a general sense of tribal control.

37. "Agency" in this context refers to the degree to which we believe our thoughts control our actions, and, more specifically, that we can positively affect our beliefs, motivation, and academic performance (North Central Regional Educational Laboratory, December 2003, www.ncrel.org).

38. "Conscientizacão" is a Freirian term that refers to the development of critical social consciousness, wherein dialogue and analysis serve as the foundation for reflection and action.

Chapter Three

Red Land, White Power

We [environmentalists] admire Indians so long as they appear to remain what we imagine them and desire them to be: ecologically noble savages symbolizing a better way of life than we ourselves find it practical to live. We respect their traditions so long as they fit our preconceived notions of what those traditions should be.

—O. Douglas Schwartz

Through our conceptual domestication of nature, we extinguish wild otherness even in the imagination. As a consequence, we are effectively alone, and must build our world solely of human artifacts. The more we come to dwell in an explained world, a world of uniformity, a world without the possibility of miracles, the less we are able to encounter anything but ourselves.

—Neil Evernden

Everyone remembers the image of the stoic, long-black-haired, tough-skinned Indian shedding a single tear as he witnessed the horror of highway littering. The tagline "Keep America Beautiful" graced the televisions screen as the camera zoomed in for a close-up, tracing his tear as it traveled through the crevasses of his brown, weathered cheek. Perhaps more than any other, this image etched the notion of the Indian-as-ecologically-noble-savage into the consciousness of modern Americans, marking (and marketing) the age-old juxtapositions of primitive and modern, red man and white man, nature and civilization. Though this advertisement ran over thirty years ago, such significations are still employed by contemporary environmentalists working to call attention to the unsustainability of a consumerist culture. The idea is to disrupt the drone of colonialist destruction by importing the image and ostensible message(s) of peoples who have seemingly escaped the cages of modernity[1] (i.e., American Indians).

In their crusade to conscript Indians to "the cause," environmental educators, activists, and scholars have relegated the discourse on Indians and the environment to questions of identity and authenticity. Academic debates commence as if the central concern of Indian communities is whether they live up to the whitestream fantasy of Indians living in harmony with nature. Indeed, scholars have made careers out of advocating a position on this matter. Some advocate the stereotype of the Indian-as-ecologically-noble-savage upholding "real Indians" as peoples with an inherent "at-oneness" with nature (e.g., Bierhorst 1994; Bowers 2003; Durning 1992; Hughes 1983; Piacentini 1993). Within this camp, an exoticized sense of indigenous peoples is perpetuated; Indians are held in fascination for their unspoiled, pure, and harmonious relationship with the land. On this viewpoint environmental scholar Douglas Buege (1996, 76) remarks:

> To many in the environmental movement, a way of life such as that lived by the allegedly ecologically noble savage sounds ideal. When we compare our way of life with the images associated with the [ecologically noble savage] we do not find ourselves to be . . . responsible people. . . . We persevere be dreaming that there are people out there living the lives that we believe we should live, possible leaders for us to follow. We cling to the hope that our way of life is not inevitable.

In opposition to this point of view are scholars who question the existence and veracity of the "ecologically noble savage," advocating instead the idea of Indian as "miscast ecologist" (e.g., Edgerton 1993; Gill 1987; Guthrie 1971; Krech 1999; Martin 1978).[2] They argue that there is and never has been any fundamental difference between the ways "Indians" and "whites" think about and relate to nature. Furthermore, such scholars maintain that historically the only differences have been in population size and access to destructive technologies. In support of their claims, they cite incidents of overgrazing, overkilling, and other forms of environmental "abuse" to evidence that Indians were just as environmentally destructive as other peoples. In the end they assert that all humans, regardless of culture, are essentially the same, all of us enacting the common destiny of the human race—domination over the natural world.

While the debate over the environmental purity of indigenous peoples constitutes a marginally interesting academic exercise, it ultimately diverts attention away from the more pressing issue of exploitation—both cultural and environmental. Specifically, exploitation manifests through the marginalization and exclusion of the voices of indigenous peoples, through the singular focus on the "White man's Indian," and through the preoccupation with "pre-contact" Indians.

As "anti-Indian" environmentalists pour through archival materials, searching for documentation of waste and overkill, and "pro-Indian" environmentalists obsess over ancient Indian myths, rituals, and traditions for windows into the magical and mystical powers of the Native eco-guru—the contemporary struggles of Native peoples are virtually ignored. One of the primary effects of the contemporary environmental debate is that it obfuscates the real environmental struggles of indigenous peoples (access to and control over tribal lands and resources) and the real source of environmental destruction (colonization and the ill-effects of its consuming habits).[3] In a time when the dominant patterns of belief and practice are being widely recognized as integrally related to the cultural and ecological crises, the need for understanding other cultural patterns as legitimate and competing sources of knowledge is critical. In this context, the voices of indigenous and other non-Western peoples become increasingly vital, not because such peoples categorically possess any kind of magical, mystical power to fix countless generations of abuse and neglect, but because non-Western peoples and nations exist as living critiques of the dominant culture, providing critique-al knowledge and potentially transformative paradigms.

This chapter thus aims to reframe the discourse on Indians and the environment, regrounding it in issues of tribal sovereignty and self-determination while reengaging a thorough examination of the ongoing affects of colonization. It also operates on the assumption that central to the development of a Red pedagogy is an analysis of the daily threats imposed by a capitalist society and consumerist culture intent on appropriating indigenous lands and resources. In terms of the Indian-as-ecologically-noble-savage debate, I take the position that the stereotype functions mainly as a homogenizing trope that negates the complexity of indigenous peoples. I also reject the whitestream logic that "we are all the same," arguing that it not only denies the "difference" of indigenous cultures and belief systems, but also tacitly reduces indigenous peoples to the status of whites-without-technology. Finally, I (re)assert American Indians as twenty-first-century peoples and nations struggling against the global capitalist forces of encroachment, appropriation, commodification, and colonization, and for further recognition of tribal sovereignty.

The relevance of critical pedagogy in constructing such a Red pedagogy is apparent. Its explanatory frameworks provide ample context for understanding the power dynamics of colonialist forces. For example, a critical analysis of the "crying Indian" campaign reveals it as an exercise in capitalist exploitation. The ad was actually the dreamchild of corporate executives in the bottling industry launching a preemptive strike to derail legislation aimed at mandating greater corporate environmental responsibility. The intention was to undermine the proposed legislation by launching a media campaign that shifted the burden of responsibility for environmental damage from corporate America to individuals. The tagline "People start pollution, people can stop it," said it all (Cronin and Kennedy 1997). The frameworks of critique, thus, not only help to draw important connections between global capitalist forces and the struggles of colonized peoples but also to reveal the deep inadequacies of an environmental discourse centered on image, identity, and authenticity.

While critical pedagogy provides the tools for constructing a more potent and overtly challenging critique of the colonialist project, it should be evident by now that it remains deeply informed by Western theory. Specifically, critical theories of education operate on the assumptions of individualism, rationality, anthropocentrism, and progressivism, which contribute not only to the cultural crisis but also to the ecological crisis. The central concern here is whether critical pedagogy's Western roots preclude it from disrupting the structures of a colonialist discourse dependent on the continued robbing of nature.

As such, this chapter begins with an examination of the "the deep structures of colonialist consciousness" and its implications for schooling. Next, some of the landmark cases documenting the struggle of American Indian tribes to gain access to and control over their own resources are described. The precepts of revolutionary critical pedagogy are then examined for the ways in which they both disrupt and sustain the ecological crisis. Specifically, I ask whether the new critical democracy envisioned by revolutionary scholars presumes the construction of nature as "serviceable other."[4] Included in this analysis is an examination of contemporary environmentalist critiques, which aim to keep alive the "White man's Indian," fetishizing indigenous cultures and their ecological nobility. The problematics of this discourse are discussed in terms of its failure to acknowledge the complexities of contemporary indigenous struggles and the colonialist context within which they operate. Finally, I argue that any educational project that fails to recognize the inherent contradictions between human emancipation, capitalist exploitation, and the ecological crisis will also fail to produce pedagogies for (ecological) sustainability. In contradistinction to such theories, a Red pedagogy theorizes "nature" as sovereign entity, acting in symbiotic relationship with human subjectivity and the struggle for self-determination.

THE SEEDS OF EMPIRE: THE DEEP STRUCTURES
OF COLONIALIST CONSCIOUSNESS

Indigenous and nonindigenous scholars from a variety of disciplines argue that the tensions between modernist and traditional societies are rooted in the adherence to different and competing ontological systems.[5] Tariq Banuri (1990, 78), for example, articulates this tension in terms of "personal" and "impersonal" maps. The personal map represents cultures with intimate relationships between knowledge and people, where identity is so deeply embedded within these realms that the very notion of the "individual" is virtually incomprehensible; the impersonal map represents cultures with disconnected relationships among knowledge and people. Since all cultural systems integrate aspects of each map, Banuri maintains that it is not the presence or absence of either that defines a culture, but the uniqueness of the balance between them (1990, 74).[6]

Morris Berman (1981) similarly discusses the difference between modernist and traditional cultures in terms of their ontological relationships, describing them as "disenchanted" and "enchanted," respectively. With respect to traditional cultures, he states: "The view of nature which predominated in the West down to the eve of the Scientific Revolution was that of an enchanted world. Rocks, trees, rivers, and clouds were all seen as wondrous, alive, and human beings felt at home in this environment. In short, the cosmos was a place of belonging" (Berman 1981, 2). In contrast, Berman describes the story of the modern epoch as one of progressive disenchantment where the individual is no longer an active participant in, but rather a detached observer of, life. There is no "ecstatic merger" between human beings and the rest of nature (Banuri 1990, 3).[7]

What Banuri and Berman describe as personal/impersonal and enchanted/disenchanted can also be expressed in terms of "sacred" and "secular."[8] In addition to differing relationships between the human, nonhuman, and *supra*human worlds, sacred and secular societies are defined by their differing orientations toward space and time.[9] Anthony Giddens (1990, 38), for example, contends that "most of the situations of modern social life are manifestly incompatible with religion as a pervasive influence on day-to-day life. In modernist cultures, religious cosmology (sacred) is supplanted by reflexively organized (secular) knowledge, governed by empirical observation and logical thought, and focused upon material technology and socially applied codes." In addition, where religion and tradition were once closely linked, Giddens argues that tradition is more thoroughly undermined since it stands in greater opposition to the reflexivity of modernity (1990, 38). Vine Deloria, Jr. concurs with this observation, articulating further:

> Judgment inevitably intrudes into the conception of religious reality whenever a temporal definition is used. Almost always the temporal consideration revolves around the problem of good and evil, and the inconsistencies that arise as this basic relationship is defined turn religious belief into ineffectual systems of ethics. But it would seem likely that whereas religions that are spatially determined can

create a sense of sacred time that originates in the specific location, it is exceed-
ingly difficult for a religion, once bound to history, to incorporate sacred places
into its doctrines. Space generates time, but time has little relationship to space.
(Deloria 1994, 71)

In other words, the reflexive and temporal assumptions of Western culture
can, in some respects, accommodate "religious reality" but not the spatially
determined realities of tradition and traditional peoples. As such, Deloria asserts that the *primary* distinction between modern (Western) and traditional
(indigenous) cultures is their differing orientations around space and time.

American Indians hold their lands – places – as having the highest possible
meaning, and all their statements are made with this reference point in mind . . .
(and) when one group is concerned with the philosophical problem of space and
the other with the philosophical problem of time, then the statements of either
group do not make much sense when transferred from one context to the other.
(Deloria 1994, 63)

Furthermore, this inherent linkage between space (land) and "religion" (the
sacred) determines the shape of indigenous epistemological systems, rendering their moral and intellectual claims virtually indecipherable to societies
concerned with the "philosophical problem of time."

Complicating matters further, the temporality of modernist/secular societies is defined by a distinctly *Christian* view of time (one that identifies a
precise beginning and prophetic end) and, as Deloria (1994) notes, Christians
do not have a sacred attachment to land and nature. Rather, the Christian
foundation of Western thought perpetuates a view that not only legitimates
human supremacy but also underwrites a general "disconnection," promoting
transience as a more advanced state of being. The construction of a grand narrative organized around change as progress and progress as change not only
legitimates the path of whitestream "history" but also sustains the hegemonic
goals of capitalism (wealth accumulation) and colonization (appropriation of
property).[10]

Indeed, while whitestream environmentalists debate the "purity" of Indian
ecological ideology and practice, they generally agree on the severe lack of
an "eco-consciousness" within Anglo-European ideology and practice. Cultural and environmental critics have long argued that the virulent forces of
modern industrialism have not only left society disparate and alienated but
also the planet exhausted. As such, they advance a critique of the overdevel-
oped, overconsumptive, and overempowered first-world nations and their environmentally destructive ontological, axiological, and epistemological systems. Though it is beyond the parameters of this chapter to engage in a full

discussion of the assumptions of modernist societies, extensive critiques of its relationship to the cultural and ecological crises are abundant. For the purposes of this discussion, however, an operational definition of the modernist worldview, or what I refer to as the deep structures of colonialist consciousness, is provided below. It is drawn as an aggregate from various critiques and analyses of the modern, Western cultural project.[11]

The Deep Structures of Colonialist Consciousness:

1. *Belief in progress as change and change as progress.* Both progress and change are measured in terms of material gain (e.g., more education, more income, more production, more status) to be acquired through economic and technological growth, and to which there is no preconceived limit. The ensuing quest for more breeds a fierce, though often tacit, competitive ethic whereby individuals rival for the control of limited resources and power.

2. *Belief in the effective separateness of faith and reason.* The separation of the physical and spiritual worlds establishes scientific and other rationally based ways of knowing as the preeminent intellectual authority and replaces religion as the definer, judge, and guardian of the cultural worldview. The bases of modern epistemology are positivistic and empirical, where reason is perceived as culture-free, and technology as neutral. "Objective" "expert" knowledge is elicited to solve problems and address crises and traditional knowledge (defined by its nonrational, subjective nature) is viewed as irrelevant or distortional to the objective understanding of the world.

3. *Belief in the essential quality of the universe and of "reality" as impersonal, secular, material, mechanistic, and relativistic.* The material entities of the cosmos are perceived entirely as the product of mechanistic principles having no special relationship with human existence or divine reality. Likewise, any divine attributes are recognized as being only the effect of primitive superstition.

4. *Subscription to ontological individualism.* This assumption is most often linked to the Cartesian idea of the self-constituting individual whereby the self is viewed as the basic social unit. Individuals in possession of high degrees of independence and autonomy are considered to be the ideals of "health," and concepts such as self-governance, self-determination, and self-actualization are viewed as goals toward which individuals are encouraged to strive.

5. *Belief in human beings as separate from and superior to the rest of nature.* Human beings are perceived to have dominion over nature and all beings incapable of rational thought. This assumption also functions to generate

other modern dualisms such as body/soul, man/cosmos, and subjective/ objective.

Richard Tarnas, author of *The Passion of the Western Mind* (1991, 282), summarily describes the human manifestation of this consciousness:

> [Sometime] between the fifteenth and seventeenth centuries, the West saw the emergence of a newly self-conscious and autonomous human being—curious about the world, confident in his own judgments, skeptical of orthodoxies, rebellious against authority, responsible for his own beliefs and actions, enamored of the classical past but even more committed to a greater future, proud of his humanity, conscious of his distinctness from nature, aware of his artistic powers as individual creator, assured of his intellectual capacity to comprehend and control nature, and altogether less dependent on an omnipotent God.

Implications for Schooling

According to Gregory Smith (1992), while socialization to modern consciousness is facilitated by a variety of cultural, economic, and political institutions, public schools have served as one of the primary vehicles, replacing "more localistic and sectarian forms of morality with a set of secular universal values constructed . . . to subsume all traditions." (Smith 1992, 48) Schools accomplish this not by *inducting* children through any explicit means, but rather by habituating them to specific forms of social organization and behavioral patterns. Such patterns are embedded in hidden curriculums that *initiate* children to the formal and impersonal relations associated with market societies (Smith 1992, 45–49). Cultural critics of the ecological crisis (e.g., Bernard Bailyn, Gregory Bateson, C.A. Bowers, Fritjof Capra, David Orr, Gregory Smith) moreover argue that while all societies may work to shape the biology and consciousness of children, modernist societies and their attendant institutions shape consciousness in ways that are profoundly destructive and unsustainable. In short, they maintain that "the more our social practices are based upon the core values and ideas of the modernist worldview, the more we contribute to the deepening of the cultural and ecological crises." (Bowers 1993, 57)

The following are points drawn from the work of Robert Dreeben (1968) and Gregory Smith (1992), highlighting further details of the relationship between schooling and the modernist worldview.

Schooling and Colonialist Consciousness

1. *Independence*. Children are expected to be self-reliant, to complete school tasks on their own, and accept personal responsibility for one's behavior.

The value of independence is so highly regarded that students themselves become suspicious of cooperative efforts as potential impediments to their own academic achievement and personal success. Similarly, relationships in school are largely characterized by formality and impersonality. Teachers retain caring but detached relations with students and actively discourage personal interaction. "Appropriate," on-task behavior is measured by the degree to which students behave as if they were in solitude, even though they are not. A good student acts as if he or she is "alone in a crowd."

2. *Achievement.* Students are encouraged to make an impact on their environment. Success and individual worth are measured by abstract and impersonal standards of excellence whereby students are aware of being in direct competition with each other. The impersonality of evaluation encourages the development of instrumental attitudes toward achievement and work; the process is perceived as a means for achieving greater ends.

3. *Humanism.* Students are expected to accept the tenets of secular humanism as essential truth—they are encouraged to believe that they are the masters of their own destinies, and that through technology and scientific inquiry nature's unknowns can become knowable. Implicit in these assumptions is the rejection of religion and spirituality as being purely ideological (if not irrelevant) and distortional to the objective understanding of the world.

4. *Detachment from sources of local and personal knowledge.* The knowledge conveyed in school is usually the knowledge of those who have accepted and benefited from the tenets of the modern worldview. Children and the reservoirs of local knowledge with which they come to school are not perceived as sufficient or valid foundations of real or universal knowledge.

5. *Detachment from nature.* The world is studied at a distance; contact with the earth, animals, and plants is severely limited. Students discover through inference that real learning occurs indoors and is composed of knowledge bases separate from life and the natural world. When it does occur, environmental education usually does so within the realms and confines of the established curriculum and with little impact on the underlying goals of American education.

As a result, Smith argues that, through school, children are encouraged to develop as progressive, competitive, rational, material, consumerist, and anthropocentric individuals. They are, moreover, compelled to learn through a "particular intellectual curriculum" that legitimates dominant definitions of reality and the associated vocabulary, setting the socially sanctioned boundaries for both discourse and reflection (Bowers 1993, 6).

Summary

The delineation of the difference between modern (secular) and traditional (sacred) societies and their competing views of land and nature helps to explain the persistence of severe conflict between such societies. Unlike secular societies—where land signifies property, property signifies capital, and capital signifies wealth, status, and power—land in "sacred" societies signifies connection to family, tribe, and ancestors. Land is furthermore thought of in connection to sacred sites, burial grounds and medicinal plants. More significantly, these distinctions are not merely inscribed as differences but rather reified as deficiencies within the hierarchical structures of Western hegemony. Specifically, the sacred is viewed as subordinate to the secular, space as subordinate to time, and tradition as subordinate to progress. Such significations have proven insoluble as they continue to mark the divide between whitestream and indigenous nations, becoming ever more virulent as the forces of colonization mutate into increasingly insidious forms. The stated "difference" of sacred societies determines that legitimate efforts to protect and extend tribal sovereignty must not only champion tribal control of land and resources but also work to dismantle the cages of modern consciousness, particularly as legitimated through American schools.

CONTEMPORARY STRUGGLES

While the "whole" of the colonialist project is far greater than the sum of its parts, the following sample of contemporary struggles exemplify the inner workings of colonialist power, or what Jorgé Luis Borges (cited in Torres 1998) refers to as the "secret adventures of order."[12] Each struggle illustrates, in rather disturbing terms, the ways in which the United States works to protect its empire, controlling its internal colonies with overt power and subterfuge. Specifically, I review three cases: the Navajo–Hopi land dispute, the Indian Land Trust Fund, and the Quechan nation's struggle against open-pit gold mining.[13] Though the potential pool of cases is limitless, these particular cases were chosen because of their notoriety as well as their ability to illustrate the magnitude of corruption and the degree to which colonialist forces continue to operate and define Indian–white relations. They also demonstrate the deeply deficient, if not racist assumptions of a discourse organized around the question of Indian ecological purity. In contradistinction to this discourse, each case is articulated in terms of how the forces of whitestream hegemony, institutional racism, corporate greed, and political entities are all complicit in maintaining the colonialist project.

Trouble on Big Mountain

While land disputes were not absent among "precontact" Indians, the disaster that is the Navajo–Hopi land dispute could have unfolded only in an imperialist system defined by the hegemonic values of colonization, especially capitalist accumulation and private property. In other words, the dispute reeks of the embers of conquest. On one side are American Indians fighting against a white power structure with contempt for tribal rights and traditions and, on the other hand, an unseemly cast of corporations and political benefactors, allied in an effort to erode sovereignty and procure indigenous resources for private gain.

While the very nature of the colonialist project renders it impossible to determine the source of any particular struggle, the beginning of this encounter can roughly be cited as early as 1868, when Navajo survivors of Kit Carson's death marches began to return from their concentration camps at Fort Sumner. Conditions for their release were delineated in the "Navajo Treaty," which was also the mechanism by which the Department of the Interior established the "Navajo Reservation." As might be predicted, reservation borders were drawn without any correlation to historical usage or occupancy. Twenty years later, in 1882, ostensibly in an effort to distinguish the Hopi from the Navajo land base, U.S. president Chester A. Arthur issued an executive order establishing the Hopi Reservation. Once again borders were drawn in a manner that completely disregarded established Hopi land use and occupancy. In 1884, Hopi elders wrote to the president, challenging his authority to delineate any boundaries for the Hopi peoples since, unlike the Navajo, they never had a treaty with the United States. The boundaries of both reservations were not only carelessly drawn but also delineated in a manner that directly contradicted the Navajo and Hopi's own sense of their lands, thus, commencing the so-called Indian land dispute.

While the hazards of empire building provided ample fuel for the territorial dispute, once valuable resources and corporate greed were added to the mix, the struggles ignited to monumental proportions. Specifically, in 1909 the U.S. Geological Survey discovered billions of tons of coal under Black Mesa, an area that lies at the center of the land dispute. The reserves went untapped in the first few years after discovery, as corporations were stymied in their abilities to access resources on reservation land. By the late 1930s, tribal governance structures had been sufficiently decimated by the Indian Reorganization Act, paving the way for corporate and government infiltration. It was around this time that the Peabody Coal Company was "fighting for its life," fending off the impact of heavy losses and talks of corporate merger.[14] In 1951, the BIA appointed John Boyden—an attorney for the Peabody Coal Company—to resurrect the "Hopi Tribal Council,"[15] empowering them to act on behalf of the tribes' resource and mineral interests. Under Boyden's administration, the so-called Hopi Council granted a thirty-five-year lease to the Peabody Coal Company to mine Black Mesa.

Similarly, in 1922, oil was discovered on the Navajo reservation. Standard Oil of California was eager to lay claim but had no legal means by which to lease the land from the tribe. At the time the Navajo did not have a centralized governing body and leadership was dispersed among several local "headmen." Not to be deterred, Standard Oil pressured the U.S. government to organize the headmen for the sole purpose of persuading them to sign off on leasing applications. After such overtures were rejected, Secretary of the Interior Albert Fall, of New Mexico, took it upon himself to invent "a series of legal fictions to facilitate oil leasing." Specifically, Fall created a "Navajo Business Council," comprised of a mere three tribal members. Though Fall established it as a general business council, the only action the council was authorized to take was to sign and approve oil leases on behalf of the tribe.[16]

In 1923, under continued pressure from Standard Oil, the BIA "legally" formed the first official Navajo Tribal Council to replace the "inefficient" conglomerate of tribal headmen. The new council authorized the U.S. Department of Interior official to negotiate all future oil and gas leases, which he did, often approving leases against the will of the Navajo people. In 1934, the Indian Reorganization Act[17] was passed, and shortly afterward, both the Navajo and Hopi[18] nations had their traditional governments definitively replaced by "tribal councils." The combination of puppet tribal governments, greedy corporations, and corrupt federal officials formed a complex web of political relations ideal for protecting corporate and government interests.

In the following decades the boundaries between the Navajo and Hopi Nations were drawn and redrawn depending on the shifting tides of power and corruption. Throughout the entire process, factions of the Navajo and Hopi tribes have resisted the forces at work, publicly insisting that the original terms of shared usage were mutually agreeable, that there was no "dispute" among their peoples, and that, left unto their own, all outstanding conflicts could be resolved. In the meantime, Arizona congressmen with much to gain from lucrative corporate deals were busy lobbying Congress, convincing them that the "land dispute" was becoming a "bloody range war" in dire need of government intervention. As a result, in 1974 Congress instituted the Navajo–Hopi Land Settlement Act (P.L. 93-531), which definitively divided the Joint Usage Area (JUA) into Navajo and Hopi halves. In addition to ostensibly settling the "dispute," the act cleared up coal and water rights in the JUA, paving the way for more rapid energy development and real estate speculators.

Since the law was passed, members of both tribes have continued to express their mutual resistance to government and corporate intervention.[19] As a result, protestors have endured numerous arrests, livestock confiscations, forced removals, assaults, and even murders. Similarly, complicit government and corporate officials have endured everything from idle threats to assassinations. The most corrupt have been forced to resign, indicted for racketeering, held in contempt of court, and accused of a variety of illegal financial dealings.

As the struggle persists tribal members increasingly come to view the corporate machinations for what they are—divide and conquer tactics. They have come to realize, more specifically, that the most significant threat to their mutual survival is not each other but the depletion of clean resources (at the rate of three billion gallons a year) and the contamination of underground aquifers, both of which threaten the tribes' access to clean water.

While the above narrative clearly implicates the colonizer, the very definition of hegemony requires that people participate in their own oppression, and the Navajo and Hopi are no exception. Specifically, the (omni)presence of Peabody and its pervasive impact on indigenous lands has forced local tribes into relations of economic dependency (read: exploitation), cultivating an unhealthy reliance on the revenues and jobs generated from the mining industry. Nevertheless, the tribes have managed to maintain a steady campaign of resistance, standing firm in their contention that Peabody not only is responsible for polluting their air and creating respiratory problems but also for the destruction of sacred sites and medicinal plants. As such, Hopi Lillian Hill laments that the tribes "feel strongly that Peabody is threatening the culture of our people" (Miller 2002). In one of their more recent public demonstrations of resistance, Hopi and Dine runners conducted a prayer run in Flagstaff, Arizona (in April 2002), sending a unified message to the government and energy corporations that the wonton waste of irreplaceable drinking water for industrial purposes must end.

The Original Enron

From the very moment the Dawes Act was enacted in 1887, newspapers began reporting that Indians were getting cheated out of their money.[20] Even so, it was decades (1929) before the General Accounting Office (GAO) publicly admitted that trust fund books were in absolute disarray, making it impossible to determine whether Indians received "the full measure of benefit to which they [were] entitled." Rather than organize their financial affairs, however, the GAO was satisfied to report that while expenditures from the trust fund did not go directly to Indians, they were used for purposes that, by a "very broad interpretation . . . was to the benefit of Indians" (Brinkley 2003). Such a lack of accountability led to several more years of neglect and mismanagement. Indeed, it wasn't until 1992 that a congressional report entitled "Misplaced Trust: The Bureau of Indian Affairs Mismanagement of the Indian Trust Fund" recognized the long history of indiscretions, characterizing the management of the trust as "a dismal history of inaction and incompetence."

In 1996, Elouise Cobell, a Montana banker and member of the Blackfoot Nation,[21] filed a suit against the federal government, asserting that it had been cheating Indians out of billons of dollars since the Indian Land Trust was first established in 1887. Based on evidence from their own records, the tribes claimed that the U.S. government owes them in excess of $137.2 billion dollars in lost revenues for the roughly eleven million acres of Indian land held in trust.[22] The suit also calls for control over the individual accounts to be taken away from the Department of Interior and placed in receivership, to be managed by officers who would report to the Justice Department. Ex-Interior Secretary Gail Norton adamantly opposes this, arguing instead for a new internal accounting system (still under her supervision) called the Bureau of Indian Trust Asset Management—a proposal developed with virtually no input from tribes.

Predictably, Norton's bureau did little to ameliorate the injustices and much to confound them. In an almost unprecedented move in the history of Indian–white relations, federal judge Royce Lambreth indicted Secretary Norton for gross mismanagement and for the submission of falsely positive progress reports to the Court. Clinton administration interior secretary Bruce Babbitt and treasury secretary Robert Rubin were also found in contempt for their failure to establish an effective accounting system. Regarding this indictment, Elouise Cobell stated, "I think [Judge Lambreth] heard six years of lying, and he's just tired of it. . . . Now he knows what it is like to be an Indian, except we've been lied to for one hundred years" (Cohen 2001). Despite the mounting evidence, the cases were eventually dismissed.

While Gail Norton and the others escaped the contempt charge, their trials helped to expose the depth of mismanagement, neglect, and abuse enacted by the government and its corporate sponsors. Among other transgressions, court investigators found evidence of massive document destruction and distortion and in certain incidences it was found that the government "failed" to collect any money from profit-reaping companies. This "failure" not only further complicated accounting efforts but also negatively skewed estimates of the total monies owed to Indians. All told, the trials revealed that government officials engaged in a myriad of specious tactics in their effort to hide billions in lost, stolen, and misappropriated funds, and to support their claim that a full accounting of the fund is not likely since "too many of the records have been lost or destroyed over the years."[23] In response to such shady practices, Representative Tom Udall (D-NM) remarked, "The way these trust fund holders have been treated is a national disgrace. If 40,000 people were cut off from Social Security, there would be an uproar in Congress."

Perhaps most unsettling is that there is no justice in sight, as current undersecretary of the interior for the Bush administration J. Steven Griles recently remarked, "I am not settling a case with taxpayer money for billions of dollars when there is no supporting evidence that the money they say they lost ever existed." Moreover, Norton and her congressional junta continued to look for ways to avoid responsibility. Specifically, they proposed an amendment to the 2003 Department of the Interior appropriations bill, which would forbid any accounting of the Indian Trust prior to 1985, citing the exorbitant cost of an audit dating back to 1887 ($ 2.4 billion) as compared to one dating to 1985, which would cost $907 million. This development caused Representative Nick Rahall (D-WV) to dub the Interior Department "the Enron of federal agencies." Perhaps the ultimate irony is the hypocrisy of an administration that celebrates "free enterprise" at the same time it fails to honor its own financial commitments to the First Americans.

Imperialist Mining

Colonization came to the Quechan in 1603 with Spanish invasion. It took them over one hundred years, but eventually the Quechan managed to mount a rebellion against their colonizers in 1781, killing, capturing, and ultimately expelling them from their land (Wullenjohn 2003). While the Spaniards never returned, the tribe was decimated by colonization, the final blow coming after the Mexican–American War. Specifically, even though the Quechan had never been subject to Mexican law, never had Mexican troops stationed in their lands, never had taxes collected by the Mexican government, and Mexican citizens never had any rights on their land, the United States gained "ownership" of Quechan territories as a result of the Treaty of Guadalupe Hidalgo in 1848 (Forbes 1965).

Over 150 years later, the Quechan are still struggling to defend their way of life against the U.S. government; this time, against the Bush administration and a multinational mining corporation. On October 25, 2001, the Department of Land Management announced that it was modifying the agency's surface mining regulations. Among other things, this "modification" paved the way for the ironically named Glamis Imperial Corporation to pursue development of a 1,650-acre open-pit gold mine in a region of the Quechan nation that contained sacred and ancestral sites. These sites are supposed to be protected by the Native American Graves Protection Act, leading the Advisory Council on Historic Preservation to comment on the potentially devastating effects of this project: "If implemented, (it) would be so damaging to historic resources that the Quechan tribe's ability to practice their sacred traditions as a living part of their community life and development would be lost."

In a deeply cynical public relations ploy, the Bush administration attempted to pass off this assault on Indian religious freedom as an effort to enhance the department's ability to "protect the environment, public land resources, and public health." Contrary to these pronouncements, the Bush administration's "modification" of the mining regulations actually dropped the "irreparable harm standard" initially employed by the Clinton administration. More significantly, the change required Interior Solicitor William G. Myers to reverse an interpretation of the Federal Land Policy and Management Act (FLPMA)[24] that included the protection of American Indian cultural and religious sites.

This is an ironic stance for an administration that has threatened to cut off Title 1 funds to public schools failing to aggressively enforce the rights of students to pray on school grounds. In the words of Quechan tribal member Lorey Cachora, "President Bush has often spoke about his goal of upholding religious freedom for all Americans . . . this must include American Indians." Apparently President Bush does not view the degradation of Indian cultural and religious sites as a similar affront to the sanctity of religious freedom, especially when Native spiritual life gets in the way of corporate interests.

The legal foundation of Bush's disregard for Indian religious freedom was established in the unfortunate *Lyng v. Northwest* decision (1988), in which the Court rejected the notion that land viewed by Indians as sacred qualified for protection under the First Amendment (Brown 1999). Ironically, the majority opinion, written by Sandra Day-O'Connor, concedes that development would irreparably harm Quechan religious practices. It reads: "[T]he logging and road building projects at issue in this case could have devastating effects on traditional Indian religious practices . . . virtually destroying the Indians ability to practice their religion" (Brown 1999, 150). Ultimately, however, the Court relied on an interpretation of the Free Exercise Clause of the First Amendment that protects religious practices only when the government makes outright prohibitions on the exercise of religion, allowing for "incidental" effects of government programs. Justice Brennan, writing in dissent, made a passionate case for the protection of Indian religion and foreshadowed many of the pending issues in the Quechan case:

> The area of worship cannot be delineated from social, political, cultural and other aspects of Indian lifestyles . . . a pervasive feature of this lifestyle is the individual's relationship with the natural world; this relationship, which can accurately though somewhat incompletely be characterized as one of stewardship,

forms the core of what can be called, for lack of better nomenclature, the Indian religious experience. . . . In marked contrast to other religions, the belief systems of Native Americans do not rely on doctrines, creeds or dogmas. . . . Where dogma lies at the center of western religions, Native American Faith is inextricably bound to the use of the land. The site-specific nature of Indian religious practice derives from the Native American perception that the land is itself a sacred, living being. . . . Rituals are performed in prescribed locations not merely as a matter of traditional orthodoxy, but because land, like all other living things, is unique, and specific sites possess different spiritual properties and significance. (cited in Brown 1999, 150)

The ideological, political, and financial force behind efforts to turn Quechan land into a gold mine are backed by the "Wise Use Movement," a special interest group initiated by the Center for the Defense of Free Enterprise in Reno, Nevada. The movement, funded by ranchers, miners, loggers, real estate developers, and gas and oil companies, is hostile to the concept of land as anything other than an economic resource, aggressively asserting the notion that "proprietary interest is the fundamental conception defining human relationship with land" (Brown 1999, 2). Among other causes, the movement's advocates lobby for opening national parks, wildlife refuges, and wilderness areas to oil and gas drilling; clear cutting ancient forests; and amending the Endangered Species Act to exclude species that impede human progress (Brown 1999).

The Wise Use belief that land exists in servile status to human "landlords" provides the ideological justification for myriad harmful acts, including the destruction of sacred Indian cultural and religious sites. Indeed, Wise Users perceive American Indian religious freedom and sovereignty as mere nuisances to the naturally ordained pursuit of progress. In short, the Wise Use movement functions as a polished twenty-first-century version of manifest destiny in which corporate interests are dressed up to look like divinely inspired "natural rights" (Brown 1999). Unfortunately, given the current composition of the Supreme Court, and the precedent established in *Lyng v. Northwest*, a legal remedy for the Quechan seems highly improbable.

Unwilling to be deterred by the long political odds, however, tribal leaders and their allies are developing a comprehensive legislative and public relations strategy to convince lawmakers and the public that mining or developing sacred places is analogous to bulldozing a church. Among their more prominent allies is U.S. senator Barbara Boxer (D-CA) who stated in an address to Congress: "We would never destroy a church, or a temple or a mosque. Unfortunately, there is no underlying law to ensure that Indian sacred sites are protected . . . so we find ourselves having to pass a law every time we want to protect an individual site" (Pearson 2003). Vowing continued resistance, Quechan tribal council president Mike Jackson Sr. characterized the efforts of the Bush administration an "affront to all American Indians," pledging to fight interminably for Quechan religion, traditions, and history.

Sadly, the cases of the Navajo, Hopi, Blackfoot, and Quechan nations constitute a meager fraction of an endless list of offenses levied against tribal peoples. Indeed, virtually every tribe in the United States is embroiled in a litany of lawsuits and community struggles against continued erosion of their sovereign rights. This cold reality exposes the gross negligence of tactics to limit the environmental discourse to questions of American Indian identity and authenticity. They also raise the imperative for educators to develop pedagogical interventions that can inform indigenous struggles against colonialist forces that are determined to consume their lands and resources.

REVOLUTIONARY CRITICAL PEDAGOGY
AND THE COLONIALIST PROJECT

As the Western notion of "progress" continues to devour life-sustaining ecosystems, it is vital that indigenous peoples and their allies, including critical scholars, struggle for political, economic, and educational reforms that recognize the inherent connection between the cultural and ecological crises. While the tools of revolutionary critical pedagogy elicit a powerful critique of whitestream capitalism and other hegemonic forces undermining tribal sovereignty, the question remains whether the Western (particularly Marxist) roots of revolutionary critical pedagogy preclude it from disrupting the deep structures of a colonialist discourse dependent on the "continued robbing of nature." As Bowers (2003) notes, though Marx was a critic of capitalism, he shared many of its deep cultural assumptions, including:

> [t]he need to think in universal terms, the disdain for peasant and indigenous cultures as backward and thus in need of being brought into the industrial age, a linear view of progress that also assumed the West's leading role in establishing the new revolutionary consciousness that would replace the backward traditions of other cultures—and in supplying the elite vanguard of theorists an anthropocentric way of thinking that reduced Nature to an exploitable resource (in the interests of the masses rather than for profit).

As such, Bowers is among the chief critics of revolutionary critical pedagogy and its lack of attention to the ecological crisis, arguing that it shares the same cultural assumptions as Western colonialism. He particularly indicts the following "core cultural assumptions" of revolutionary critical pedagogy as Eurocentric, rendering it indistinguishable from other Western pedagogies. According to Bowers:

1. Critical pedagogy assumes that critical reflection or what Freire calls "conscientization" is the only approach to "nonoppressive knowledge and cultural practices" (Bowers 2003, 13). And further, that the imposition of "[e]nlightenment ways of thinking with all its culturally specific baggage, is no different from universalizing the Western industrialized approach to food production and consumption, forms of entertainment, and consumer-based subjectivity" (Bowers 2003, 14). Moreover, the emphasis on critical reflection undermines the "mythopoetic narratives" that serve as "the basis of a cultures moral system, way of thinking about relationships, and its silences."
2. Critical pedagogy presumes that change is "a progressive force that requires the constant overturning of traditions." The directives to "rename" and "transform" are equivalent to injunctions to replace "local traditions of self-sufficiency with a worldview that represents change and individual autonomy as expressions of progress." Moreover, the "emphasis on change, transformation, liberatory praxis, and the continual construction of experience," has led critical theorists to ignore what needs to be conserved and the value of "intergenerational knowledge" (a.k.a. tradition) (Bowers 2003, 14).
3. Critical pedagogy is "based on an anthropocentric view of human/nature relationships" that "contributes to the widely held view that humans can impose their will on the environment and that when the environment breaks down experts using an instrumentally based critical reflection will engineer a synthetic replacement" (Bowers 2003, 15).
4. Critical pedagogy presumes a "Western approach to literacy" that "reinforces patterns of social relationships not found in oral-based cultures." In "oral-based cultures, participation is the central feature of life rather than the analytical and decontextualized judgment that fixed texts make possible" (Bowers 2003, 15).

While Bowers is right to caution against the unconscious and unilateral imposition of "enlightenment ways of thinking," the frameworks of revolutionary critical pedagogy are malleable by design, rendering the overall tone of his critique somewhat unwarranted. Indeed, Peter McLaren himself (Bowers's chief target) concedes, "I am certainly aware of the implications of a creeping Eurocentrism slipping through the textual fissure of any theoretical discourse . . . and that the conceptual space of any work . . . is open to many forms of colonization" (McLaren 1991, 463). In addition to overgeneralizing the intentions of critical theorists, Bowers underestimates the capacities of indigenous teachers and scholars, basing much of his critique on the assumption that they share his own expectations for critical pedagogy, namely, that it functions as a one-size-fits-all pedagogical elixir. Despite these shortcomings, Bowers raises some incisive and important points that compel closer examination.

First, while critical theorists undoubtedly place a premium on critical reflection, any close reading of revolutionary pedagogies reveals that the primary emphasis is on *meaning*. This emphasis renders Bowers's claim that such theorists advocate critical reflection as *the only* viable approach to nonoppressive knowledge and cultural practices unfounded. Such theorists are, moreover, clear that their pedagogies (including the adherence to marxism) are intended to serve as guides to action not as "a set of metaphysical dogmas" (Bowers 2003, 29). According to McLaren (2003, 29), critical theories require that "symbolic formations" be analyzed "in their spatio-temporal settings, within certain fields of interaction, and in the context of social institutions and structures so that teachers have a greater sense of how meanings are inscribed, encoded, decoded, transmitted, deployed, circulated and received in the arena of everyday social relations." The emphasis on "symbolic formations" (as opposed to the more limited category of text) conceivably includes expressions of meaning that are nontextually based (e.g., dance, ceremony, song)—ones that Bowers identifies as the definitive features of "mythopoetic cultures."

Bowers's second claim, that critical pedagogy presumes change as a progressive force requiring "the constant overturning of traditions," is perhaps more warranted. Indeed, the discourse is littered with references to social and self-transformation. Specifically, critical theorists posit an action-oriented pedagogy with the objective of encouraging students and teachers to utilize "critical knowledge that is *transformative* as opposed to *reproductive,* (and) *empowering* as opposed to *oppressing,"* asking the question, "what is the relationship between our classrooms and our effort to build a better society?" (Bowers 2003, xv, xxxiv). The end goal is to encourage "students beyond the world they already know [and] to expand their range of human possibilities" (Giroux 2001, 24).

While any pedagogy with a root metaphor of "change as progress" presents specific challenges to indigenous cultures rooted in tradition and intergenerational knowledge, revolutionary theorists do not categorically advocate change as *inherently* progressive. Rather, they are very definitive in their distinction between change that emancipates and change that merely furthers the dictates of market imperatives. McLaren, in particular, is candid in his advocacy of change as defined by Marxist imperatives to act against imperialism and exploitation. "[M]illions from aggrieved populations worldwide stand witness to the law governed process of exploitation known as capital accumulation, to the ravages of uneven development known as 'progress,' and to the practice of imperialism in new guises called 'globalization'" (McLaren 2003, 13). Moreover, McLaren agrees with Eric Fromm's positioning of "revolutionary humanism" at the center of Marx's philosophy: "Marx's aim was that of the spiritual emancipation of man, of his liberation from the claims of economic determination, of restituting him in his human wholeness, of enabling him to find unity and harmony with his fellow man and with Nature" (cited in McLaren 2003, 13). While such sentiments reveal a pedagogy that is clearly concerned with change and social transformation, it is not unconcerned (as Bowers contends) with the interconnection between economic oppression and environmental destruction.

A more pertinent question is to what degree the acts of interrogation and transformation themselves encode the same sociotemporal markers of a colonialist consciousness intent on extinguishing "traditional" (sacred) ways of knowing with ostensibly more "progressive" (secular) understandings of the world. For instance, Giddens (1990) identifies one of the distinguishing features between modernist and traditional cultures as their differing approaches to knowledge. He maintains that in traditional cultures "the past is honored and symbols are valued because they contain and perpetuate the experience of generations," making tradition "a mode of integrating the reflexive monitoring of action with the same time-space organization of the community."[25] In contrast, modernist cultures sever the connection between daily life routines and the past. Giddens argues that reflexivity in this context takes on a wholly different character as "it is introduced into the very system of production, such that thought and action are constantly refracted back upon one another" (Giddens 1990, 38). Although Giddens concedes that even in the most modern cultures tradition continues to play a role, he maintains that the role is greatly diminished since it receives its identity only from the reflexivity of the modern and "justified tradition is tradition in sham clothing" (1990, 38). In other words, it is the tendency of modernity to reject the sanctioning of any practice on the grounds that it is simply traditional and to appropriate instead only those traditions "justified" through "the light of knowledge [that] is not itself authenticated by tradition." This process, according to Giddens, inherently transforms, if not destroys, the very nature of tradition, reducing it to a "sham."

Thus, where revolutionary theorists challenge the moral imperatives of modern consciousness they may inadvertently maintain its epistemic codes, reinforcing the bias toward "reflexively organized knowledge"—the same means by which "tradition" is undermined. Consider, for example, the following commentary on the role of tradition as expressed by McLaren (1991):

> I do not object to tradition itself. What I do object to is the concealment of cultural uncertainties in the way that tradition gets ideologically produced . . . [and]

while I agree that there are ecologically, morally, politically, enabling aspects to mythic, religious, and familial traditions, and that such traditions can be empowering to the extent that they locate subjectivity in a reciprocal relationship to the larger environment, critical pedagogy concentrates on the process of demythologization. That is, I am concerned with uncovering the social contradictions that are ideologically resolved or harmonized to preserve existing relations of power—relations which have debilitating effects on certain groups.

And thus, he goes on to ask:

Why shouldn't all aspects of culture be problematized? To problematize culture does not guarantee that everything "traditional" will be condemned or rejected . . . what it does mean is that we can recover from such traditional cultural texts and practices those aspects which empower and discard or transform those which don't. (McLaren 1991, 469)

Thus (contrary to Bowers's reading), while McLaren does consider the effect of revolutionary pedagogies on traditional knowledge, he may be too dismissive of the cultural codes embedded in the act of social transformation. It is, for instance, highly unlikely that the "pedagogical negativism" required of such emancipatory pedagogies can be wielded with the degree of surgical precision revolutionary theorists confidently express—teaching students to doubt everything but also believe in and take seriously the truth claims of their own traditions. In other words, the process of interrogation itself may encode the same sociotemporal markers of a colonialist consciousness that incites movement away from "sacred" ways of knowing toward increased secularization. In response to McLaren, rather than asking why all aspects of culture shouldn't be problematized, we, as critical educators, should ask how the processes of problematizing itself may serve as a homogenizing force, muting and domesticating the distinctiveness of traditional ways of knowing.

That does not, however, preclude such processes of interrogation from being an integral part of a Red pedagogy, particularly as indigenous communities remain threatened and deeply compromised by colonialist forces. Bowers's dismissal of the need for social transformation within indigenous communities is not only shortsighted but also patronizing. For example, while he admires with romantic fascination, "how the Quechua people have resisted European colonization," he does not specify which Quechua peoples he is referring to—those in Paramus, New Jersey; Hartford, Connecticut; Ayacucho, Peru; or Quito, Ecuador? Like other indigenous nations, the Quechua are profoundly diverse, and while many continue to resist the forces of colonization, it remains evident to all that such "resistance" comes at tremendous cost to both the individual and the community. Specifically, such costs can manifest in the compromising of one's mental and physical health, education, employment, and social status, with organized resistance bringing the price of increased economic and political oppression. While indigenous cultures have, for centuries, managed to retain their traditions in the face of imperialism—resisting and selectively employing facets of Western culture as they see fit—they can resist only what they fully know. When engaged with caution and restraint I believe the tools of revolutionary pedagogy can prove invaluable, particularly in revealing the inner sanctums of power and hidden structures of domination. Consider, for example, how a revolutionary critical pedagogy could assist Navajo, Hopi, Blackfoot, and Quechan students struggling to make sense of their nations' respective battles against colonialist forces.

Bowers's third claim, that revolutionary critical pedagogy is "based on an anthropocentric view of human/nature relationships" is perhaps the most accurate. Consider for example the (anthropocentric) questions that McLaren and Farahmandpur (2001) position at the center of "revolutionary critical pedagogy": What does it mean to be human? How can we live humanely? What actions or steps must be taken to be able to live humanely? While such questions could be answered in a manner that de-centers human beings (i.e., to be "human" means living in a way that accounts for the deep interconnection between all living entities), McLaren and Farahmandpur both choose to reassert the primacy of Marxist theory in their responses. Specifically, they confirm and concur with Marx's radical assertion of a profoundly human-centered world quoting the following declaration made in *Capital* (vol. 1): "A spider conducts operations which resemble those of a weaver and a bee would put many a human architect to shame by the construction of its honeycomb cells. But what distinguishes the worst architect from the best of bees is that the architect builds the cell in his mind before he constructs it in wax" (Marx 1977, 284).

In response to this quote McLaren and Farahmandpur (2001, 307) write, "[i]n other words, the fundamental distinction between humans and other species is that humans are endowed with a social imagination, one that operates as a tool for transforming their social conditions," underscoring the primacy of consciousness as "a powerful mediating force in transforming the existing social and economic structures that constrain it." Thus, following Marx, they insist that the "question of what it means to be human" is "conditioned by the specificity of the socio-historical conditions and circumstances of *human* society," believing that "the purpose of education is linked to men and women realizing their powers and capacities" (McLaren and Farahmandpur 2001, 305, emphasis added).

Such expressions of profound anthropocentrism are not only unnecessary to the imperatives of the critical project but also weaken its validity. To begin, it simply isn't true that humans are the only species to actively transform their social conditions. Primates, for example, both choose and "dethrone" leaders based on qualities they find desirable, and it is probable that many other species operate in similar ways not yet understandable to our limited imaginations. McLaren and Farahmandpur's maintenance of the hierarchy between human beings and nature thus not only prohibits us from learning from "all our relations," but also reinscribes the colonialist logic that conscripts "nature" to the service of human society. Indeed, McLaren (2003, 31) seconds Joel Kovel's notion that "the transition to socialism will require the creation of a usufructuary of the earth." While Mclaren contends that a "usufructuary" implies "restoring ecosystemic integrity" so that "ecocentric modes of production" are made accessible to all, the model exists for the sole purposes of transferring assets "to the direct producers" (i.e., worker ownership and control). The value of nature is therefore only derived in terms of its ability to serve as a distinctly human resource, carrying no inherent worth or subjectivity.

While Bowers's final claim, that critical pedagogy presumes a "Western approach to literacy" that reinforces a "pattern of social relationships not found in oral-based cultures" is rather self-evident, it is unclear what kind of pedagogy (a Western construct) would not presume literacy as its basis. Moreover, indigenous cultures engaged in institutionalized forms of schooling are just as concerned with students' literacy as other cultures. Indeed, the value of revolutionary pedagogies is that the concept of "literacy" is reformed to take on meaning beyond a simple depoliticized notion of reading and writing. Specifically, it takes on a *politics* of literacy that recognizes it as being "socially constructed within political contexts: that is, within contexts where access to economic, cultural, political, and institutional power is structured unequally" (Lankshear and McLaren 1993, xviii). Lankshear and McLaren further comment on the notion of critical literacy:

> In short, literacies are ideological. They reflect the differential structured power available to human agents through which to secure the promotion and serving of their interests, including the power to shape literacy in ways consonant with those interests. Consequently, the conceptions people have of what literacy involves, of what *counts* as being literate, what they see as "real" or "appropriate" uses of reading and writing skills, and the way people actually read and write in the course of their daily lives—these all reflect and promote values, beliefs, assumptions, and practices which shape the way life is lived within a given social milieu and, in turn, influence which interests are promoted or undermined as a result of how life is lived there. Thus, literacies are indicies of the dynamics of power. (1993, xviii)

Such a definition neither limits "literacy" to purely Western conceptions nor advocates an unconscious approach that merely "enables producers to get their message to individual consumers," as Bowers contends. On the contrary, critical theorists aim to disrupt the unconscious processes of "language" acquisition and communication. While the question regarding the homogenizing effects of critical literacy reemerges, indigenous cultures have been navigating the impact of such forces since the time of contact. Furthermore, knowledge of the oppressor and the oppressor's language is essential to the processes of resistance, particularly in a context where the vast majority of indigenous students are schooled in whitestream institutions.

In summary, Bowers's critique of critical theory identifies significant points of tension but it is limited by both its inaccurate reading of such theories and its essentializing of indigenous cultures. In perhaps the final irony, Bowers's own outline for an eco-conscious education employs the same precepts of critical pedagogy that he discounts. Specifically, he calls for a pedagogy that helps students: (1) understand the causes, extent, and political strategies necessary for addressing environmental racism; (2) clarify the nature of the ideological and economic forces that are perpetuating the South by the North; (3) revitalize noncommodified forms of knowledge, skills, and activities within the communities represented by the students in the classroom; and (4) recognize the many ecologically informed changes in individual lifestyles and uses of technology that will help ensure that future generations will not inherit a degraded environment (Bowers 2003, 18). Such precepts clearly presume some of the cultural assumptions of critical pedagogy, namely, the importance of critical reflection, an orientation toward (emancipatory) change, and a mastery of critical forms of literacy that enable such reflection and change.

TOWARD A NEW RED PEDAGOGY

For over five hundred years, an unsavory alliance of Christians and capitalists has engaged in a holy war against American Indians, imposing their own gospels of salvation. As a result, whole tribes have been eradicated and dispossessed of their land—their tribal, communal, and democratic ways of life undermined in every conceivable way. Throughout it all, however, indigenous peoples have resisted with countless numbers of indigenous peoples choosing to live in ways consistent with their traditional values. They refuse to succumb to a value system that elevates humans above all other creatures and treats nature as a hostile entity to be exploited, subdued, and abandoned. Nevertheless, those with the greatest stake in sovereignty for indigenous peoples—that is, indigenous people themselves—need more than a spirit of resistance, they need a pedagogical structure that provides methods of inquiry and analysis that expose, challenge, and disrupt the continuing colonization of their land and resources.

Revolutionary pedagogies have the potential to provide such a structure as they have the analytical robustness and ideological inclination needed to sort through the underlying power manipulations of colonialist forces. They also have the potential to understand that people raped of their land are no more liable for their suffering than other rape victims. Moreover, the emphasis on structural analysis also avoids the narrow, tangential questions of identity and the ecologically "purity" of Indians, which only serve to deflect attention from the vital issues of tribal sovereignty.

Yet, as noted by Bowers and other critics, critical pedagogy is born of a Western tradition that has many components in conflict with indigenous cosmology and epistemology, including a view of time and progress that is linear and an anthropocentrism that puts humans at the center of the universe. Moreover, one of its primary informants, marxism, is prone to promulgating its own oppressive grand narratives by dismissing indigenous cultures as "primitive" or precapitalist entities. If, however, critical pedagogy is able to sustain the same kind of penetrating analysis it unleashes on capitalism, it may evolve into an invaluable tool for indigenous peoples and their allies, fighting to protect and extend Indian sovereignty over tribal land and resources.

NOTES

1. For the purposes of this text, "modernity" refers to the ideological system that emerged out of the complex intermingling of the Western cultural epochs known as the Renaissance, the Reformation, and the Scientific Revolution. This ideological system serves as the basis for the modern project, or that project which arose in Western industrialized nations, where all of reality was divided into inner experience and outer world and where objectivity and science became the new faith (Tarnas 1991, 223).

2. The term "miscast ecologist" comes from Calvin Martin (1981).

3. As previously defined, "colonization" refers to a multidimensional force underwritten by Western Christianity, defined by white supremacy, and fueled by global capitalism.

4. The term "serviceable other" is used by Edward Sampson (1993) to differentiate members of the dominant group to those on the margins. He argues that for every social construction of reality operating in a given society there are those who do the constructing and those who are constructed. Furthermore, throughout the history of modern Western society, the primary constructors have been white, educated males of the dominating class. Sampson maintains that the dominant groups give priority to

their own experiences and construct "serviceable others," or others constructed to be in service to the dominant group's needs, values, interests, and points of view.

5. While it is not within the purview of this chapter to engage in a deep discussion of competing ontologies, a rough outline of the fundamental difference(s) or orientation(s) of indigenous and nonindigenous societies is drawn as a means of articulating what is inherently multifarious and complex in more basic terms.

6. Banuri maintains that modernist cultures hold impersonal relations as being inherently superior to personal.

7. Though only Banuri and Berman are discussed here, the fundamental dualisms inherent in their models are also reflected in Louis Dumont's individualism/holism; Emile Durkheim's contractual/organic solidarity; and Donald Oliver and Kathleen Gershman's ontological/technical knowing.

8. While "the sacred" in whitestream society is generally limited to things associated with the practice of formal religion(s), I employ this metaphor to refer to all that lies beyond human capacity and understanding to an overall sense that such *supra*human forces guide the universe. An indigenous society that is deeply informed by the sacred is, thus, not the same as a theocracy (where one "religion" or "god" rules and governs all practice), but is, rather, one that operates on the understanding that human beings exist in deep relationship to the nonhuman and suprahuman worlds. Similarly, a secular society is not only governed by "nonreligious" precepts but also operates on the implicit understanding that human beings are the preeminent source of knowledge and power.

9. Giddens (1990, 38) argues, for example, that where traditional (sacred) cultures make no distinction between time and sociospatial markers, modern (secular) cultures disconnect time and space.

10. Indeed, the notion of "manifest destiny" made colonization and profit seeking a holy, god-mandated project. This mandate is reflected in the infamous words of Horace Greeley: "God has given this earth to those who will subdue and cultivate it, and it is vain to struggle against his righteous decree."

11. See Gary J. Coates (1981), Joan Galtung (1986), Michael Ignatieff (1984), and Donald Oliver and Kathleen Gershman (1989).

12. Carlos Alberto Torres (1998) discusses Jorgé Luis Borges's metaphor of "the secret adventures of order" as "a symbol of intricate relations between the state, power, and education."

13. It should be noted that the details of each of these cases could themselves constitute a separate book. As such, only the barest of facts are provided here to give the reader a sense of the presenting problems. For more information on the Navajo–Hopi Land Dispute see, David Brugge (1999), Suzanne Gordon (1973), and John Sherry (2002). For more information on the Indian Land Trust Fund, see Joel Brinkley (2003), Richmond Clow and Irme Sutton (2001), and PBS Online Newshour (http://www.pbs.org/newshour/bb/fedagencies/july-dec02/indiantrusts_12-18.html [December 18, 2002]). For further information on Quechan mining see Robert L. Bee (1981) and Jack Forbes (1965).

14. The language "fighting for its life" is used in the section under "Growth" on the company's own website: www.peabodyenergy.com [accessed February 2004].

15. The original Hopi Council was a product of the Indian Reorganization Act and was never really functional as the Hopi staunchly resisted "reorganization."

16. "Navajo Nation Council," online: www.lapahie.com/index.cfm [accessed February 2004].

17. To reiterate, the Reorganization Act replaced traditional forms of tribal governance with tribal councils, their structures modeled after whitestream notions of "representation" and "democracy." In practice the councils functioned as puppet governments of the United States and its corporate envoys, providing Congress easy access to Indian decision-making bodies with the "power" to initiate actions favorable to industry. Indeed, Gordon (1973) maintains that had "traditional systems remained intact" tribal decisions "would have required the consent of each village chief, a difficult, if not impossible thing to obtain."

18. The Hopi managed to resist the reorganization for several years. So that while a "tribal council" was officially formed in 1936, it was not recognized by any tribal authority and virtually collapsed shortly afterwards. The "Council" was resurrected in 1951 by John Boyden, a BIA appointed attorney for Peabody Coal, and former archbishop of the Mormon Church.

19. For example, in 1979, a traditional Navajo council of elders issued a "Declaration of Independence" disassociating itself from the prodevelopment Tribal Council. In 1981, a delegation from Big Mountain Diné and traditional Hopi traveled to Geneva, Switzerland, submitting their case to the U.N. Human Rights Commission; such claims have consistently been brought before the commission ever since.

20. Under Dawes, "surplus" Indian land was leased to private interests. The "royalties" gained from such ventures (oil, coal, etc.) were to be accounted for and held "in trust" by the U.S. government.

21. The Blackfoot Nation consists of four distinct Blackfoot nations who share a historical and cultural background but have separate leadership: the Siksika (which means Blackfoot), the Akainawa (also called Kainai or Bloods), the Pikanii (variously spelled Piikani, Pikani, Pikuni, Piegan, or Peigan), and the Blackfeet. The first three nations are in Alberta, Canada, and the fourth is in Montana. ("Blackfeet," though the official name of this tribe, is actually a misnomer given to them by white authorities; the word is not plural in the Blackfoot language, and some Blackfoot people in Montana resist this label.)

22. PBS Online Newshour. December 18, 2002. Broken Trust? http://www. pbs.org/newshour/bb/fedagencies/july-dec0s/indiantrusts1 2-18.html.

23. http://mytwobeadsworth.com/Indian TrustFund.html

24. The Federal Land Policy and Management Act mandated the secretary of the interior to take preventative action against any "unnecessary or undue degradation of the lands."

25. Giddens, moreover, recognizes that tradition is not wholly static but rather reinvented, to some degree, by each new generation, rendering traditional cultures not as ossified relics of some mythic past but rather as cultures working to limit the terms by which change takes on meaningful form (1990, 37).

Chapter Four

American Indian Geographies
of Identity and Power

Until Indians resolve for themselves a comfortable modern identity that
can be used to energize reservation institutions, radical changes will not be
of much assistance.

— Vine Deloria Jr. and Clifford M. Lytle (1984, 266)

Our struggle at the moment is to continue to survive and work toward a
time when we can replace the need for being preoccupied with survival
with a more responsible and peaceful way of living within communities
and with the ever-changing landscape that will ever be our only home.

— Robert Allen Warrior (1995, 126)

*While I entered the academy quite certain of my identity and positionality I
quickly became entangled in the abyss of identity politics, forced to answer
the proverbial question, who am I? and the more political question, who are
you? As I worked on honing my responses to these questions, I began to realize that I was not alone in this quest and Native academics everywhere were
feeling besieged by the rancor of identity politics. Indeed, the debate over who
are the "real" Indians, the new Indians, the wannabes and the "frauds" rages
with great fury. The more I paid attention to the debate, the more I became
paralyzed by compulsions to claim every-thing, one-thing, and no-thing, and
haunted by the prospect that I might inadvertently construct a "mistaken"
identity. I feared that what I had to contribute to the academic world would
be viewed as immaterial in comparison to whether or not I claimed the proper
identity cache and assumed the correct (read: most authentic) voice. As a result, for the first couple of years of my postdoc status I lived in a state of ar-
rested development, obsessing myself into private turmoil and public silence.*

*Ironically, I found salvation from this discursive nightmare in the intoler-
ance of the nondiscursive world. That is, in spite of my "mixed blood" status,
I am a dark-skinned woman with undeniably "Indian" features and, thus, inherit and incite all the prejudices, stereotypes, and racist assumptions that
such a persona elicits. On any given day, introspective musings over my identity portfolio are invariably interrupted by some random act of racist ignorance—kids donning Chief Wahoo gear and "whooping" as I pass by, New
Agers stalking me in search of "authentic" Indian wisdom, or by the more serious permutations of institutional racism. Once I was asked in a faculty
meeting to defend American Indian history as an integral part of "American"
history. Needless to say, the struggle to exist in a climate where such a claim
is not readily recognized was a daily one. Thus, in the end, the real existing
world never afforded me the luxury of academic perseveration.*

The broad aim of this chapter is to reveal how the current obsession with
questions of identity and authenticity obscures the sociopolitical and material
conditions of American Indian communities. Indeed, questions of who or
what is an American Indian, who should be allowed to speak from the authority of that voice, who can conduct research on behalf of American Indian
communities, and what counts as the "real" Indian history dominate the discourse in a manner that suggests to the non-Indian world that the primary
struggle of American Indians is the problem of forging a "comfortable modern identity." By displacing the real sites of struggle (sovereignty and self-
determination), the discourse of identity politics ultimately obfuscates the
real sources of oppression—colonialism and global capitalism.

The connection between identity politics and capitalist imperatives is perhaps most readily seen in the context of higher education, where battles over
authenticity are waged in the for-profit arenas of admissions, faculty recruit-
ment, affirmative action, and scholarship. Allegations of otherwise "white"
individuals committing "ethnic fraud" further muddy the waters of an already
impossible debate. Regrettably, as the academy preoccupies itself with ferret-
ing "fraudulent" Indians and debunking bogus research, continued assaults on
American Indian lands, cultures, and communities proceed with little public
notice and even less public outrage.

The discourse of "authenticity" is underwritten by "essentialist" theories of
identity. That is, theories of identity that treat race (and other aspects of identity) as a stable and homogenous construct, as if members of different racial
groups possessed "some innate and invariant set of characteristics" that set
them apart from each other as well as from whites (McCarthy and Crichlow
1993, xviii). Critical scholars critique such essentialist theories, contending
that they grossly undertheorize identity, muting its inherent complexities and

contradictions. They not only reject the notion that group membership can be reduced to lists of essential characteristics but also contest such practices as, at best, inaccurate, and, at worst, racist.

In contrast, critical scholars advocate theories of difference firmly rooted in the "discourses of power, democracy, social justice and historical memory" (McLaren and Giroux 1997, 17), liberating "identity" from the specious discourse of "authenticity" and re-centering it in the context of power. In so doing, they replace the relatively static notion of "identity" (a fixed, passively inherited entity that one is endowed with) with the more fluid concept of "subjectivity" (the active and continuous "product of human work") (Said 1993, xix). The postmodern discourse of subjectivity spawned a whole new language among critical scholars, with a variety of constructs emerging to express the profound contingency of "identity": border cultures, border-crossers, mestíza, *Xicanisma*, postcolonial hybridities, cyborg identities, and *mestizaje* are just some of the emergent concepts formulated to explain and bring language to the experience of multiplicity, relationality, and transgression as they relate to identity (Anzaldúa 1987; Delgado Bernal 1998; Castillo 1995; Harraway 1991; Darder, Torres, and Gutiérrez 1997; McLaren and Sleeter 1995; Valle and Torres 1995).

Such constructs posit subjectivity as being radically contingent, continually shifting along axes of race, class, gender, and sexuality, and aggressively dismissing the notion that one "is" anything. In other words, in the borderlands of subjectivity, the only normative standard is hybridity, wherein the modernist "borders" of identity are contested, particularly those that have been placed in binary opposition: self/other, male/female, black/white, heterosexual/homosexual, and organism/machine. Indeed, critical scholars advocate the dissolution or disregard for borders of any sort, calling for subjects to actively contest these artificial boundaries, to "border-cross" and transgress,[1] embracing the "spaces-in-between." Such acts are viewed as democratizing contestations wherein the implosion of center and margin creates a space of "intersection," a space of possibility where new cultures can be created—*una cultura mestizo* (Anzaldúa 1987). As such, the postmodern notion of subjectivity not only contests essentialist constructions of identity but also the hegemony of whiteness as the normative standard for all subjects.

For critical scholars, the development of more complex and inclusive understandings of identity is crucial to the democratic project. Through rupturing the concretized categories of identity, critical theorists imagine a new social order wherein transgression and *mestizaje* dismantle the old social order and therefore the existing relations of exploitation. In short, transgression is linked to the creation of greater possibilities for political solidarity and solidarity to the hope of democracy.

The persistent belief in the superiority and emancipatory powers of democracy, even among radical scholars, indicates the degree to which whitestream America has never really understood what it means to be Indian and even less about what it means to be tribal. This ignorance has deep historical roots and even wider political implications. Indeed, as previously discussed, the uncompromising belief in the superiority of Western social and political structures—that is, democracy and citizenship—was the motivating force behind the numerous expurgatory campaigns exacted against indigenous peoples. The Civilization Act of 1819, the Indian Removal Act of 1830, the General Allotment Act of 1887, the Indian Citizenship Act of 1924, the Indian Reorganization Act of 1934, and the Indian Civil Rights Act of 1968 are just a sample of the myriad legal mechanisms imposed on tribal America in the name of "democracy."

While critical theorists contest the hegemonic forces that eventuated this "imposition," they also continue to presume the normalcy of the democratic order. This presumption fails to account for the "difference" of American Indian tribal identity—specifically, what it means to be sovereign, tribal peoples within the geopolitical confines of the United States. Native scholars, thus, remain skeptical of the "new" political project, viewing it as simply the latest in a long line of political endeavors aimed at absorbing American Indians into the prevailing model of the "democratic citizen."

In response, indigenous scholars have worked hard to articulate the "difference" of tribal identity, distinguishing it, both legally and culturally, from mainstream conceptions of identity. Such efforts have been, in some ways, shaped by the need for a collective indigenous response to the dehumanizing and racist depictions of Indian-ness put forth by whitestream America. As such, the emergent counterhegemonic discourse generated antiracist and highly idealized constructions of American Indian identity and culture. Warrior (1995) notes the mid-1980s as the height of when idealized images of American Indians flooded the marketplace with writings about the benevolent "Indian worldview" dominating the discourse. Of this era Warrior states, "such a commitment to essentialized indigenous worldviews and consciousness became . . . a pervasive and almost requisite feature of American Indian critical writing" (1995, xvii).

Though a cadre of indigenous scholars have always expressed resistance to essentialist depictions of American Indian culture and identity (e.g., Chrytos, Deloria, Durham, Forbes, Vizenor, and Warrior), they continue to hold sway. In particular, communities struggling to fetter the impact of colonialist forces—specifically, identity appropriation ("ethnic fraud"), cultural imperialism, and corporate commodification—are compelled by essentialist definitions of Indian-ness and the clearly demarcated lines between "us" and "them." The project of defining a contemporary Indian identity is, thus, highly mediated by whitestream forces, particularly the homogenizing effects of global capitalism. This reality exposes the perceived existential crisis of identity as in actuality a crisis of power. Specifically, the power to name, shape, and control the products and conditions of one's life and particularly one's labor.

As a result, the "crisis" of American Indian identity is perhaps better articulated as an identity paradox. That is, at the same time the relentless cadence of colonialist forces necessitates American Indians to retain more closed or "essentialist" constructions of Indian-ness, the challenges of their own "burgeoning multiculturalism" requires the construction of more open, fluid, and "transgressive" definitions of Indian-ness. This paradox or the tension between the urgency to border-cross and impulse to border-patrol is one of the central themes of this chapter. More specifically, I aim to reveal how the rancor of identity politics has not only deeply compromised the power of American Indians to mediate the forces of colonialism and global capitalism but also how dominant modes of educational theory have failed to construct models of identity that effectively interrogate and disrupt the project of colonization.

The discussion begins with an examination of the legal and political forces that have shaped the historical formation of American Indian identity. Then, a contemporary model of "the difference of tribal identity" is articulated as a by-product of these historical forces. Next, the dominant modes of identity theory—left-essentialism and postmodernism—are examined in terms of their intersection with current formations of American Indian identity. This analysis reveals how whitestream theories of identity have not only failed to interrogate and disrupt the project of colonization but have also provided the theoretical basis and intellectual space for its continuance. More specifically, the colonialist forces of corporate commodification, identity appropriation, and cultural imperialism are discussed as the consequences of a geographic and political terrain that aims to absorb indigenous peoples.

Finally, concepts that emerge from critical theories of identity—specifically the construct of *mestizaje* and other models of hybridity—are examined as potential tools for developing a counterdiscourse of American Indian subjectivity. The chapter concludes with a discussion of the need for an indigenous theory of identity—one historically grounded in indigenous struggles for self-determination, politically centered in issues of sovereignty, and spiritually guided by the religious traditions of American Indian peoples. The aim is to develop an emancipatory theory—a new Red pedagogy—that acts as a true counterdiscourse, counterpraxis, counterensoulment[2] of indigenous identity.

THE HISTORICAL FORMATION OF AMERICAN INDIAN IDENTITY: TOWARD A MODEL OF TRIBAL IDENTITY

The "discovery" of natives in the so-called New World offered one of the greatest challenges to Europeans' accepted notions of self, personhood, and culture. Hayden White (1976, 133) notes that their encounter with a race of "wild men" created a crisis of category for the general notion of "humanity" developed in Western philosophy, igniting a debate between two opposing views of Indians:

> On the one hand, natives were conceived to be continuous with the humanity on which Europeans prided themselves; and it was this mode of relationship that underlay the policy of proselytization and conversion. On the other hand, the natives could be conceived as simply existing contiguously to Europeans, as representing either an inferior breed of humanity or a superior breed, but in any case being essentially different from the European breed; and it was this mode of relationship that underlay the policies of war and extermination which the Europeans followed throughout the seventeenth and most of the eighteenth century.

At stake for the colonizers was not only the prospect of acquiring religious converts but also of defining the terms of political engagement—were the natives "the same" and therefore deserving of equal rights or were they inferior deserving of no rights at all? Such questions were critical for a young democracy working to build its notion of democratic citizenship on the "truths" of individualism and private property.

The bloody encounter between these operational truths and those of the Indian nations came to a head in 1887 with the passage of the General Allotment Act. As discussed in chapter 2, Senator Henry Dawes spearheaded a campaign to rid the nation of tribalism through the virtues of private property, allotting land parcels to Indian heads of family. Before allotments could be dispensed, however, the government had to determine which Indians were eligible, igniting the official search for a federal definition of Indian-ness. The task of defining "Indian-ness" was assigned to the Dawes commission, a delegation of white men who facilely embraced the prevailing racial purity model, expressing Indian-ness in terms of blood-quantum.

Satisfied with their quantifiable definition of Indian-ness, Dawes commissioners dispersed into the field, interviewing thousands of Indians about their "origins." Much to their dismay, federal officials found that "after forced relocations, intermarriages, absconded parents, informal adoptions, and civil wars" many Indians had only fuzzy ideas of their origins and little knowledge of their blood-quantum (Malcomson 2000, 16). Since there was no "scientific" means of determining precise bloodlines, commission members often ascribed blood status based on their own racist notions of what it meant to be Indian—designating full-blood status to "poorly assimilated" Indians and mixed-blood status to those who most resembled whites. As a result, a significant number of Indians refused to comply with the process of racial categorization (Malcomson 2000). Unfazed, the Dawes Commission published the first comprehensive tribal rolls neatly listing names in one column and blood quanta in another; designating F for "full-blood" and 1/2, 1/4, or 1/8 for "mixed bloods."

Land parcels were dispensed according to the lists and followed their same racist logic. That is, "full-blooded" Indians (considered legally incompetent), received relatively small parcels of land deeded with trust patents over which the government retained complete control for a minimum of twenty-five years. "Mixed-blood" Indians, on the other hand, were deeded larger and better tracts of land, with "patents in fee simple" (complete control), but were also forced to accept U.S. citizenship and relinquish tribal status (Churchill and Morris 1992; Stiffarm and Lane 1992). In perhaps the most controversial turn, Indians who failed to meet the established criteria were effectively "detribalized," deposed of their American Indian identity and displaced from their homelands, discarded into the nebula of the American "otherness."[3]

Its myriad indiscretions arguably make Dawes the single most destructive U.S. policy. All told, the act empowered the U.S. government to: (1) legally preempt the sovereign right of Indians to define themselves; (2) implement the specious notion of blood-quantum as the legal criteria for defining Indians;[4] (3) institutionalize divisions between "full-bloods" and "mixed-bloods";[5] (4) "detribalize" a sizable segment of the Indian population;[6] and (5) legally appropriate vast tracts of Indian land. Indeed, so "successful" was this aspect of the "democratic experiment" that the federal government decided to retain—or rather, further exploit—the notion of blood-quantum and federal recognition as the means for dispensing other resources and services such as health care and educational funding.

An Operational Definition of Indian-ness

While five centuries of imperialist strategies may have decimated the traditional societies of preinvasion times, modern American Indian communities still resemble traditional societies enough so that, "given a choice between Indian society and non-Indian society, most Indians feel comfortable with their own institutions, lands and traditions" (Deloria and Lytle 1983, xii). Despite the persistent divide between "Indian" and "non-Indian" societies, however, defining tribal America has remained curiously difficult.[7] To tease out, name, and assign primacy to certain aspects of Indian-ness as "the definition" would not only grossly oversimplify the complexity of American Indian subjectivity (forcing what is fundamentally traditional, spatial, and interconnected into the modern, temporal, and epistemic frames of Western theory), but also reenact the objectification of Indians set in motion by the Dawes commission over a century ago. Accordingly, the following rubric merely calls attention to the "difference" of tribal identity as conceived through some of the legal indicators of what it means to be American Indian in U.S. society.[8] It is not meant to represent some mythic view of a unified indigenous culture or objectified view of American Indian identity.

The Difference of Tribal Identity
- *Sovereignty vs. Democracy*: American Indians have been engaged in a centuries-long struggle to have what is legally theirs recognized (i.e., land, sovereignty, treaty rights). As such, indigenous peoples have not, like other marginalized groups, been fighting for inclusion in the democratic imaginary, but rather for the right to remain distinct, sovereign, and tribal peoples.
- *Treaty Rights*: These rights articulate the unique status of Indian tribes as "domestic dependent nations." A dizzying array of tribal, federal, and state laws, policies, and treaties creates a political maze that keeps the legal status of most tribes in a constant state of flux. Treaties are negotiated and renegotiated in a process that typically reduces tribal rights and erodes traditional structures (Deloria and Lytle 1984; Fixcio 1998).
- *Dual Citizenship*: The Indian Citizenship Act of 1924 extends the rights of full citizenship to American Indians born within the territorial United States insofar as such status does not infringe upon the rights to tribal and other property. It is a dual citizenship wherein American Indians do not lose civil rights because of their status as tribal members and individual tribal members are not denied tribal rights because of their American citizenship (Deloria and Lytle 1984).[9]
- *Federal Recognition*: Federal law mandates that American Indians prove that they have continued to exist over time as stable, prima facie entities to retain federal recognition as tribes. Acknowledgment of tribal existence by the Department of the Interior is critical, as it is a prerequisite to the protection, services, and benefits made available by the federal government to Indian tribes by virtue of their status as tribes. Therefore, a tribe's existence is contingent upon its ability to prove its existence over time, to provide evidence of shared cultural patterns, and to prove "persistence of a named, collective Indian identity" (Bureau of Indian Affairs, USD, 83, 7).

- *Economic Dependency*: American Indians continue to exist as nations within a nation wherein the relationship between the U.S. government and Indian tribes is not the fictive "government to government" relationship described in U.S. documents, but, rather, one that positions tribes as fundamentally dependent on the federal government.[10]
- *Reservations*: Almost two-thirds of American Indians continue to either live on or remain significantly tied to their reservations and, as such, remain predominantly "tribally oriented" as opposed to generically Indian (Joe and Miller 1997).

The above indicators position American Indians in a wholly unique and paradoxical relationship to the United States. They also illuminate the inherent contradictions of modern American Indian existence: the paradox of having to prove "authenticity" to gain legitimacy as a "recognized" tribe, while simultaneously having to negotiate a postmodern world in which all claims to authenticity are dismissed as essentialist (if not racist). This reality not only conscripts American Indians to a gravely dangerous and precarious space but also points to the gross insufficiency of models that treat American Indians as simply another ethnic minority group.

Specifically, the identity paradox of American Indians deeply problematizes the postmodern insistence that we move beyond concretized categories and disrupt the "myth" of prima facie indicators of identity. For American Indians, such notions only reflect whitestream reality. For instance, it currently remains a fundamental truth of Indian reality—no matter how you define it—that the titles to Indian land remain in the hands of the U. S. government. Moreover, the U.S. government—not tribes—retains the right to confer "federal recognition" and therefore the power to enable self-determination. Indeed, the criteria required for federal recognition are constructed to protect the rights and interests of the government and not those of Indian tribes. According to the *Indian Definition Study* (1980), the inner contradictions of the current criteria create the following impossible paradox for tribes:

1. An American Indian is a member of any federally recognized tribe. To be federally recognized, an Indian tribe must be comprised of American Indians.
2. To gain federal recognition, an Indian tribe must have a land base. To secure a land base, an Indian tribe must be federally recognized.[11]

So, five hundred years after the European invasion, "recognized" and "unrecognized" American Indian communities repeatedly find themselves engaged in absurd efforts to prove (in whitestream courts) their existence over time as stable and distinct groups of people.

Thus, contrary to postmodern rhetoric, there are in fact, stable markers and prima facie indicators of what it means to be Indian in American society. Within this context, indigenous scholars cannot afford to perceive essentialism as a mere theoretical construct and may, in fact, be justified in their understanding of it as the last line of defense against capitalistic encroachment and last available means for retaining cultural integrity and tribal sovereignty. The question therefore remains whether contemporary theories of identity are able to provide any valuable insights to the paradox of American Indian identity formation.

(LEFT) ESSENTIALISM: AMERICAN INDIAN IDEATIONS AND CAPITALIST CRAVINGS

Left-essentialism is basically a permutation of essentialist theories. While left-essentialism rejects the biologic determinism of essentialist theories, it similarly downplays the variability and historical contingency of race, favoring more simplistic constructions that limit racial identity to its most essential and/or stereotypical features. In short, left-essentialism employs a kind of sociocultural determinism built around the notion of authenticity. Specifically, identity is formed on the bases of romanticized ideals and nationalistic pride wherein "purity" functions as a hallmark of legitimacy and authenticity. Aside from this distinction, left-essentialism differs from its counterpart in terms of its politics. Specifically, essentialist theories are driven by the whitestream desire to define "otherness" while left-essentialist theories are employed by subaltern peoples, as a tool of political empowerment.

Joe Kincheloe and Shirley Steinberg (1997) maintain the politics of left-essentialism can be quite authoritarian. The implication is that purity or "essence" produces a form of moral superiority or "oppression privilege" where only authentically oppressed people are viewed as possessing moral agency. For example, in a conversation about sexism, a woman's perspective would be seen as carrying a greater degree of moral authority over a man's, and in a conversation about racism, a person of color's over a white person. Kincheloe and Steinberg (1997) maintain such logic forces one to "submit proper credentials before offering an opinion," arguing that the politics of location privileges an unexamined set of authentic experiences as the foundation for authority. In other words, "truth" is constructed as a function of identity.[12]

In the academy, (left-essentialist) identity politics plays out in a manner that sutures social location to discursive power so that a person's "physical proximity to the oppressed or their own location as an oppressed person" provides "a special authority from which to speak" (McLaren 1995). Such a "pedigree of voice" typically pits white scholars against scholars of color in the final battles of the war against centuries of intellectual hegemony and academic colonialism. In the field of Native studies, battle lines have been drawn between American Indian scholars working to claim intellectual sovereignty and non-Indian scholars working against the essentialist grain to sustain and reassert the validity of their own scholarship, raising the question of who has the right to conduct research and publish findings on Indian Country.[13] A report issued by the American Indian Studies Center at UCLA[14] had this to say about the ensuing battles:

> Just as the exploitation of American Indian land and resources is of value to corporate America, research and publishing is valuable to non-Indian scholars. As a result of racism, greed, and distorted perceptions of native realities, Indian culture as an economic commodity has been exploited by the dominant society with considerable damage to Indian people. Tribal people need to safeguard the borders of their cultural domains against research and publishing incursions. (American Indian Studies Center UCLA 1989, 6)

While the deficiencies of left-essentialism are apparent, it is worth noting that the charge of "identity politics" by whitestream liberals often gets levied in the same manner that charges of "political correctness" get exacted by conservatives. Both charges conjure pictures of overpowered minorities and disempowered whites and transmute the efforts of subaltern peoples to expose the inner workings of white privilege to acts of reverse discrimination. It is therefore important to distinguish the left-essentialist tactics employed by subaltern peoples for the purposes of political empowerment from discriminatory tactics employed by conservative forces intent on returning to the days of eugenics. More significantly, it is important to recognize both theoretical strategies as being borne of the colonialist project.

Indeed, various critical scholars have revealed "essentialism" as an integral part of the overall project of domination working to hold American Indians (and other subaltern peoples) to the "polemical and creative needs of whites" (Berkhofer 1978; Deloria 1970; P. Deloria 1999; Mihesuah 1996). With respect to Native peoples, Deloria (1970) argues that the predominant image of the American Indian—the nature-loving, noble savage—persists to serve the whitestream need to escape the deadening effects of modernity. He writes: "[Whites] are discontented with their society, their government, their religion, and everything around them and nothing is more appealing than to cast aside all inhibitions and stride back into the wilderness, or at least a wilderness theme park, seeking the nobility of the wily savage who once physically fought civilization and now, symbolically at least, is prepared to do it again" (1970, 34). Deloria's somewhat cynical reference to the "wilderness theme park" describes the propensity of whitestream America to satisfy its need for "authenticity" via climate-controlled, voyeuristic tours through the lives and experiences of "authentic" peoples. In this instance, "discontented" whites maintain psychological control over the overconsumption of modern society by requiring Indians to remain nature-loving primitives. The parasitic relationship between whitestream desire, capitalist imperatives, and American Indians does not end here. Indeed, while the American Indian intellectual community has managed to wrest a degree of control over the question of "who is Indian," it has yet to muster the capability to fetter the powers of capitalism. Thus the impact of capitalist desire on the intellectual sovereignty of indigenous peoples remains significant, particularly in the academy.

For example, indigenous scholar Elizabeth Cook-Lyn (1998, 121) questions why the same editors and agents who solicit her "life story" also routinely reject her scholarly work. She writes: "[W]hile I may have a reasonable understanding why a state-run university press would not want to publish research that has little good to say about America's relationship to tribes . . . I am at a loss as to explain why anyone would be more interested in my life story (which for one thing is quite unremarkable)." The explanation, of course, is that the marketable narrative is that which subscribes to the whitestream notion of Indian as romantic figure, not Indian as scholar and social critic—a predisposition that works to favor cultural/literary forms of indigenous writing over critical forms. As Warrior (1995, xx) observes, the current discourse is more interested in "the Charles Eastman [Sioux] who grew up in a traditional Sioux home than in the Charles Eastman who attended Mark Twain's seventieth birthday party or who read a paper at the First Universal Races Conference with W.E.B. Dubois."

Indeed, the marketplace is flooded with the tragic stories of American Indians as lost cultures and lost peoples. Moreover, such stories are told and retold as history, as part of America's dark and distant past. Within the contexts of whitestream history the consequence of genocide is typically depicted as an egregious but perhaps unavoidable consequence of the country's belief in manifest destiny. While I would never argue that stories depicting the tragedy of genocide (e.g., Indian boarding schools, the Trail of Tears) are not centrally important in the telling of American history, their prominence in the discourse becomes problematic when considered in the wider context of whitestream consumption. In other words, why are these stories upheld as the prime-time programs in the commodified network of Indian history? What is gained from the proliferation of essentialist portrayals of whitestream domination and Indian subjugation?

Such stories, in fact, serve several purposes, none of which contribute to the emancipatory project of American Indians. First, by propagating romanticized images of American Indians as perpetual victims while simultaneously marginalizing the work of indigenous intellectuals and social critics, whitestream publishers maintain control over the epistemic frames of the discourse and thus over the fund of available knowledge on American Indians. The desire for such control is underwritten by the understanding that critical scholarship threatens the myth of the ever-evolving democratization of Indian–white relations. Second, essentialist accounts of Indian history (framed in good- vs. bad-guy terms) allow the consumer to fault rogue groups of dogmatic missionaries and wayward military officers for the slow but steady erosion of indigenous life, thereby distancing themselves and mainstream government from the ongoing project of cultural genocide. Third, the virtually exclusive focus on Indian history allows the whitestream to ignore contemporary issues facing American Indian communities. As a result, Indians as a modern people remain invisible, allowing a wide array of distorted myths to flourish as contemporary reality: that all the "real" Indians are extinct, that all surviving Indians are either alcoholics or gaming entrepreneurs. Meanwhile, as these images are circulated, the intensive, ongoing court battles over land, natural resources, and federal recognition are relegated to the margins of the discourse, fueling the great lie of the twenty-first century—that America's "Indian problem" has long been solved.

While there has been some public commentary by American Indian intellectuals on the limitations of market imperatives, many have been complicit in the authenticity game, bamboozled into legitimating the colonialist discourse of identity politics.[15] The conundrum goes something like this: at the same time American Indian scholars are held to the "publish or perish" rule of the academy they are held captive to market imperatives that demand easily digestible, readily accessible texts, prepackaged for whitestream consumption. These contradictory forces create the following "options" for indigenous scholars: (1) to produce scholarship-lite (work deemed publishable by whitestream presses) and gain "wide" (read: "mainstream") recognition, thereby increasing chances for tenure and promotion; or (2) publish critique-al scholarship with smaller Native presses, thereby retaining one's integrity as a scholar but risking the denial of tenure and promotion on the basis of limited publication with "highly competitive" (read: whitestream) journals and presses. In other words, the game is rigged. The space for American Indian intellectualism is conscripted by academic colonialism and the essentialist fascination with "authentic" subjectivities. Therefore, "the American Indian story" becomes more about the perpetuation of whitestream fantasies than about the political, economic, cultural, and social subjugation of America's first nations.

In response to this dilemma, many American Indian scholars have resorted to occupying a sort of intellectual middle ground, a space where relatively safe and easy questions can be asked of controversial subjects, often cleverly disguising critique behind the literary mask of fiction and poetry. This is perhaps why bookstore shelves are brimming with Native legends, poems, novels, and short stories relatively barren of critique-al studies of contemporary American Indian life. In short, the obsession with identity politics has pressured American Indian intellectuals to succumb to the vision of who they are supposed to be instead of who they are. Such pressures have limited the frames of indigenous inquiry, raising the question: How has the conscription of indigenous scholarship to the "traditional" realms of art and culture impacted contemporary American Indian peoples struggling to negotiate an increasingly complex global-capitalist world?

All told, essentialism fails the American Indian community. It fails to theorize the relational character of identity by denying the historicity and social comprehensiveness of American Indian subjectivity. It fails to account for the ways indigenous peoples are forced to negotiate incoherent and other conflicting pressures on identity formation. And, perhaps most important, it fails to provide an explanatory critique of the persistent colonialist forces that undermine tribal life and consequently to provide the transformative knowledge needed to disrupt their hegemonic effects.

Pedagogical Implications of Essentialism

Essentialist theories of identity theory have undoubtedly impacted educational practice, shaping the way teachers view students and, perhaps more important, the way students view themselves. American Indian students have indeed internalized the invisible but powerful borders demarcating "authentic" Indian-ness. On some level, they understand that the problem of forging a contemporary Indian identity is, in part, a problem of resisting the images and fantasies of whitestream America. This is evident in some students' resistance to occupying the social and political spaces associated with "acting white."

As John Ogbu (1986, 25–26) has noted, "blacks and similar minorities (e.g., American Indians) believe that in order for a minority person to succeed in school academically, he or she must learn to think and act white."[16] Thus, as a result of their subordinate position, Ogbu argues that blacks have constructed an identity system that is not merely different from but *formed in opposition to* the social identity of whites. Furthermore, he argues that within the black community itself there are formal and informal sanctions against those who cross over into what is generally regarded as the "white cultural frame of reference." As such, Ogbu posits that students from "castelike" mi-nority groups may actively *resist* school achievement, as it is often associated with "acting white."

Though there are clear differences between blacks and American Indians, their shared positionality as subordinate groups in the United States maps a terrain of common experience. Like black students, the majority of Ameri-can Indian students find themselves in white-controlled institutions with agendas of assimilation and therefore vulnerable to the hegemonic norms of identity. In more concrete terms, insofar as everything from high achieve-ment to learning classical violin is associated with "acting white," American Indian students and their teachers often render such aspirations off-limits. As such, students faced with the dilemma of choosing between "academic suc-cess" and "cultural suicide" become unwitting but active participants in their own "failure." McLaren (1998), therefore, theorizes resistance as part of the overall process of hegemony, pointing out that students who actively contest the colonizing effects of the dominant culture ultimately limit their own life chances.

While Ogbu and other critical scholars (e.g., Fine 1989; Weis 1985; Willis 1977) have examined the role of resistance in minority identity formation few have investigated this concept as it relates, more directly, to American Indian students. Among these works (Wax and Dumont 1989; Wolcott 1967; Deyhle 1995) the analyses of Donna Deyhle is arguably the most important. While much of her work confirms the deep impact of racism and hegemony in schools, her broad focus on Navajo students, schools, and families sheds great insight to the difference of American Indian-ness. Specifically, she found that "traditional" Navajo students, or those most secure in their identity as "In-dian," did not experience the same compulsions to "resist" as Ogbu's other "caste-like" minorities. On the contrary, Deyhle found that the "failure" of such students was more a factor of "racial warfare" in both school and soci-ety (1995, 6). Indeed, she concludes, "the more Navajo students resist assim-ilation while simultaneously maintaining their culture, the more successful they are in school" (1995, 8). Deyhle's analysis not only illuminates the in-adequacies of Ogbu's theory for American Indian students, but also illumi-nates the danger of absorbing indigenous peoples into the frameworks of other "minorities." Moreover, her astute theorization of the complex and con-tradictory terrain of power in schools leads her to underscore McLaren's (2003) observation that "school failure is both structurally located and cul-turally mediated."

Thus, as we struggle to map the terrain of American Indian identity we must keep in mind that domination is no longer signaled by overt exploitation and legal discrimination, but has become increasingly codified in the systems of global capitalism. As Sleeter and McLaren (1995, 9) note, "the motor force of capitalist domination rests on the tacit collusion of the oppressed in their own lived subordination." For example, the fact that the practice of dividing indigenous peoples according to their status under colonial law (e.g., full-blood, mixed-blood) is replicated within and legitimated by American Indian communities speaks to the insidious power of the broader legitimating structures within colonialist society. The insidious nature of colonialist power determines that American Indian students experience its hegemonic effects on a visceral, subconscious level. In this context, resistance is clearly the manifestation of subjugation and the impulsive desire to act in opposition to hegemonic absorption. Such courageous but misguided acts of defiance indicate the need for a politics of difference that not only asserts the positivity of group difference but also ruptures the "sacredotal status of universalist claims to unity that demonize certain groups" as malignant others (McLaren 1998, 255). In constructing such a politics, it is important to situate groups *in relation* (not in binary opposition) to each other, thereby avoiding the translation of difference to mean exclusion and dominance and the subsequent impulse to act or behave oppositionally. In short, what is needed is a form of critical agency that moves beyond the "either-or" logic of assimilation and resistance (McLaren 1998).

It is incumbent upon American Indian intellectuals to assist students in overcoming the dilatory effects of resistance and its coconspirator, essentialism. In short, American Indian intellectuals must be careful, in their own assertions of what constitutes American Indian-ness, to avoid reenacting the divisive logic of colonialist domination—one that not only pits Indian against non-Indian, but also Indian against Indian and tribe against tribe. Thus, while the clearly defined categories of essentialism provide the necessary protection against cultural encroachment and colonialist absorption, it is important to recognize that they also confine American Indian students to narrowly prescribed spaces, ossifying indigenous subjectivity to the chasms of the whitestream imagination.

POSTMODERNISM AND AMERICAN INDIAN IDENTITY: OPEN BORDERS OR OPEN SEASON?

In response to the multiple aporias of essentialism, postmodernists abandon the notion of a rational, unified subject in favor of a socially de-centered and fragmented subject, maintaining that "identity" is shaped and determined by social and historical contingencies, not by some checklist of innate, biological, or primordial characteristics (de Lauretis 1989). Identity, in other words, is viewed as a highly relative construct, one resembling "a theater of simulation marked by the free play of images, disembodied signifiers, and the heterogeneity of differences" (Ebert 1991, 15). Within this "theater" identity is viewed as both fluid and shifting, fed by multiple sources and embodied in multiple forms (Kumar 1997).

Insofar as postmodern theories have stripped away the "epistemological scaffolding" used to prop up essentialist claims to authenticity—peeling away the shroud of legitimacy that once protected positivist assertions of truth and objectivity—postmodernism has had an emancipatory effect. More specifically, postmodernists have helped to uncover the ways in which such "universalist" theories have operated to normalize whiteness. Thus, through its rejection of origin and authenticity, postmodernism provides a theoretical path away from the parochial and limiting effects of essentialism, mapping instead the hidden trajectories of power within the politics of identity.

That being said, postmodern constructions of identity as "free-floating" also create a new set of problematics for American Indians. As articulated in chapter 2, American Indians are not like other subjugated groups struggling to define their place within the larger democratic project. Specifically, they do not seek greater "inclusion"; rather, they are engaged in a perpetual struggle to have their legal and moral claims to sovereignty recognized. The duration and severity of this struggle for American Indians removes the question of identity from the superficial realm of cultural politics to the more profound arena of cultural survival.

Thus, contrary to postmodern analyses, American Indians do not exercise essentialist tactics in order to establish hierarchies of "authenticity," but rather as a means of resisting wholesale appropriation of Indian culture and identity. Specifically, indigenous peoples work to fend off the global capitalist forces that crave indigenous cultures at the same time such forces operate to destroy all that sustains indigenous communities (i.e., land bases, natural resources).[17] Therefore, while it is important to recognize the way essentialism works to undermine the emancipatory project, it is also important to be aware of the dangers of postmodern constructions of identity as they interface with American Indian realities.

To facilitate better understanding of the specific ways postmodernism and cultural imperialism work together to undermine the integrity and viability of American Indian communities, the phenomena of identity appropriation and cultural encroachment are discussed below. Though examined discretely, both forces emanate from the political project of colonization, the social project of postmodernism, and the insatiable, if not cannibalistic, desire of capitalism to consume all that it produces.

Identity Appropriation

Ever since we entered the post–*Dances with Wolves* era, it has become increasingly popular to be American Indian. Joane Nagel, a sociologist and expert in the politics of ethnicity, attests that between 1960 and 1990 the number of Americans reporting "American Indian" as their racial category in the U.S. Census more than tripled. Researchers attribute this growth to the phenomenon of "ethnic switching," a process by which individuals previously identifying as "non-Indian" now claim "Indian" as their racial affiliation. Nagel (1995) identifies three factors as contributing to the practice of ethnic switching: changes in federal Indian policy, changes in American ethnic politics, and increases in American Indian political activism.

The changes in federal Indian policy referenced by Nagel are the termination and relocation policies of the 1960s and 1970s that led to the growth of urban Indian populations and the various land-claims settlements of the 1980s, which also led to increases in certain tribal populations.[18] The changes in ethnic politics are those that reverberated from the civil rights and Red Power movements that ostensibly made American Indian identification "a more attractive ethnic option." The increased political activism from these movements also helped to raise American Indian ethnic consciousness, encouraging individuals to reclaim their Native American ancestry (Nagel 1995, 956).

While Nagel makes strong arguments for the three factors she identifies, she ignores the possibility that part of the resurgence may also be due to increasing incidents of identity appropriation or "ethnic fraud"—the practice of claiming an Indian identity based on the recent discovery of real or imagined residuals of Indian blood in one's distant ancestry. While there is nothing inherently wrong with "claiming" one's ancestral background, when such claims are opportunistically used to cash in on scholarships, set-aside programs, and other affirmative actions intended to correct centuries of unequal treatment it becomes highly problematic. For example, studies conducted at UCLA in 1988–1989 and 1993 reveal that of the enrolled 179 American Indian students, 125 did not or could not provide adequate documentation of their tribal affiliation, and that, on average, less than 15 percent of American Indian students were enrolled in federally recognized tribes (Machamer 1997). More important, a significant number of students who initially identified themselves as American Indian to gain admission ultimately relinquished that identity by the time of graduation, suggesting that economic incentives aside, "new Indians" eventually reclaimed their whiteness (Machamer 1997). Such practices indicate that it is not only popular but also *profitable* to be "Indian" in postmodern America.

These so-called fraudulent Indians have also found ways to profit in the publishing world as their (highly romanticized) work is often favored over that of "legitimate" American Indian scholars. Deloria (1998) observes that what passes in the academic world as legitimate scholarship on American Indians is either the product of average (whitestream) scholars advocating a predetermined anti-Indian agenda[19] or that of "fraudulent Indians" who cater to whitestream notions of Indian-ness, moving him to ask: "Who is it that has made such people as Adolph Hungry Wolf, Jamake Highwater, Joseph Epes Brown, Su Bear, Rolling Thunder, Wallace Black Elk, John Redtail Freesoul, Lynn Andrews, and Dhyani Ywahoo the spokespeople of American Indians?" He responds by naming whitestream America as both patron and peddler of the Hollywood Indian, adding, "They [the fraudulent Indians] represent the intense desire of whites to create in their own minds an Indian they want to believe in" (1998, 79).

In addition to outright identity fraud, American Indian communities also endure the more superficial but equally problematic phenomenon of "ethnic vogueing." Every summer there is a seasonal influx of tour buses, church groups, and do-gooders that discharge a veritable wave of whiteness into Indian communities. Armed with their own constructions of Indian-ness, the interlopers appropriate and try on various elements of Native culture, voyeuristically touring reservation communities like cultural predators loose in Indian theme parks. They stay for as long as their experience meets their needs and then they leave, completely dysconscious[20] of the fact that their adventures have conscripted Native culture as fashion, Indian as exotic, and the sacred as entertainment.[21]

All told, the practice of identity appropriation has become so widespread that some American Indian organizations have felt compelled to devise statements and enact policies against its proliferation.[22] Even the federal government has acknowledged the impact of ethnic fraud, passing Public Law 101-644, or what is commonly referred to as the Indian Arts and Crafts Act (IACA).[23] In an effort to "protect" Native craftspeople, the federal government passed legislation that forbids any one other than a "certified Indian" to display for sale or sell any good that is suggested to be "Indian produced." Individuals found to be in violation of this law are subject to penalties of up to one million dollars and fifteen years in prison (P.L. 101-644, 1990).

While such legislation appears to protect the interests of American Indian artists, the IACA ultimately does more to protect whitestream consumers against the purchase of "fraudulent" goods. As a result of the legislation, countless "legitimate" Indian artists from over two hundred federally unrecognized tribes (and other adequately "blooded" Indians who refuse to comply with the federal "blood-certifying" system) found themselves out of work, now criminalized for practicing their own trades (Jaimes 1992). In addition to being exclusionary, the IACA undermines the political and economic power of tribes by stripping them of their sovereign right to control their own labor and means of production.

While measures such as the IACA may appear reasonable in theory, in practice they become problematic. The reliance on essentialist logic rarely "protects" Indian interests and often backfires to undermine them. Furthermore, insofar as compliance with "ethnic fraud" policies requires the formation of an Indian Identity Police,[24] enforcement becomes a dubious enterprise, inviting even more scrutiny from outside federal and private agencies.

Cultural Imperialism

"Indian Country" persists as both a metaphoric space and a geographic place, one that profoundly shapes the subjectivities of those who traverse it. Specifically, the relationship between American Indian communities and the surrounding (white) border towns not only shapes the ways Indians perceive and construct the whitestream but also their views of themselves. Thus, while reservation borders exist as vestiges of forced removal, colonialist domination, and whitestream greed, they are also understood as marking the defensive perimeters between cultural integrity and wholesale appropriation. They are the literal dividing lines between "us" and "them," demarcating the borders of this nation's only internal sovereigns. Though the power of this status is continually challenged, American Indians have retained enough of their plenary powers to establish tribal courts, tribal governments, and tribal police forces; the borders of such communities are thus material realities and not simply "signifiers" of Indian Country.

That being said, tribal sovereignty remains deeply fettered by the fact that most reservation economies are only sustainable with the infusion of outside capital (Deloria and Lytle 1984). This dependency on outside capital generates a subordinating effect, often leaving American Indians at the mercy of venture capitalists and whitestream do-gooders. Emissaries of white justice, private entrepreneurs, and New Age liberals thus descend on reservation communities, forging lucrative careers at the same time they engage in "charitable" practices. Indeed, most of the business people, teachers, principals, doctors, and health care professionals in reservation communities are white and most of the laborers, minimum-wagers, underemployed, and unemployed are American Indian. Safely bivouacked in their internal and external compounds, they wield power and broker services by day and, by night, retreat back into the comforts of their bourgeois border towns.

Though the social and political impact of "do-gooders" is significant, culture vultures and venture capitalists wreak even more damage as they aim to sell everything Indian, from Native art and music, to spirituality and DNA. Indigenous scholar Laurie Ann Whitt (1998) faults late-capitalist views of ownership and property for sustaining cultural imperialism, which she sees as "the central historical dynamic mediating Euro-American/indigenous relations." In particular, she identifies the following two central assumptions of property and ownership as underlying relations of imperialism: (1) the belief that ownership is individually held; and (2) the belief that individual owners have the right to privacy, in both the maintenance and the economic management of their property. Whitt maintains that these "politics of property" have provided the premise under which U.S. imperialists have seized everything from American Indian lands to spiritual traditions and cultural practices (1998, 148).

Specifically, the first assumption—that ownership is individually held—is used to negate tribal (collective) "ownership" over Indian lands, spiritual practices, and cultural traditions: If (a) ownership of such "goods" cannot be traced back to a single individual; then, (b) no "one" must own them. This logic is insidiously and explicitly employed by whitestream proprietors to transfer commonly held indigenous "property" to the realm of public domain. Once American Indian "property" is reclassified as material of the public domain, the second assumption of U.S. property law comes into effect, that is, that any individual can claim property formerly in the "public domain" and that such claim bestows private and exclusive ownership thereafter, with all the privacy rights inherent to such ownership. In other words, once the music, art, spiritual, and cultural traditions of American Indians are deemed to be part of the "public domain," they become fair game to anyone seeking to pilfer, copy, and re-create such goods and practices, reaping considerable profits in a capitalist marketplace that craves the exotic and authentic. Therefore, the whitestream politics of property not only fails to discourage the commodification of American Indian goods and traditions but also actively encourages it.

The latest and perhaps most egregious form of capitalist profiteering to impact indigenous communities is the quest for genetic materials set in motion by the Human Genome Diversity Project (HGDP). Burrows (1994) reports that indigenous opposition to the project has been extensive and emphatic, and that, in 1993, the Annual Assembly of the World Council of Indigenous Peoples unanimously resolved to "categorically reject and condemn HGDP as it applies to [indigenous peoples'] rights, lives, and dignity" (Burrows 1994, 33). In addition, Whitt (1998) reports that indigenous representatives at the 1993 session of the U.N. Commission on Sustainable Development (CSD) called for a stop to the HGDP. As representatives of those who have been subjected to ethnocide and genocide for five hundred years, delegates questioned why the only alternative to "saving" indigenous peoples being discussed was the collection and storage of indigenous DNA. The delegates argued that such a strategy was just a more sophisticated version of how the remains of indigenous peoples have been collected and stored in museums and scientific institutions for centuries. They argued: "Why don't they address the causes of our being endangered instead of spending $20 million for five years to collect and store us in cold laboratories? If this money will be used instead to provide us with the basic social services and promote our rights as indigenous peoples, then our biodiversity will be protected" (Tauli-Corpus 1993, 25).

Whether it is land, spiritual practice, or genetic material that is being mined, appropriated, and sold, the logic of domination remains the same—in the eyes of U.S. law and policy the collective rights and concerns of indigenous peoples are considered subordinate to individual rights. Thus, the extension of marketplace logic to the realms of cultural and intellectual property not only extends the power of the whitestream but also diminishes the power of indigenous communities, continuing the project of cultural imperialism that began over five hundred years ago.

In view of the above, it is clear to see how postmodernism—the notion of fluid boundaries, the relativizing of difference and negation of grand narratives—primarily serves whitestream America. The *multiphrenia* of postmodern plurality, its "world of simulation" and obliteration of any sense of objective reality, has given rise to a frenetic search for the "authentic" led by culture vultures and capitalist bandits fraught with "imperialist nostalgia."[25] In response, American Indian communities have restricted access to the discursive spaces of American Indian culture and identity and the nondiscursive borders of American Indian communities. In short, the notion of fluidity has never worked to the advantage of indigenous peoples. Federal agencies have invoked the language of fluid or unstable identities as the rationale for dismantling the structures of tribal life. Whitestream America has seized upon the message of relativism to declare open season on Indians, and whitestream academics have employed the language of signification and simulation to transmute centuries of war between indigenous peoples and their respective nation-states into a "genetic and cultural dialogue" (Valle and Torres 1995, 141). Thus, in spite of its "democratic" promise, postmodernism and its ludic theories of identity fail to provide indigenous communities the theoretical grounding for asserting their claims as colonized peoples, and, more important, impede construction of transcendent emancipatory theories.

Despite the pressures of cultural encroachment and cultural imperialism, however, indigenous communities continue to evolve as sites of political contestation and cultural empowerment. They manage to survive the dangers of colonialist forces by employing proactive strategies, which emphasize education, empowerment, and self-determination, and defensive tactics that protect against unfettered economic and political encroachment. Thus, whatever else the borders of indigenous communities may or may not demarcate, they continue to serve as potent geographic filters of all that is non-Indian—dividing between the real and metaphoric spaces that differentiate Indian country from the rest of whitestream America.

Pedagogical Implications of Postmodern Theories

As students learn to navigate the plurality of difference, it is equally important to avoid falling into the (postmodern) trap of relativism. A postmodern theory of difference that insists on impartiality masks the power and privilege that underpins whitestream culture and perspectives. In other words, American Indian students do not enter into a social space in which identities compete with equal power for legitimacy; rather, they are infused into a political terrain that presumes their inferiority. For example, postmodern musings of subjectivity as disembodied and free-floating ignore the fact that American Indian students, along with other indigenous peoples, are "engaged with the state in a complex relationship in which there are varying degrees of interdependency at play" (Alfred 1999, 85). As such, American Indian students are neither free to "reinvent" themselves nor able to liberally "transgress" borders of difference, but, rather, remain captive to the determined spaces of colonialist rule. These students experience the binds of the paradox inherent to current modes of identity theory and it becomes increasingly evident that "neither the cold linearity of blood-quantum nor the tortured weakness of self-identification" (both systems designed and legitimated by the state) will provide them any relief (Alfred 1999, 84). Thus, while postmodern theorists rightly question the whole notion of origins and work to disrupt the grand narrative of modernism, its hyperelastic and all-inclusive categories offer little to no protection against the colonialist forces of cultural encroachment and capitalist commodification.

CRITICAL THEORIES OF SUBJECTIVITY: POSTCOLONIAL CONSTRUCTS AND COLONIZED BODIES

A cost-benefit analysis of both essentialist and postmodern discourse indicates the dire need for a revolutionary theory and praxis that addresses the political need for sovereignty and the socioeconomic urgency for building a transnational agenda. In these efforts, it is critical that American Indians work to maintain their distinctiveness as tribal peoples of sovereign nations (construct effective means of border patrolling) while, at the same time, move toward building political solidarity and coalition (construct effective means of border patrolling). Such is the promise of critical or "revolutionary" formations of subjectivity.

In a postmodern world where "everything is everything," critical scholars critique the practice of framing questions of "difference" exclusively in terms of the cultural and discursive (e.g., language, signs, tropes), cutting them off from the structural causes and material relations that create "difference." They argue that reducing political struggles to discursive arguments not only displaces explanation—knowledge for social change—with resignification but also authorizes a retreat from social and political transformation. According to McLaren (1998, 242) such postmodern tactics promote "an ontological agnosticism" that not only relinquishes the primacy of social transformation but also encourages a kind of "epistemological relativism" that calls for the tolerance of a wide range of meanings without advocating any single one of them. Therefore, critical scholars contest the overblurring of boundaries, the reduction of difference to matters of discourse, and the emphasis on local over grand narratives, contending that such "tactics" serve to obfuscate and, in effect, deny the existing hierarchies of power.

In response, critical scholars advocate the postcolonial notion of *mestizaje* as a more effectual model of multisubjectivity (Darder, Torres, and Gutiérrez 1997; McLaren and Sleeter 1995; Kincheloe and Steinberg 1997; Valle and Torres 1995). While incorporated into wider usage by the academic Left, the counterdiscourse of *mestizaje* is rooted in the Latin American subjectivity of the mestízo/a—literally, a person of mixed ancestry, especially of American Indian, European, and African backgrounds (Delgado Bernal 1998).

Chicana scholar Gloria Anzaldúa's seminal text *Borderlands, la Frontera: The New Mestíza* (1987) infused the cultural terrain of the Northern Hemisphere with the language and embodiment of mestíza consciousness. Anzaldúa (1987, 79) states: "The new mestíza copes by developing a tolerance for contradictions, a tolerance for ambiguity. She learns to be an Indian in Mexican culture [and] to be Mexican from an Anglo point of view." Since the publication of Anzaldúa's *Borderlands* text, mestíza has come to signify a new feminist Chicana consciousness that "straddles cultures, races, languages, nations, sexualities, and spiritualities" and the experience of "living with ambivalence while balancing opposing powers" (Delgado Bernal 1998).

More recently, critical education scholars searching for a viable model of multisubjectivity have incorporated the spirit of the Chicana mestíza, viewing it as the postcolonial antidote to imperialist notions of racial purity (di

Leonardo 1998). The emergent discourse of *mestizaje* embodies the mestíza's demonstrated refusal to prefer one language, one national heritage, or one culture at the expense of others, asserting instead a radically inclusive construct that "willfully blurs political, racial, [and] cultural borders in order to better adapt to the world as it is actually constructed" (Valle and Torres 1995, 149). McLaren articulates *mestizaje* as "the embodiment of a transcultural, transnational subject, a self-reflexive entity capable of rupturing the facile legitimization of 'authentic' national identities through (the) articulation of a subject who is conjunctural, who is a relational part of an ongoing negotiated connection to the larger society, and who is interpolated by multiple subject positionings" (1997, 12). In other words, *mestizaje* crosses all imposed cultural, linguistic, and national borders, refusing all "natural" or transcendent claims that "by definition attempt to escape from any type of historical and normative grounding" (McLaren and Giroux 1997, 117). Ultimately, the critical notion of *mestizaje* is itself multifunctional. It not only signifies the decline of the imperial West but also de-centers whiteness and undermines the myth of a democratic nation-state based on borders and exclusions (Valle and Torres 1995).

Insofar as the notion of *mestizaje* disrupts the jingoistic discourse of nationalism it is indeed crucial to the emancipatory project. As McLaren notes, "Educators would do well to consider Gloria Anzaldúa's (1987) project of creating *mestizaje* theories that create new categories of identity for those left out or pushed out of existing ones" (1997, 537). In so doing, however, he cautions "care must be taken not to equate hybridity with equality" (McLaren 1997, 46).[26] Coco Fusco (1995, 46) similarly notes: "The postcolonial celebration of hybridity has (too often) been interpreted as the sign that no further concern about the politics of representation and cultural exchange is needed. With ease, we lapse back into the integrationist rhetoric of the 1960s." In the wake of transgressing borders and building postnational coalitions, these words caution us against losing sight of the unique challenges of particular groups and their distinctive struggles for social justice. In taking this admonition seriously, it is important to consider the ways in which transgressive subjectivity—*mestizaje*—both furthers and impedes indigenous imperatives of self-determination and sovereignty.

The Postcolonial *Mestizaje* and Indigenous Subjectivity

Though the postcolonial construct of *mestizaje*—rooted in the "discourses of power"—differs from "free-floating" postmodern constructions of identity, an undercurrent of fluidity and displacedness continues to permeate, if not define, *mestizaje*. As such, it remains problematic for indigenous formations of subjectivity and the expressed need to forge and maintain integral connections to both land and place. Consider, for example, the following statement on the nature of critical subjectivity by McLaren (1997, 13–14):

> The struggle for critical subjectivity is the struggle to occupy a space of hope—
> a liminal space, an intimation of the anti-structure, of what lives in the in-
> between zone of undecidedability—in which one can work toward a praxis of
> redemption. . . . A sense of atopy has always been with me, a resplendent place-
> lessness, a feeling of living in germinal formlessness. . . . I cannot find words to
> express what this border identity means to me. All I have are what Georges
> Bastille calls *mots glissants* (slippery words).

Though McLaren speaks passionately about the need for a "praxis of redemption," the very possibility of redemption is situated within our willingness to not only accept but also flourish in the "liminal spaces," border identities, and postcolonial hybridities inherent to postmodern life. In fact, McLaren perceives the fostering of a "resplendent placelessness" itself as the gateway to a more just and democratic society. In other words, the critical project of *mestizaje* maintains the same core assumption of the "politics of property." That is, in a democratic society, human subjectivity—and therefore emancipation—is conceived of as inherently a rights-based as opposed to land-based project.

While indigenous scholars embrace the anticolonial aspects of *mestizaje*, they require a construct that is both geographically rooted and historically placed. Consider, for example, the following commentary by Deloria (1994, 278, 281) on the centrality of place and land in the construction of American Indian subjectivity:

> Recognizing the sacredness of lands on which previous generations have lived
> and died is the foundation of all other sentiment. Instead of denying this dimen-
> sion of our emotional lives, we should be setting aside additional places that
> have transcendent meaning. Sacred sites that higher spiritual powers have cho-
> sen for manifestation enable us to focus our concerns on the specific form of our
> lives. . . . Sacred places are the foundation of all other beliefs and practices be-
> cause they represent the presence of the sacred in our lives. They properly in-
> form us that we are not larger than nature and that we have responsibility to the
> rest of the natural world that transcend our own personal desires and wishes.
> This lesson must be learned by each generation.

Gross misunderstanding of this connection between American Indian subjectivity and place, and more important, between sovereignty and land has been the source of myriad ethnocentric policies and injustices in Indian Country.

Consider, for example, the impact of the Indian Religious Freedom Act (IRFA) in 1978. Government officials never anticipated that passage of this act would set up a virtually intractable conflict between property rights and religious freedom. But, American Indians viewed the IRFA as an invitation to return to their sacred sites. Since several sites were on government lands and being damaged by commercial use, numerous tribes filed lawsuits under the IRFA, alleging mismanagement and destruction of their "religious" sites. At the same time, whitestream corporations, tourists, and even rock climbers filed their own lawsuits accusing federal land managers of illegally restricting access to Indian sacred sites. They argued that since such restrictions were placed on "public sites" that the IRFA violated the constitutional separation of church and state. This history alone points to the central difference of American Indian and whitestream subjectivity, whether articulated through the theoretical frames of essentialism, postmodernism, or postcolonialism.

To be clear, indigenous and critical scholars do share a common ground, namely, they envision an anti-imperialist theory of subjectivity; one free of the compulsions of global capitalism and the racism, classism, sexism, and xenophobia it engenders. But where critical scholars ground their vision in Western conceptions of democracy and justice that presume a "liberated" self, indigenous scholars ground their vision in conceptions of sovereignty that presume a profound connection to place and land. Thus, to a large degree, the seemingly liberatory constructs of fluidity, mobility, and transgression are perceived not only as the language of critical subjectivity but also as part of the fundamental lexicon of Western imperialism. Deloria (1999, 247) writes:

> Although the loss of land must be seen as a political and economic disaster of the first magnitude, the real exile of the tribes occurred with the destruction of ceremonial life (associated with the loss of land) and the failure or inability of white society to offer a sensible and cohesive alternative to the traditions, which Indians remembered. People became disoriented with respect to the world in which they lived. They could not practice their old ways, and the new ways which they were expected to learn were in a constant state of change because they were not part of a cohesive view of the world but simply adjustments which whites were making to the technology they invented.

Thus, insofar as American Indian identities continue to be defined and shaped in interdependence with place, the transgressive *mestizaje* functions as a potentially homogenizing force that presumes the continued exile of tribal peoples and their enduring absorption into the American "democratic" whitestream.[27]

While critical scholars clearly aim to construct a very different kind of democratic solidarity that disrupts the sociopolitical and economic hegemony

of the dominant culture around a transformed notion of *mestizaje* (one committed to the destabilization of the isolationist narratives of nationalism and
cultural chauvinism), I argue that any liberatory project that does not begin
with a clear understanding of the difference of American Indian-ness will, in
the end, work to undermine tribal life. In this light, the very notion of transgression runs deeply counter to the roots of *indígena*. So while there may be
support for the notion of coalition within the Indian community there is
also a great deal of expressed concern over the potential for its mediator—
transgressive subjectivity—to ultimately mute tribal differences and erase distinctive Indian identities. The above tensions indicate the dire need to develop
a language that operates at the crossroads of unity and difference that defines
this space in terms of political mobilization *and* cultural authenticity,[28] expressing both the interdependence and distinctiveness as tribal peoples.

The above analysis points to the need for an indigenous theory of subjectivity, one that addresses the political quest for sovereignty, the socioeconomic urgency to build transnational coalitions, and creates the intellectual
space for social change. In these efforts, it is critical that American Indians
work to maintain their distinctiveness as tribal peoples of sovereign nations
(construct effective means of border patrolling) while, at the same time, move
toward building inter- and intratribal solidarity and political coalition (construct effective means of border crossing). Such a Red pedagogy would not
only view the personal as political but the political as deeply informed by the
structures of colonialism and global capitalism, transforming the struggle
over identity to evolve not apart from, but in relationship with, struggles over
tribal land, resources, treaty rights, and intellectual property. A Red pedagogy
also aims to construct a self-determined space for American Indian intellectualism, recognizing that survival as an indigenous scholar not only depends
on one's ability to navigate the terrain of the academy but to theorize and negotiate a racist, sexist, marketplace that aims to exploit the labor of signified
"others" for capital gain. Finally, a Red pedagogy is committed to providing
American Indian students the social and intellectual space to reimagine what
it means to be Indian in contemporary U.S. society, arming them with a critical analysis of the intersecting systems of domination and the tools to navigate them.

NOTES

1. In the critical discourse the notion of transgressive identity begins with the postmodern notion of subjectivity, that is, identity as a highly fluid construct, intersecting
along the perceived stable categories of race, class, ethnicity, sexuality, and gender.

Critical scholars build upon this definition arguing that beyond "intersection" there is indeed "transgression" (strategies of resistance) between and among categories working to destabilize "identity." In other words, it is not only that race, class, gender, and sexuality intersect but also that these ostensibly stable categories are themselves highly contested spaces. As such, "transgression" is viewed as an inherently subversive and destabilizing construct where there is constant resistance to any fixed notion of identity.

2. American Indian scholar Greg Cajete defines "ensoulment" as the expressed affective–spiritual relationship indigenous peoples extend to the land (Cajete 1994).

3. It is important to note that this category included Indians who refused to accept the terms established by the government, regardless of blood-quantum.

4. Insofar as blood-quantum has been retained as the legal marker of "legitimacy," it has been used to not only undermine the unity and cultural integrity of American Indian communities but also to further extend and embolden the power of the federal government.

5. The contrived division between "mixed-bloods" and "full-bloods" has not only served to threaten unity within Indian communities but also to prevent the likelihood of political solidarity emerging between tribal and detribalized, and/or reservation and nonreservation Indians.

6. Though the Dawes Act is typically recognized as the primary instigation of divisions between tribal and detribalized Indians, the history of detribalization actually precedes Dawes. This discussion focuses exclusively on American Indian "tribal" identity and does not include the history of detribalized Indians. Though I recognize the historically contrived and arbitrary nature of this division, to be a member of a federally recognized tribe remains an important legal distinction in the United States as well as carries a particular legal status, warranting special consideration. The eventual aim, however, is to reveal the colonizing effects of such "traditional" categories of Indian-ness and to propose a more comprehensive and complex understanding of American Indian identity.

7. Preeminent American Indian scholar Vine Deloria Jr. has written over eighteen books and one hundred articles in an effort to delineate the political, spiritual, cultural, and intellectual dimensions of American Indian tribal life. His expansive body of work alone testifies to the complexity of defining tribal life and suggests the impossibility of encompassing its multiple dimensions in a single work.

8. It should also be noted that these "legal indicators" exist as a consequence of colonization, each representing numerous treaties, legislative acts, executive orders, and Supreme Court decisions.

9. It should be noted that the "protection" proffered by citizenship rights (i.e., civil liberties) worked to erode traditional structures of tribal life, sometimes pitting Indian against Indian and tribe against tribe. For a more complete discussion of the distinction between that which is civic and that which is tribal see Deloria and Lytle (1984) and Denis (1997).

10. As presently constructed, tribal governments retain many powers of nations, some powers greater than those of states, and some governing powers greater than local non-Indian municipalities (Deloria and Lytle 1984). In spite of their "sovereign"

status, Indian tribes currently rely on the federal government for their operating funds, for the right to interpret and renegotiate their own treaty rights, and for access and control of natural resources on their own lands.

11. Native American Consultants, Inc., *Indian Definition Study*, contracted pursuant to P.L. 95-561, Title IV, Section 1147, submitted to the Office of the Assistant Secretary of Education, U.S. Department of Education, Washington, D.C., January 1980.

12. For example, in terms of American Indians, being born on "the Rez" and speaking one's language serve as markers of "authenticity," and the more one fits this ideal type (essence), the more authority one is granted to speak on "the American Indian experience."

13. In addition to these struggles, turf wars have also ensued between and among American Indian scholars. Here, the pedigree of voice situates "half-breeds," "mixed-bloods," and urban Indians in subordination to "full-blood" and reservation-grown scholars. While it is often publicly acknowledged that such divisions only serve to replicate the contrivances of colonization, it is difficult to exorcise such logic from the private discourse, especially when it continues to be institutionally reinforced by whitestream America.

14. As part of the National Dialogue Project on American Indian Education, the American Indian Science and Engineering Society (AISES) and the College Boards' Educational Equality Project sponsored a research project that examined what educational changes American Indians want for American Indian youth. Seven regional dialogues were conducted wherein American Indian educational leaders, educators, parents, and students not only served as informants but also as principal investigators. A report of the dialogues was developed by AISES and written by Indian staff and graduate students of the American Indian Studies Center at UCLA.

15. It is, however, always important to view such acts of complicity within the broader context of domination.

16. In his work, Ogbu identifies several categories that constitute what it means to "act white," including speaking Standard English, working hard in school to get good grades, and being on time.

17. For further insight to the marketing of Native America see Laurie Ann Whitt's "Cultural Imperialism and the Marketing of Native America" Mihesuah (1998).

18. For example, after land claims in Maine were settled in the 1970s many Indians returned to their reserves not only to reclaim their homeland but also their identities as Indian peoples. Similar processes have followed wherever land claims have been settled.

19. Deloria (1998) includes among such scholars James Clifton, Sam Gill, Elisabeth Tooker, Alice Kehoe, Richard deMille, and Stephen Farca.

20. Joyce King (1991) defines dysconscious racism as an uncritical habit of mind; a form of racism that tacitly accepts white norms and privileges. She contends that such unintended racism does not reflect the absence of consciousness, but rather an impaired or distorted way of thinking about race.

21. While there is a measure of complicity on the part of American Indians who sell their culture, the overlay of colonialism renders such behaviors as the products of

lost culture, lost economic vitality, and a lost sense of being, and not necessarily as a crass indicator of Indian capitalism.

22. For example, in response to the growing phenomenon of "ethnic fraud," the Association of American Indian and Alaska Native Professors has issued a position statement urging colleges and universities to follow specific guidelines in their considerations of admissions, scholarships, and hiring practices. Those guidelines are as follows: (1) require documentation of enrollment in a state or federally recognized nation/tribe with preference given to those who meet this criterion; (2) establish a case-by-case review process for those unable to meet the first criterion; (3) include American Indian/Alaska Native faculty in the selection process; (4) require a statement from the applicant that demonstrates past and future commitment to American Indian/Alaska Native concerns; (5) require higher education administrators to attend workshops on tribal sovereignty and meet with local tribal officials; and (6) advertise vacancies at all levels on a broad scale and in tribal publications. Contrary to the backlash that this statement received, the association does not promote "policing," nor do they employ exclusionary tactics within their own organization but rely instead on self-identification and disclosure. www.niti.net/michael/AIANP/fraud.htm

23. In addition to these sanctions, galleries, museums, and other private venues displaying the work of individuals not meeting the federal definition of Indian-ness are subject to a fine of up to $5 million.

24. The term "Indian Identity Police" is used by M. Annette Jaimes Guerrero.

25. Renato Rosaldo uses the term "imperialist nostalgia" to refer to the paradoxical condition of deliberately altering forms of life, only to nostalgically long for the past, regretting that things have not remained the same. "[I]n any of its versions imperialist nostalgia uses a pose of 'innocent yearning' both to capture peoples imaginations and to conceal its complicity [in the] brutal domination" (Rosaldo 1993, 70).

26. Critical scholars Cameron McCarthy (1988, 1995), John Ogbu (1977), Chandra Mohanty (1989) and Henry Giroux (1992) similarly caution against equating hybridity with equality.

27. The notion of *mestizaje* as absorption is particularly problematic for indigenous peoples of Central and South America where the myth of the *mestizaje* (belief that the continent's original cultures and inhabitants no longer exist) has been used for centuries to force the integration of indigenous communities into the national mestízo model (Van Cott 1994). According to Roldolfo Stavenhagen (1992), the myth of *mestizaje* has provided the ideological pretext for numerous South American governmental laws and policies expressly designed to strengthen the nation-state through the incorporation of all "nonnational" (read: indigenous) elements into the mainstream. Thus, what Valle and Torres (1995, 141) describe as "the continents unfinished business of cultural hybridization," indigenous peoples view as the continents' long and bloody battle to absorb their existence into the master narrative of the mestízo.

28. In contrast, McLaren and Gutiérrez (1997) admonish educators to develop a concept of unity and difference as political mobilization *rather than* cultural authenticity.

Chapter Five

Whitestream Feminism and the Colonialist Project: Toward a Theory of *Indigenísta*

This chapter began as an exercise in self-education and discovery. Like many indigenous women, I come from a long tradition of strong, capable, and powerful women. Therefore, feminism was anathema to me. Though I never took the time or harnessed the energy to educate myself on the intricacies of feminism, I was very self-satisfied to reject it on the basis of two observations: (1) that the vast majority of women engaged in feminism were white; and (2) that there remained varying degrees of resistance among white feminists to the ideas and lived experiences of women of color. Once I entered the academy, however, it became increasingly difficult to dismiss feminism out of hand. Sexism was alive and well in the institution and I began to listen and learn from some of my colleagues' articulations of its manifestations and of the changing face of feminism. Eventually, I decided it was time to educate myself on the theories and praxis of feminist scholars. I engaged the enterprise with the hope of discrediting my own long-held assumptions and of finding a truly multivocal, multifarious feminism that aimed for the decolonization of all women. Unfortunately, I mostly encountered feminisms that confirmed my sense of the feminist project as a whitestream project. Duly frustrated, I penned my articulations of the feminist aporias, particularly as they interfaced with the lived realities of indigenous women. Though I made what I believed to be astute observations, I couldn't find a feminist journal interested in what I had to say. Specifically, the argument that feminism remained a whitestream project was dismissed as "well rehearsed" and "passé." Interestingly enough, anytime I presented portions of this chapter at education conferences it was always met with great enthusiasm, especially from women of color. So, encouraged by their voices, I have retained my faith in the message of this work and its ability to speak to colonized women.

I feel compelled to begin by stating: I am not a feminist. Rather, I am *indí-gena*.[1] While, like other indigenous women, I recognize the invaluable contributions that feminists have made to both critical theory and praxis in education, I also believe the well-documented failure of whitestream feminists to engage race and acknowledge the complicity of white women in the history of domination positions it alongside other colonialist discourses. Indeed the colonialist project could not have flourished without the active participation of white women; therefore, as Annette M. Jaimes notes (1992, 311–344), some American Indian women continue to hold white women in disdain as they are first and foremost perceived as constituents of the same white supremacy and colonialism that oppresses all Indians. Thus, in contrast to dominant modes of feminist critique that locate women's oppression in the structures of patriarchy, this analysis is premised on the understanding that the collective oppression of indigenous women is primarily an effect of colonialism—a multidimensional force underwritten by Western Christianity, defined by white supremacy, and fueled by global capitalism.

To begin, it is necessary to map the complex and contradictory terrain of both feminist theory and indigenous women. Just as the political space of feminism is multifarious, so is the sociocultural space occupied by women who identify as "American Indian." As Devon Mihesuah (1998) notes, American Indian women differ in everything from blood-quantum to skin color, and from religious affiliation to "opinions about what it means to be Indian." Interfaced with such diversity, however, Indian women share commonalities that extend beyond their gender—most significantly, the struggles against genocide, cultural imperialism, and assimilation.

While these common experiences do not constitute a shared American Indian history or contemporary reality, nor does the heterogeneity of experience preclude the power and existence of grand narratives (e.g., colonization, capitalism, the Enlightenment). Critical scholar Henry Giroux (1997) maintains that "grand narratives" interface with the heterogeneity of experience, providing for the historical and relational placement of different groups within some "common project." In other words, while indigenous women may indeed differ in everything "from blood-quantum to skin color," their shared experience as "conquered peoples" historically and relationally places them within the "common project" of colonization (Mihesuah 1998, 38). Furthermore, it is this placement that connects the lives and experiences of indigenous women (the colonized) to each other while it distinguishes them from white women (the colonizers).

Generally speaking, such "binaries" (colonizer/colonized) are anathema to "mainstream" feminism, dismissed as everything from essentialist and universalizing to masculinist and coercive (Lather 1998). Insofar as this dismissal erases their lived experience, indigenous women view it as a rhetorical device that not only relativizes difference but also conveniently allows white women to deny their complicity in the colonialist project. Indeed, "mainstream" feminists have been widely critiqued for failing to acknowledge their privilege and the historical significance of racial and class differences among women. Women of color, in particular, have taken issue with their presumptions of a universal "sisterhood" and unproblematized patriarchy. On this point, bell hooks (1989, 19–20) is worth quoting at length:

> Ideologically, thinking in this direction enables Western women, especially privileged white women, to suggest that racism and class exploitation are merely an offspring of the parent system: patriarchy. Within the feminist movement in the West, this has led to the assumption of resisting patriarchal domination as a more legitimate feminist action than resisting racism and other forms of domination. Such thinking prevails despite radical critiques made by black women and women of color who question this proposition. To speculate that an oppositional division between men and women existed in early human communities is to impose on the past, on these non-white groups, a worldview that fits all too neatly within contemporary feminist paradigms that name man as the enemy and woman as the victim.

hooks's critique resonates deeply for indigenous women who continue to assert the historical–material "difference" of their experiences. Indeed, this analysis joins the voices of indigenous with African-American and other "labeled women" working to create awareness of the interlocking systems of domination, particularly those forces that have empowered white women "to act as exploiters and oppressors" (hooks 1989, 603).

The historical divide between white and subaltern women suggests that what has long passed as "mainstream" feminism is actually whitestream feminism,[2] that is, a feminist discourse that is not only dominated by white women but also principally structured on the basis of white, middle-class experience, serving their ethnopolitical interests and capital investments. Currently, however, the critique of feminism as a whitestream discourse is viewed as "passé," a "well-rehearsed argument" that no longer holds validity.[3] While women of color and other marginalized women have long critiqued the racist underpinnings of whitestream feminism, I am not convinced that the discourse has fundamentally changed. Thus, on some level, this analysis serves as a test of my own doubts about this supposed transformation.

There is no mistaking that the contemporary terrain of feminism is broadly "diverse." Even a cursory examination of the field reveals a multiplicity of contemporary feminisms: liberal, postmodern, post-structural, Marxist, critical race, socialist, lesbian, womanist, and transnational feminisms. Upon closer examination, however, it becomes apparent that there is little if any intersection among these feminisms. In other words, women of color tend be the ones writing about race and feminism, lesbi-bi-transgendered women about sexuality and feminism, working-class women about class and feminism, and middle-class heterosexual women about a depoliticized feminism. Thus, it isn't that the feminist discourse has intrinsically diversified, but rather has simply evolved to be more pluralistic, "inviting" different voices at the same time the existing axes of power are retained. More pointedly, contemporary feminism is a ghettoized terrain, marked by an uneven playing field wherein whitestream feminists commandeer "the center," and subaltern women, the margins. This reality calls into question the self-proclaimed death of whitestream feminism, (re)inviting examinations of the field from a variety of perspectives.

Therefore, one of the primary aims of this chapter is to perform an autopsy on the field of contemporary feminism, investigating whether the dominant whitestream discourse has indeed given way to more complicated readings of gender and power. An official death notice will be served if the field has moved beyond the mere "inclusion" of women on the margins toward an integration of their voices, experiences, theories, and praxis. Evidence of this integration may be signified by: the theorization of "race" as a construct that emerged through colonialism and imperialism (which is to say capitalism and industrialism); a historical–materialist framework that problematizes the notion of race with questions of capitalism, labor, and economic power; and the presence of "a pedagogy of critique" that explains how exploitation operates in the everyday lives of people as well as encourages collective struggle against exploitive relations (Ebert 1996a). Indeed, a feminist discourse that engages all of the above would not only signal a retreat from whitestream feminism but also provide hope and possibility to indigenous and other colonized women, serving as a basis for revolutionary struggle and as a pedagogical home for the project of decolonization.

The examination begins with an analysis of the historical conditions under which early (first-wave) feminists initially formed relationships with American Indian women. Specifically, the various roles and attitudes of nineteenth-century moral reformists and antimodern feminists are discussed as they intersected with American Indian women. Second-wave feminists are similarly discussed in terms of the relationship between their struggles for equality and indigenous women's struggles against colonization. Finally, the third-wave or contemporary feminist terrain is examined through a variety of current texts, particularly those generated by "education feminists."

I move from this discussion to an analysis of the relationship between American Indian women and contemporary feminism, examining their long-standing resistance to the feminist project. This resistance is discussed more specifically as it emanates from two sources: (1) the widely shared belief that American Indian women do not need feminism since they have always held places of distinction within the structures of tribal life; and (2) the perceived inherent disjuncture between the indigenous project of sovereignty and decolonization and the feminist project of democratic inclusion. Taken at face value, these claims call attention to the "difference" of indigenous women and their "sisters" in struggle.

Finally, the promise of critical and revolutionary feminisms—namely, transnational and Marxist feminisms—are discussed in terms of their ability to inform the contemporary lives and struggles of indigenous women. While there are clearly tensions between this discourse and the indigenous project, a common ground emerges. From this basis, a theory of *indigenísta* is proposed: one that retains the notion of woman as warrior, woman as "Mother," and woman as spiritual leader.

THE HISTORICAL DIVIDE:
THREE WAVES OF WHITENESS

While both American Indian men and women have been subjected to the misapprehensions and objectifications of whitestream history, indigenous women have endured a double erasure—first, as indigenous peoples and, secondly, as women. Feminist scholars (Jacobs 1999; Fiske 2000; Katz 1995; Klein and Ackerman 1995; Shoemaker 1995) have called attention to this erasure, holding white European and Euro-American men responsible. In their analyses they construct the white European and Euro-American man as both the colonizer of indigenous peoples and the oppressor of American Indian women. For instance, Deirdre Almeida (1997, 757) notes, "in their roles as missionaries, Indian agents, folklorists, and ethnographers" white men were the ones to collect and interpret American Indian narratives, establishing themselves as the "leading experts" on everything Indian, including Indian women. Undoubtedly, intellectual imperialism was an important factor in the colonialist project, especially as it impacted American Indian women.

Indeed, prior to the mid-eighteenth century, American Indian women were virtually ignored as viable subjects (objects) of study, excluded from historical texts and documentation as a means of disempowering them vis-à-vis their structural invisibility (Almeida 1997). In addition, what little has been documented in terms of indigenous women's history was written from the standpoint of the colonizer, reflective of their prevailing racist and patriarchal views. As a result, a variety of erroneous and degrading portrayals of American Indian women proliferated. As Katz (1995, 5) notes: "[M]isperceptions of Indian women were rampant because they were held up to the patriarchal model. Euroamericans expected men to be the providers and defenders of the family while women were supposed to be adjuncts to their husbands, dependent and frail." Nancy Shoemaker (1995, 3) similarly asserts that "from Columbus's initial descriptions of 'India' up through the twentieth century, most of the available written records . . . produced by Euro-American men" depicted Indian women as either "squaw drudges . . . bowed down with overwork and spousal oppression, or 'Indian Princesses,' voluptuous and promiscuous objects of white and Indian men's sexual desire." While the racism and sexism inherent in such images is self-evident—reflecting both the Eurocentric view of Indians as subhuman and the phallocentric view of women as subservient to men—they have remained the dominant image of American Indian women (Albers and Medicine 1983; Almeida 1997; Fiske 2000; Green 1983; Jaimes 1992; Klein and Ackerman 1995).

The feminist analysis of the treatment of American Indian women as "sexist" serves as the basis of their perceived solidarity. Moreover, at the same time white men are implicated as the colonizers of American Indian women, white feminists tend to uphold themselves as primary agents in their "liberation." Shoemaker (1995, 3), for example, credits feminist anthropologists with bringing the "woman question" to the forefront of research on American Indians, contending that their "early ethnographic studies (and) feminist theories of anthropology in the 1970's . . . established the parameters of the debate on gender in Indian cultures and posed many of the questions that still concern us today."[4] While feminist analyses of white male dominance are indisputable, the implicit denial of white women's participation in the colonialist project warrants further examination.

Though the field is replete with works that examine the role of white women in the colonial era, there are scant few that examine this role through a critical lends. Even feminists who theorize the implications of whiteness seem to hold on to a view of early (white) American women as the foremothers of contemporary feminism—fighting for the rights of all women—overlooking their role as harbingers of colonialist rule. In this context, Margaret Jacobs's text *Engendered Encounters: Feminism and Pueblo Cultures 1879–1934* (1999) almost stands alone. She examines Indian–white relations at the turn of the century, documenting the early relations between Pueblo Indian and white American women through a critical lens. Though Jacobs focuses on their history, she maintains that the attitudes and relationships that developed between these women played a significant role in shaping the overall perceptions of Indian-white relations. Jacobs writes, "indeed, by the late twentieth century, many of the assumptions that white women writers made about the Pueblo Indians in the 1920's have become accepted truths about all Native Americans" (1999, 183). As such, the following examination of "first-wave" feminists and their impact on the lives of American Indian women borrows heavily from her work.

Single, White, Female: Feminist Foremothers and the "Wild West"

In the late 1800s through the mid-1900s two distinctive groups of first-wave feminists besieged the Southwest: moral reformers and antimodern feminists. While the women shared common beliefs in manifest destiny, white superiority, and feminist utopias, the differences in their politics and personal presentation warrants separate discussion.

Moral Reformers

The women known as "moral reformers" were the poster women of the nineteenth-century "true woman"—an iconic figure that exemplified the qualities of Christian piety, sexual purity, submissiveness, and domesticity (Welter 1966).[5] Emboldened by the superiority of their "civilized" ways, moral reformists banded together to pressure the U.S. government to modify its program of cultural genocide against American Indians, advocating instead an assimilationist agenda that featured the total overhaul of tribal gender relations as its centerpiece (Jacobs 1999). Thus, while it is often discussed as a repressive discourse, the notion of "true womanhood" enabled white women to promote their class interests and standards of morality on American Indian women.

Specifically, reformists worked together with the BIA to enact a social reform program that identified the American Indian family as ground zero in the cold war against "Indian savagery." In these efforts, reformists served as the principal agents in the reeducation of American Indian women. Viewed through their ethnocentric and racist lenses, reformists perceived these women as "victims of paganism, immorality, [and] forced subservience" (Jacobs 1999, 1). As such, they fixated on the "plight" of American Indian women, committing to "uplift" them to the standards of "true womanhood." Large troops of white women answered this call to duty, mobilizing to the southwest to serve the cause in a variety of capacities: as BIA schoolteachers, field matrons, and missionaries.

In their role as schoolteachers, reformists not only taught academic subjects but also provided Protestant religious instruction and "morality" lessons on the superiority of white middle-class standards of conduct between men and women. In so doing, they wittingly reenacted and enforced the existing gendered divisions of labor and power in colonialist society. Thus, as American Indian boys were schooled for public life and self-sufficiency, Indian girls were schooled for domesticity.

This "education" transcended the walls of the school building, extending into the field through work-study programs also known as "outing systems." Specifically, American Indian students were placed in Euro-American homes for the summer under the rationale that a change in environment would provide white women the optimal setting to "school" Indian girls in the finer points of "ladylike behavior" (Almeida 1997). In addition to these cultural exchanges, field matrons visited American Indian women in their homes, providing instruction in the proper deportment of cleanliness and hygiene, the essential duties of food preparation, and the daily chores of housekeeping. In so doing, they endeavored to do for American Indian women "what farmers and mechanics [were] supposed to do for Indian men"—that is, institutionalize "women's work for women," and thereby ease their assimilation to white society (Jacobs 1999, 26).

Finally, reformists served as missionaries, performing their duty to "invalidate the totality of Indian life and replace it with Christian values," transforming their "pagan households" into good Protestant homes (Deloria 1999, 23). Reformists were particularly concerned with the perceived lack of sexual morality and blatant "sacrilege" of American Indian religious and ceremonial practices, condemning Pueblo traditional dances as public demonstrations of "gross obscenity and debauchery" and traditional healing practices as "witchcraft." They faulted these and other traditional practices as impediments to Indian "progress" (Jacobs 1992, 30).

All told, moral reformists enacted a full-scale program of colonization. As BIA schoolteachers they asserted the superiority of Western knowledge; as missionaries they proselytized the virtues of Christianity and monotheistic patriarchy; and as proprietors of white middle-class households, they reaped the benefits of Indian women's labor and servitude. Remarkably, despite their efforts, the project of moral reform failed. Though there are multiple reasons for this "failure," one of the primary causes was their inability to see beyond themselves, especially their belief in the existence of a universal patriarchy. Their myopia rendered them blind to the matrilineal structures of Pueblo society, causing them to grossly misread Pueblo sexual relations, gendered divisions of labor, and religious practices as degrading and disempowering to American Indian women.

Reformists correlated the matrilineal organization of Pueblo society with the sexual domination of American Indian women. Their logic reflected the prevailing racist notion that "savages" only determined descent through the mother because of an inability to determine paternity, linking matrilineality with sexual promiscuity and immorality (Jacobs 1999, 12). While reformists wholly adopted this notion, they incorporated their own feminist riff, explaining the "free sexuality" of American Indian women by implicating Pueblo men "as sexual predators" who forced themselves on "vulnerable Indian women" (Jacobs 1999, 13). Reformists, thus, vehemently worked to disabuse Pueblo women of the practice of matrilineality, preaching instead the patriarchal family as a more "civilized" form of male–female relations.

The sexual division of labor among the Pueblos also incurred the ire of the moral reformers. Specifically, they interpreted these divisions as expressions of male dominance and female subordination, failing to consider that outside patriarchal rule such divisions might not indicate imbalances in power. Indeed, as several scholars note, such "imbalances" often worked to enhance rather than diminish American Indian women's status, positioning men and women in different but equally powerful and complementary roles[6] (Jacobs 1999).

Lastly, reformists indicted traditional Pueblo religious practices as one of the key components in the oppression of American Indian women. In keeping with the imperialistic logic of the time, they dismissed the religious beliefs of Indians as everything from "utterly inane" to "devil worship," viewing Indians' religious beliefs, in any form, as inconsequential. Indeed, they were so dumbfounded by the expressed resistance of Pueblo women to Christian conversion that they imagined it must be some implicit effect of patriarchy. Specifically, they speculated that since the adoption of white medicine and spirituality meant a loss of control and economic power for tribal medicine men, that Pueblo resistance was more about male greed than their religious convictions (Jacobs 1999).

Ultimately, the reformist's failure to perceive American Indian women as respected and "empowered" members of their own communities exposes their project as one shaped more by racism than by their feminist ideals. In contrast, American Indian women were well aware of racial power structure. In *Cultivating the Rosebuds: The Education of Women at the Cherokee Female Seminary (1851–1909)*, Devon Mihesuah notes that Cherokee women were very conscious of the fact that they could not "realistically aspire to the ideal of 'true womanhood' because [it] could only be attained by white women and those Indian women who looked white" (Mihesuah 1994, 37-40). Their awareness of the prevailing racial order indicates that American Indian women not only resisted assimilation from a purely "cultural" standpoint but also from a recognition that the racial divide was intractable. Indeed, many Indian women found that their training not only failed to "assimilate" them into whitestream culture but also prepared them for little else beyond a life of domestic servitude in white women's homes (Lomawaima 1994, 81).

Though the project of "moral reform" failed, the miseducation of American Indian women at the hands of white women inflicted serious damage, not only devastating individual women but also their families and tribal communities. The physical removal of women from their homes was especially disruptive as it prevented women from serving their traditional roles: as warriors, tribal leaders, cultural proprietors, and clan mothers. In addition, many women found that they had to work hard to regain the trust of tribal members who had grown skeptical of returning "students" as the new oppressors (Almeida 1997). Overall, the extreme isolating effects of removal and assimilation forced once autonomous Indian women into increasingly dependent relationships, particularly with the U.S. government—the impact of which is still being felt today (Jaimes 1992).

Antimodern Feminists

By the 1920s another group of women, the antimodern feminists, joined the "save the Indian" campaign. Contrary to the reformist ideal of the "true woman," antimodernists advocated the more progressive "New Woman"—a young, independent, well-educated, sexually liberated woman who valued self-development, self-expression, and personal satisfaction (Jacobs 1992). These "new women" traveled in the same circles as the "Greenwich Village radicals," known for their strident critiques of industrial life and capitalism. Indeed, it was their disdain for "modernity" that drove these women to the "Wild West."

As the antimodernists descended into reformist territory, they found their sisters in struggle to be less than welcoming. On the contrary, they were met with derision, ridiculed as a bunch of "rich women who graduated from Birth Control and the Soviet Union to find a thrill in Native Art"; turning from "feminism, free love and flaming books" to the "refreshment of primitive life" (Jacobs 1992, 57). Cattiness aside, there were significant differences between reformists and antimodernists, principally their competing ideas on how to save the Indian. Where reformists aimed to "civilize" Indians through the imposition of white middle-class values, antimodernists sought to "preserve" American Indian culture, protecting it from what they perceived as the corrupting influences of modern Anglo society.

More specifically, antimodernists critiqued modern society as patriarchal, individualistic, spiritually barren, overindustrialized, and engendered, and idealized "primitive society" as matriarchal, communal, sexually expressive, deeply religious, and anti-industrial. Antimodernists essentially seized upon the fantasy of the free and "wild" Indian as the primitive antidote to the restrictions of white society. Indeed, their intense desire for a way of life that both rejected the trappings of modernity and celebrated women's independence and sexual liberation led them to imagine the Pueblos as living in "feminist utopias" and the Southwest as the "land of women's rights." The matrilineal structures and matriarchal features of Pueblo society particularly enamored the antimodernists, who envied Pueblo women for being raised in such a "utopia."

Given their predilection to uphold American Indian women and culture as models for white society, antimodernists have historically been viewed by whitestream feminists as the "foremothers" of equality, helping to "recast" the prevailing racial and gender hierarchies of their time. Jacobs (1991, 59), for example, not only credits antimodernists with challenging the notion of white superiority but also with championing the equal treatment of Indians through efforts to secure Indian "rights" to land, religion, and citizenship.[7]

While it is true that antimodern feminists rejected the inherent racism of the reformists' civilizing campaign, they also enacted a more insidious form of racism. Specifically, they had become so personally invested in their search for a feminist utopia that their desires to "preserve" American Indian culture led them to fetishize white notions of Indian purity. Their obsessions grew so acute that they ultimately became more wedded to the Indian of their imagination than to "real" Indians, demonstrating "little sympathy" for those "who did not conform to their image of the primitive" (Jacobs 1999, 103).

For example, antimodernists came to greatly admire the nonmechanized farming methods of the Pueblos, codifying such methods as markers of their "authenticity." In their view, "real" Indian men rejected modern technology for the more "traditional" scythe and sickle. Thus, even as it became increasingly difficult for Pueblos to maintain their subsistence economy in an ever-changing modern world, antimodern feminists insisted that they maintain their "traditional" practices and reject modern technologies—contorting such essentialist logic into the rhetoric of (Indian) "rights." Moreover, contrary to prevailing depictions of the naïve Indian, the Pueblo were well aware of the racism inherent to the antimodernist doctrine. For example, after antimodernist Mabel Dodge Luhan made a plea for Indians to "stick to the old ways" in a local paper, a young Indian boy suggested that Luhan "trade houses with him and live without electric lights, running water, or a toilet" (Jacobs 1991, 104).

It is important to note that antimodernists did not "unconsciously" engage in essentialist thinking but rather deliberately and opportunistically wielded the ideology to suit their needs. For instance, whenever their "save the Indian" campaign brought them to Washington, D.C., or on national fund-raising tours, antimodernists were sure to bring American Indian models that best typified the stereotypic image of the long-haired, dark-skinned Indian. They not only insisted that their Indian "delegates" wear "traditional" dress but also embellished their regalia with what they perceived to be "generic" but "authentic" accessories (Jacobs 1999).

In addition to staging such performances of "Indian culture," antimodernists wholeheartedly embraced the essentialist notion of blood-quantum as the primary indicator of Indian-ness (Jacobs 1999). They believed that the more "pure" and "undiluted the blood" the more authentically primitive the individual or tribe (Jacobs 1999). As such, they were staunchly against interracial marriage for American Indian women, viewing it as a tragic dilution of Indian "purity." Of course, this did not preclude antimodernists from engaging in interracial relationships with American Indian men, and some, including Mary Dodge Luhan, married Indian men.

Other women believed so deeply in the blood criteria as an indicator of "purity" that they felt compelled to claim some distant ancestry—in effect, "purifying" their own souls through the enactment of ethnic fraud. Mary Austin, for example, alleged that she was called to be among Indians by some "uncorrupted strain of ancestral primitivism, a single isolated gene of that far-off and slightly mythical Indian ancestor of whose reality I am more convinced by what happened to me among Indians than by any objective evidence" (Jacobs 1999, 98). Still others, not quite convinced of distant blood ties, were content with "playing" Indian, borrowing freely from Pueblo religious practices and cultural traditions. They not only donned the hairstyle, dress, and mannerisms of Pueblo women but also pilfered their ceremonial practices. In perhaps the most flagrant demonstration of white power and privilege, feminist anthropologist Elsie Clews Parsons appropriated a Hopi "identity" (by changing her name) for the sole purpose of increasing her access as a researcher (Jacobs 1999, 102).

Though the moral reformers and antimodern feminists proceeded by different means and aspired to different goals, they ultimately achieved the same end—power through the subjugation of American Indian women. In particular, their ethnocentric reading of the lives of American Indian women imposed both racist and classist frames of intelligibility on their experiences. The moral reformists' ideological vigilance for abuses of patriarchal power caused them to grossly misread Pueblo culture and thereby subvert the power of American Indian women. On the other hand, antimodern feminists enacted a more insidious form of racism, privileging an essential "primitive" over the "modern," and created polarities that proved even more rigid and enduring than those of the reformists (Jacobs 1999, 83).

This is the "women's history" that is shared from generation to generation of indigenous women, helping to keep alive the racial divide. It is a history that shatters the notion of a unified sisterhood, locating the source of oppression in the broader structures of colonization and not in some universal patriarchy. While many whitestream feminists argue that first-wave feminists were merely operating within the given restrictions of a patriarchal society, the construction of such women as "at once totally dominated and essentially good" does little to further the project of long-term political struggle (Newton and Rosenfelt 1985, xvii). In fact, the insistence on a unified culture of sisterhood may actually inhibit more substantive explorations of the class and racial divisions among women, divisions that must be encountered before any authentic political sisterhood can be established. The question remains whether the work of contemporary feminists abandons or furthers the suffocating whitestream trope of "sisterhood."

CONTEMPORARY FEMINISM(S): SECOND-WAVE BORDERS AND THIRD-WAVE GHETTOS

In the early days of the second wave of feminism, whitestream feminists essentially retained their unreflective belief in women's common identity and the aim of a unified sisterhood. Disillusioned with the male-dominated politics of the civil rights movement, they began to organize their own "consciousness raising groups" (Brooks 1997, 212). While these groups raised consciousness about how racial and class differences informed women's experience, "movement women" rationalized that the fight for equal rights necessitated a de-emphasizing of difference. Thus, operating under the rally cry "the personal is political," second-wavers pressed on, working for the removal of social barriers and structural impediments, demanding a "sex-neutral society" where all citizens are afforded the equal opportunity to shape his or her life regardless of sex (Mandle 2003).

While second-wave feminists are attributed with making important strides in the struggle for women's equal rights, the question has been consistently raised: At whose expense? More specifically, women of color have persisted in their claims that such gains were achieved "on the backs" of marginalized women. As such, second-wave feminists have been rigorously critiqued for their obdurate insistence on a unified sisterhood, their failure to comprehend the difference between gender-based and race-based oppression, and their continued construction of patriarchy as the universal oppression.

As the movement waned, critiques of second-wave feminism became an integral part of the discourse, chiefly emanating from three sources: (1) the political impact of women of color who drew attention to the racist and ethnocentric assumptions of largely white, middle-class second-wavers; (2) the critique of French feminist deconstructivists who highlighted the essentialism embedded in constructions of sexual difference; and (3) the emergence of postmodern, post-structural, and postcolonial theories. The ensuing discord engendered what whitestream feminists experienced as a "fracturing" of feminism.

The new (post)feminisms, emerging in conjunction with antifoundational-
ist movements (e.g., postmodernism, post-structuralism, and postcolonialism), marked a clear departure from the second-wave preoccupation with patriarchy and other metanarratives, exploring instead the multivocal,
multifarious world of difference. This departure away from universalizing
theories toward examinations of "difference" marked the transition between
second- and third-wave feminism.

Third-wave feminists view themselves as the post–equal rights generation
of feminists, seeking to complicate the old dictum of "the personal is political" by asking: Which personal? Whose politics? (Heywood and Drake 1997,
23). Perhaps the single most distinguishing feature of third-wave feminism is
its implosion of modernist constructions of the unitary subject. Following
postmodern theory, they embrace Jacques Derrida's "ordeal of the undecidable" and its obligations to openness, passage, and nonmastery (cited in
Lather 1998, 488). In this theoretical framework, sex and gender are not products of nature or definitely shaped by culture, but rather are viewed as entities that are continually produced and performed. Leading postmodern feminist Judith Butler argues that division along gender lines is simply "the
articulation of repeated performances of culturally sanctioned acts of gender,"
positing a "theory of performativity" that has come to define third-wave feminism (cited in Brooks 1997, 192). According to Butler, do not seek to cele-
brate "difference qua difference" but rather to make visible the complexities
of identity that have been made invisible by dominant discourses deeply invested in articulating a knowable subject (cited in Brooks 1997, 192).

Nevertheless, Butler's "theory of performativity" has ignited a virtual cas-
cade of feminisms preoccupied with the polyvocal, multibodied subject, em-
phasizing what Teresa Ebert (1996) refers to as the "traffic of difference."[8]
The emergent preoccupation with the subject and "difference" has instigated
a "turn to culture" or what Michéle Barrett (1992, 204) notes as the general
shift toward the processes of symbolization and representation in understanding subjectivity, the psyche, and the self. The practical implications of this
shift has been a fusion of "feminist theory" (now discussed in terms of narrative, discourse, and experience, since "theory" itself is viewed as masculinist
and patriarchal) with the discursive world of tropes, narrative, sign, popular
culture, media, film, and other "cultural spaces" that enable a feminist reading of the entire world as "text."

The response to third-wave feminisms has been greatly mixed. Indeed, the
debate between postmodern/post-structural feminists and those who theorize
their problematics of this discourse is arguably the most salient debate within
feminist theory today. Women of color and Marxist feminists play a central
role in these deliberations, leading the critique of postfeminisms as the latest

articulation of a whitestream discourse that privileges the desires and concerns of white middle-class women over the material and political struggles of "other labeled" women.

Specifically, Marxist feminists argue that while postmodern and post-structural feminists advanced knowledge of the "hidden trajectories of power within the processes of representation," they also exiled the feminist project to the world of the discursive/cultural/textual. In so doing, revolutionary theorists contend that whitestream feminists displaced "a politics grounded in the mobilization of forces against the material sources of political and economic marginalization" (Scatamburlo-D'Annibale and McLaren 2003). Peter McLaren (1998, 442–443) articulates the "questionable assumptions" that underlie this discourse:

> [Postmodernists/post-structuralists] view symbolic exchange as taking place outside the domain of value; privilege structures of deference over structures of exploitation, and relations of exchange over relations of production; emphasize local narratives over grand narratives; encourage the coming to voice of the symbolically dispossessed over the transformation of existing social relations; reduce models of reality to historical fictions; abandon the assessment of the truth value of competing narratives; replace the idea that power is class-specific and historically bound with the idea that power is everywhere and nowhere and [thereby] end up advancing a philosophical commission that propagates hegemonic class rule and reestablishing the rule of the capitalist class.

Teresa Ebert (1996a, 1996b) identifies feminist theories that operate under these assumptions as "ludic feminism," that is, theories that not only replace radical critique with "assumptions about linguistic play, difference, and the priority of discourse," but also separate feminist theory from feminist struggle and practice.

Moreover, in the context of such postmodern theories, power is dislocated, theorized as "asystematic, contingent, and aleatory" as well as marked by chance and arbitrariness" (Ebert, 1996b). In other words, just as the discursive tactics of postmodernism privilege the indeterminacy of the subject, they also construe power as indeterminate and diffuse. These theoretical underpinnings give rise to a feminist pedagogy primarily concerned with how (white) women feel and whether they are free to express and act upon how they feel. (Ebert, 1996a). Ebert maintains that such postmodernist machinations allow white middle-class women to equate their own bourgeois desires with those of "third-world" and other colonized women since, in the realm of feeling, experience, and cultural representation, it becomes possible to equate "the oppressed" with the "distressed."

Whitestream feminists provide various rationales for privileging the personal world of text over the so-called patriarchal world of social transformation. They claim that writing in an intimate voice, about local knowledges, and with partial understanding, is an act of resistance against the "masculinist voice" of universalization and truth that depicts oppression in "essentialist" terms. However, from the vantage point of colonized women, their rejection of "totalizing" narratives serves the whitestream quest for absolution and desire more than it serves the projects of emancipation or decolonization. Indeed, feminist pedagogies that merely assert the equality of female power and desire function as accomplices to the colonialist project.

Thus, while third-wave feminism may provide a much-needed corrective to the aporias of second-wave feminism, the issues of white women's racial privilege and complicity in the colonialist project remain unaddressed. Indeed, rather than respond to the critique that feminism remained too exclusive, too white, and too middle class by interrogating the subjectivities of white women, it appears that whitestream feminists have chosen to: (1) decenter the subject entirely (conveniently blurring the boundaries between margin/center, oppressor/oppressed); and (2) remove feminism from the political project, rearticulating it as a struggle over language and representation. Though such discursive tactics were perhaps intended to be liberatory and progressive, women of color and other critical scholars remain skeptical, questioning them as convenient devices by which oppression can be relativized and the ubiquity of the colonialist project diminished.

In recent years, much has been made of the so-called identity crisis within feminist theory and the discord between and among various schools of feminist thought. Indeed, the debate itself has incited dramatic pronouncements that we may have entered a "post-feminist" age (Alice 1995; Brooks 1997; Faludi 1992). As such, I fully expected to find, in my own mapping of the third-wave terrain, a hopelessly fractured feminism, one so disparate and diffuse that its once clear (albeit exclusive) political project would be virtually incoherent.

On the contrary, I found that, despite the rhetoric, the feminist geography remains relatively stable: still dominated by white, middle-class women, whitestream perspectives, and the notion of patriarchy as the universal oppression. While some white scholars—Lyn Brown, Michelle Fine, Ruth Frankenberg, Margaret Jacobs, Jane Kenway, Peggy McIntosh, Mab Segrest, Valerie Walkerdine, Kathleen Weiler—have integrated theories of whiteness and antiracism into their work, such women represent the exception and not the rule in academic feminism.[9] In contrast, whitestream feminists such as Judith Butler, Patricia Carter, Drucilla Cornell, Elizabeth Ellsworth, Rita Felski, Nancy Fraser, Jane Gallop, Jennifer Gore, Elizabeth Grosz, Patti Lather, Carmen Luke, Frances Maher, Linda Nicholson, and Janie Ward continue to define the public face of feminism, committing the same aporias as their feminist foremothers. This is especially true in terms of their treatment of American Indian women, as their voices and experiences remain either glaringly absent or relegated to realms of "women's history."

Texts and Contexts: Mapping the Third Wave

The following analysis of contemporary feminism is drawn from a broad snapshot of the field as well as an in-depth look at four recent texts on educational feminism.[10] Despite their currency, the texts reveal a discourse stubbornly resistant to more complicated analyses of gender and power. Indeed, the pervasive failure of contemporary feminists to theorize race and racism in relationship to issues of production, labor, and economics—the machinery of capitalism and colonization—confirms that whitestream feminism is, indeed, live and well.

Invisibility and Marginalization

To begin, the only place where the voices and experiences of American Indian women are found with any kind of regularity is in texts on women's history of the United States. Remarkably, though, there are still texts in this genre that make little to no reference to American Indian women. In reference to such practices, hooks (1981, 138) writes: "[T]he force that allows white feminist authors to make no reference to racial identity in their books about 'women' that are in actuality about white women is the same one that would compel any author writing exclusively on black women to refer explicitly to their racial identity. That force is racism."

Though complete invisibility remains a problem, it is far more common for American Indian women to be minimally included, making cameo-like appearances in what remains white women's history. For example, in three of the most popular history texts—*Second to None: A Documentary History of American Women, from the Sixteenth Century to 1865; Women's America: Refocusing the Past;* and *Born for Liberty: A History of Women in America*—American Indian women appear almost exclusively in the first chapter, entitled in all three books something like "The First American Women." Furthermore, the lives and experiences of American Indian women are described as they interface with either a genderless colonial society (i.e., the school, the state, the government, the missionaries) or a white, male, patriarchal society. Indeed, if their lives are discussed in relationship to white women at all, the relationship is portrayed as one of alliance.

Specifically, white women are depicted in their roles as sympathetic teach-ers, enlightened activists, or mutual "sisters in oppression," struggling against the same white male patriarchy of colonialist society. For example, in Coffey and Delamont's *Feminism and the Classroom Teacher: Research, Praxis and Pedagogy* (2000), the authors champion the (white) "foremothers" of today's teachers. They write: "the women who taught in the 'Wild West,' in the vir-gin territory of Australia, and in the pioneering girls' schools like Wycombe Abbey were heroines and deserve to be remembered, not least because of the struggles they overcame and the legacies they left" (Coffey and Delamont 2000, 105). The authors' use of language such as "Wild West" and "virgin ter-ritory" to describe Indian and Aboriginal territories in the United States and Australia is nothing less than racist, reducing indigenous peoples to "wild" savages, and at the same time the authors erase them entirely from their "vir-gin" territories. Moreover, their concomitant construction of the white teach-ers as "heroines" fails to account for the fact that such women were first and foremost colonizers; middle- and upper-class missionaries working to "civi-lize" and claim indigenous lands, cultures, minds, and bodies. Indeed, such women "deserve to be remembered for the legacy they left"—that is, the deculturalization and colonization of indigenous lands and peoples.

Similarly, in her stirring account of six BIA schoolteachers, feminist histo-rian Patricia Carter (1995, 55) explicitly rejects previous depictions of these women as either pious models of self-sacrifice or colonialist invaders "force-feeding white, middle-class, Christian rhetoric to children of other races and classes." She maintains that such depictions "fail to see the deeper meaning of teacher agency, resistance, and growth through interaction with cultures other than their own." In her effort to move beyond these binaries, she uses the women's autobiographies as her primary source, hoping to provide a more "balanced" and "intimate and detailed dialogical exploration" of their experi-ence. It is interesting that in the process of working to achieve this so-called balance, Carter relies only on the white women's autobiographies. Not sur-prisingly, the ensuing "balanced" account greatly emphasizes their feelings of "helplessness, guilt, and fear" over American Indian women's experience of racism, oppression, and domination.

Moreover, while Carter easily dismisses the "dichotomous" representation of white teachers as either "savior" or "colonizer," her analysis makes facile use of the dichotomies of patriarchy—positioning white women teachers (the oppressed) against the white, male, BIA bureaucracy (the oppressor). In so doing, Carter absolves white women of their complicity, portraying them as disempowered agents forced to carry out the orders of patriarchal rule. In the end, it is white women's suffering under the conditions of patriarchy and its imposed limitations that becomes *the story,* and the universal history of

American women. Indeed, in her closing statement, Carter ponders, "it is intriguing to wonder whether the system's legacy of cultural imperialism would have been mitigated in any way had the BIA treated teachers more like professionals and allowed them to obtain the freedom and adventure they craved"—indicating that the real tragedy of this era is not the countless generations of American Indians impacted by the brutality of deculturalization, but the white women who were impeded in their desires for "freedom and adventure" (Carter 1995, 80).

Author hooks (1981) understands such actions as the result of a profound racism suppressed by narcissism, a combination that enables white women to deny two realities: "one, that in a capitalist, racist, imperialist state there is no one social status women share as a collective group; and, [two] that the social status of white women in America" has never been like that of black, American Indian, or any other women *or men* of color (hooks 1981, 136).

Epistemological Erasure: Ludic Postmodernism and the Colonialist Project

Given that American Indian women remain virtually invisible in the texts of contemporary feminism, it makes more sense to analyze the discourse on a broader level, examining whether their theories of difference leave space for the difference of indigenous women. Unfortunately, an analysis on this level also reveals a whitestream feminism defined by postmodern and post-structural theories that allow white women to deny the material significance of their power and privilege.

For example, while Coffey and Delamont (2000) examine the impact of social class on (white) women's lives, they do so in a manner that treats class as just another form of individual difference, not as a historically determined social construct. Thus, while the authors acknowledge the existence of a class-tiered system in education, they do not discuss its implications for a democratic society. Rather, they are concerned only with the mitigating effects of class on the careers and professional opportunities of white women—specifically, middle-class schools in terms of their role in creating jobs that were "socially respectable and paid a sufficient salary for a woman to live independently without the economic support of her father, or a husband" (Coffey and Delamont 2000, 95). In contrast, working-class schools are noted for their relatively poor employment opportunities and "harsh" working conditions. Indeed, the authors bemoan that middle-class women teaching in working-class schools were subjected to "Spartan" living accommodations and expected to do "domestic" work:

> Teaching in the elite schools was hard work, but the salary and status made it a reasonable choice. The pupils and students taught, and their parents, came from

a similar class and there were common values. The lives of those who taught the working classes were harder. Salaries were lower, saving less possible, the status lower, and the conditions of work much worse. Classes of forty, in dreadful buildings, with children who would smell, refuse discipline, and exhaust their teachers meant that staying in the job was a brave decision. (Coffey and Delamont 2000, 98)

Apparently, from the authors' perspectives, a "feminist analysis" of the history of teaching looks only at the working conditions of white women and the impact of such conditions on their opportunities for social and economic mobility. Missing is any structural analysis of a capitalist system that exploits members of the working class or of a colonialist system that privileges white women and their desires for equality and social mobility over the democratic imperative of extending access and equity across class and racial groups. Instead, members of the working class appear only to represent undesirable ("smelly" and "undisciplined") impediments to the feminist pursuit for adequate careers and equal pay for equal work. In this sense, Coffey and Delamont's work epitomizes whitestream feminism. They not only fail to problematize gender by examining its intersections with race and class but also maintain the distortions and aporias of a whitestream logic that privileges the desires and fantasies of the dominant class over the experiences and concerns of the culturally marginalized and politically disfranchised.

In comparison, Maher and Ward, authors of *Gender and Teaching* (2002), theorize gender as a more complex and fluid category. Specifically they take a "radical social reconstructionist" approach that takes into account the "larger cultural, social and political dynamics" of both school and society, examining how such dynamics operate to marginalize poor, working-class, gay/lesbian, female, and nonwhite students.[11] They also link these imperatives to the importance of reimagining both school and society along democratic aims, stating: "teachers must work to challenge the social inequalities that operate in each and every classroom . . . [making] sure the curriculum contains explicit references to inequality and resistance" (Maher and Ward 2002, 117).

Though Maher and Ward promote a "radical politics of difference," they ultimately adhere to a "liberal progressive" epistemology that privileges individual choice, objectivity, and impartiality over social transformation. Specifically, they provide the reader with a menu of "public arguments" on issues of gender and education, presenting each as equally tantalizing and legitimate (e.g., one item on the menu is the "conservative argument," which views feminists as antifamily, multiculturalism as the politics of victimhood, and schools as controlled by "a host of anti-white, anti-male, anti-family, and anti-religion fanatics") (Maher and Ward 2002, 76). The reader is then invited to make their selections, guided by such questions as "What aspects of this viewpoint are appealing to you?" and "What aspects do you disagree with?" While this approach may encourage development of the reader's point of view, it also ignores the ways in which such liberal approaches to pedagogy— veiled in the (whitestream) myths of objectivity and rational discourse—help to maintain repressive pedagogies by presenting them as equally legitimate alternatives.

Ebert argues that the liberal discourse of objective rationalism legitimates, among other things, "a pragmatic pluralism that tolerates exploitation as one possible free choice," ultimately privileging individual choice over radical social transformation (1996b, 17). Thus, while Maher and Ward articulate a "radical politics of difference," they fail to assert these politics as a democratic imperative, positioning the need for social transformation as merely one option among many, including the maintenance of social control by the dominant class.

Similarly, while Maher and Tetreault (2001) demonstrate adeptness at *theorizing* the intersections of gender and power in their text *The Feminist Classroom*, they do not synthesize this analysis into their conceptualization of a feminist praxis. Rather, in the real world of classrooms, the authors tacitly adhere to an essentialist definition of feminist pedagogy, one that relies upon classroom practices that are student-centered, nonauthoritarian, and collaborative/cooperative in nature. Similarly, pedagogical practices that are decidedly teacher-centered, authoritarian, and individualistic are implicitly categorized as nonfeminist or patriarchal. More significantly, though individual teachers problematize the values of "student-centered," "nonauthoritarian," and "cooperative" as being raced and classed, these values are, by the end of the text, still assumed to be universal characteristics of "feminist" praxis and "women's" ways of knowing.

In addition to these prevailing values, the authors persist in their construction of "the feminist classroom" as a space in constant flux, where all things are continually negotiated, characterizing feminist pedagogy as a praxis of indeterminacy. Similar to Maher and Ward (2002), the authors do not consider the ways in which postmodern theories of indeterminacy compromise the feminist political project. Ironically, while they observe the new generation of women faculty comparatively (politically apathetic), seeing "feminism as a theoretical position, not a political agenda," they blame this apathy on the patriarchal nature of the institution and its resistance to change. The possibility that the new generation of feminists might be disenchanted with postmodern feminism's privileging of textual analysis over a politics of engagement is not even considered. In this sense, *The Feminist Classroom* carries on in the tradition of whitestream feminism, privileging the personal over the political.

In terms of the reviewed materials, the text *Feminist Engagements: Reading, Resisting and Revisioning Male Theorists in Education and Cultural Studies* (2001) offers the best hope for liberating feminism from its whitestream roots. This edited collection is significantly different from the other texts in that it is primarily theoretical and aimed at defining the relation between feminist theory and the "intellectual heritage of men" (Weiler 2001, 3). Editor Kathleen Weiler maintains that while education feminists have been profoundly influenced by the "classic male theorists" (e.g., John Dewey, Jean-Bernard Foucault, Paulo Freire, Antonio Gramsci, and Stuart Hall), their relationship has been uneasy. As such, she poses the following critical question: "[though] our ultimate goals may be very similar . . . what do we take on if we imagine ourselves as the inheritors of these 'gender blind' theories and . . . apply them to our concerns as feminist women?" (Weiler 2001, 3).

The text essentially unfolds as a collective response to this question, with different feminist scholars articulating their particular intellectual relationship to male theorists. Though responses vary in theoretical approach, Weiler identifies "critical feminist theory" as the "stance most frequently taken by writers in the collection" (2001, 6). She defines "critical feminism" as a theory committed to "alliances across race and ethnic lines," putting forth complex readings of male antiracist theorists who articulate goals of liberation and human rights in "powerful and poetic rhetoric" but ignore "women's concerns" in the process (Weiler 2001, 6). Through this approach, critical feminists explore the dangers of "using a male intellectual tradition that has objectified or ignored women" as the foundation of a feminist critique of that same tradition. In addition, Weiler asserts that critical feminists perceive themselves as "speaking directly to white and heterosexual women about their blindness to their own privilege and their ignorance of the profundity of differences among women" (2001, 4–5).

Unfortunately, despite these initial proclamations, most of the essays in *Feminist Engagements* do not demonstrate consistent adherence to the principles of critical feminism. Only two of the nine authors are women of color—one African Caribbean Canadian woman and one African American woman—indicating that critical feminists' "commitment across racial and ethnic lines" begins and ends at the black–white divide.[12] Moreover, while some of the white women address race in their essays, it is clear that the race question is relegated to the women of color. In other words, Cally L. Waite (who writes about W.E.B. Du Bois) and Annette Henry (who writes about Stuart Hall) have clearly been designated as the theorists of color "assigned" to write about black male theorists and to confront the question of black women and education.

In addition to the racial divide, the majority of contributors also fail to problematize race through its intersections with class and the exploitative relations of capitalism and colonization. Rather, most contributors examine gender in terms of a universal and abstract patriarchy. Indeed, only two authors—Kathleen Weiler and Jane Kenway—engage a "critical feminist" analysis as defined in the introduction to the collection. Since these essays come the closest to articulating a critical and/or antiwhitestream feminist theory, a more detailed account and analysis of their theories is provided.

First, in her essay "Rereading Paulo Freire," Weiler begins by acknowledging feminism's grounding in both racist and patriarchal (Western) theories:

> The social and political goals of U.S. feminism were originally framed around liberal, Enlightenment conceptions of rights and justice for women; it has subsequently condemned patriarchal desires and practices using the Western discourses of psychoanalysis and poststructuralism. This grounding in the Western tradition has been a profound limitation for feminism, as the work of women of color and feminists outside the dominant Western tradition have so forcefully made clear. (2001, 67)

Moreover, Weiler goes on to acknowledge the dangers and limitations of essentialist feminisms, noting that "such approaches tend dangerously toward recasting the same old story of Western patriarchy, in which rationality is the province of men, and feeling and nurturance that of women" (2001, 70).

What makes Weiler's analysis unique, however, is that it moves beyond a mere critique of whitestream feminism and integrates a more complex analysis of racial and class difference into the foundation of her own theory. She begins by recognizing the privileges inherent to her own positionality (as a white middle-class woman) and examines the ways in which her "social and historical location" shapes her work and, in this instance, her critique of Freire. Indeed, she cautions against "women" positioning themselves "on the same side" as the oppressed without any regard for the differences in power and privilege among women: "the fallacy of assuming there is a single category—woman—hides the profound differences among women in terms of their race, class, nationality, and other aspects of their identities" (Weiler 2001, 75).

The real power of Weiler's critique, however, lies in the parallels she draws between whitestream feminists' failure to theorize race and class and male liberatory theorists' failure to theorize gender. Unfortunately, her analysis loses some ground when she turns to the specifics of Freire's work, holding him accountable in a tone and manner that she does not take with her feminist colleagues. Nevertheless, Weiler extends a trenchant critique of any form of liberatory scholarship that does not theorize the intersections of race, class, and gender—including feminism. Though she does not write specifically about the connection between liberatory political projects and the imperatives set in motion by global capitalism and colonialism, her work leaves open the possibility of engaging this analysis.

Where Weiler merely alludes to the importance of historical–materialist critique, Jane Kenway expressly calls for critical feminists to undertake this project. In her essay "Remembering and Regenerating Gramsci," Kenway argues that a firm grounding in materialist analysis is essential to the feminist project. She notes that while Gramsci was considered en vogue among feminists in the 1980s (e.g., Madeleine Arnot, Sandra Kessler, Patti Lather), he is no longer considered a "fashionable theorist," particularly since the emergence of postmodernism. As such, she articulates the shortcomings of this discourse and its ill-effects on feminist and other emancipatory projects:

> This [postmodern] theoretical move has seen an eroded interest in the economy and social class, an intensified concern with discourse, difference, and subjectivity and with consumption rather than production. Throughout this period there has been much more interest in mini-narratives rather than metanarratives, multiple identities rather than political identities, positioning rather than repositioning, discourse rather than politics of discourse, performance rather than poverty, inscription rather than political mobilization and deconstruction rather than reconstruction. Culture has been much more the focus of analysis than the economy—even its cultural elements—and notions of difference and plurality have held sway over the trilogy that emerged in the 1980s of class, race and gender. (Kenway 2001, 60)

In summary, Kenway views postmodern feminisms privileging of the "politics of recognition" over the "politics of redistribution" and retreat from engagement in "practical political activity" intolerable. In response, she seeks to reinvigorate feminist theory with "matters economic," replete with theories of difference that recognizes the economic exploitation, marginalization, and deprivation of subaltern women (Kenway 2001, 61).

Most important, however, Kenway insists on regrounding feminist theory in historical–materialist analysis, maintaining that such a Gramscian view of feminism would require "serious empirical attention to the relationships among the ideological processes and economic and political arrangements of contemporary, globalized times" (Kenway 2001, 61). More specifically, she calls for feminist studies that examine "present forms of economic colonization" and the new material conditions of alienation and exploitation they engender. The resulting "feminist class analysis" would theorize the ways in which struggles over meaning and identity articulate with struggles over other resources, highlighting "the multiple registers of power and injustice" (Kenway 2001, 61).

Kenway is confident that this renewed commitment to historical–materialist analysis would reinvigorate the feminist political project, rendering it "better prepared" to engage "the big issues" of our time (2001, 62). The advocacy of such an agenda places her analysis squarely at the intersection of race, class, and gender, as well as "on the same side" as analyses generated by women from subaltern groups. Unlike Weiler, who registers her unease with (white) women positioning themselves "on the same side as" the oppressed, Kenway avoids enacting the presumptions of whiteness by accounting for the complex intersections of power. Indeed, her ability to theorize these intersections and to offer an analysis that accounts for the effects of colonialism and global capitalism marks a definitive break from whitestream feminism. In this sense, Kenway's essay not only stands apart, but also alone.

Insofar as her essay marks the promise of contemporary feminism for American Indian and other colonized women, Patti Lather's essay "Ten Years Later, Yet Again: Critical Pedagogy and Its Complicities" marks the ubiquity of whitestream feminism. Specifically, Lather works to undermine the legitimacy and relevance of historical–materialist analysis for feminist work, seeking instead to "sensitize" the discourse of radical critique to the issues raised by poststructuralism" (Lather 2001, 184).[13] She maintains that critical pedagogy's concern with a conscious unitary subject, economic materialism, "totalizing categories," and positions of closure all derive from a patriarchal view of the world, creating an inherent tension between critical and feminist pedagogies. Though this tension was previously aired in a series of exchanges between education feminists and "the boys" of critical pedagogy nearly ten years ago, Lather regards the problems as still relevant, producing "the truth of critical pedagogy as a 'boy thing' and the use of poststructuralism to deconstruct pedagogy as a 'girl thing'" (Lather 2001, 184). She explains, "this is due not so much to the dominance of male authors in the field as it is to the masculinist voice of abstraction, universalization, and the rhetorical position of 'one who knows'" (Lather 2001, 184).

In contrast to the "certainties" presumed by critical pedagogy, Lather proposes a feminist praxis of "not being so sure," or one in which "questions are constantly moving and one cannot define, finish, close" (Lather 2001, 184). She asserts further that "rather than return to historical materialism . . . my interest is in a praxis in excess of binary and dialectical logic, a praxis that disrupts the horizon of already prescribed intelligibility" (2001, 189). Ultimately, she calls for a feminist praxis that attends to the "poststructural suspicions of rationality, philosophies of presence, and universalizing projects," embracing both "undecidability and the unforeseeable" (Lather 2001, 189, 190).

In short, Lather seems to call for feminism to move away from standing for something (as in being *against* exploitation and *for* emancipation) to nothing—the unknown, the undecidable, the unforeseen. Ironically, she levies this call for uncertainty and incompleteness with a great deal of certitude, adopting the voice of "one who knows" in her argument that poststructuralism is "the one right story." In so doing, Lather writes in the dominant voice of whitestream feminism—a post-Marxist, postmodern, post-structural voice that rejects the so-called patriarchal and "masculinist" theories of radical other emancipatory scholars, taking issue with the goal of emancipation itself as "messianic."

Summary: Contemporary Feminism and the Colonialist Project

The aim of this analysis was to determine the state and prevalence of whitestream feminism in the contemporary feminist terrain. As it turns out, it not only appears to be alive and well but also thriving as the dominant discourse. Indeed, the voice of whitestream feminism and its resistance to theorize at the intersection of economics, labor, production, and exploitation is so predominant that it raises the question: Who gains from abandoning the problems of labor?

One possibility is that it allows white middle-class women to deny that their increased power and access has come at the expense of poor women and women of color. This reality compels Ebert to draw a distinction between emancipatory pedagogies, which explain how exploitative relations operate in the everyday lives of people so that they can be changed, and liberatory pedagogies, which privilege the desiring subject at the center of their politics, protecting the material interests of the powerful and propertied classes.

In this light, Lather's resistance to "totalizing" and "universal" categories (and her subsequent assertions of indeterminacy) is revealed as a "legitimization of the class politics of an upper-middle-class Euroamerican feminism obsessed with the freedom of the entrepreneurial subject" (Ebert 1996b, 31). Driven by the capriciousness of postmodern and post-structural theories, such feminisms ultimately dismiss the political imperatives of radical critique and its commitment to the collective emancipation of all peoples, privileging instead the desires of the white, bourgeois, female subject. As an indigenous woman, I understand this discourse as a "theory of property holders" and until whitestream feminists "come clean" about their participation in the forces of domination, indigenous and other colonized women will continue to resist its premises.

AMERICAN INDIAN WOMEN'S RESISTANCE: TOWARD A THEORY OF *INDIGENÍSTA*

Since most indigenous women link their subjugation to colonization and recognize the integral participation of white women in this project, they have consistently voiced their misgivings about the feminist movement. Their resistance is also buttressed by the "widely shared belief that American Indian women do not need feminism" (Bataille and Sands 1984). Indeed, while patriarchy may be a salient feature in the structural oppression of women in Western societies, many indigenous societies reveal an overall de-emphasis on virtually all relations of domination and submission (Klein and Ackerman 1995). As Maltz and Archambault (1995, 247) note, in societies where relations of prestige and hierarchy are virtually absent, "the ability to dominate others does not tend to be a major basis for determining status," and "the (more specific) control of men over women is not a major theme." On the contrary, matrilineal, matrilocal, and matriarchal structures tend to be the historical norm for many indigenous societies.[14] In addition to the differences in social and political structures, indigenous societies differ in their religious and cosmological systems. Specifically, in contrast to the patriarchal structures of Christianity dominant in Western societies, indigenous belief systems demonstrate clear patterns of gender balance and female empowerment.

As a result of the above social and political structures, many indigenous women share historical memories and contemporary experiences of women as warriors, healers, spiritual leaders, clan mothers, tribal leaders, council members, political activists, and cultural proprietors, and thus, already live with a sense of their own traditional "feminist" agency. Thus, while such women may occupy a marginalized space in the whitestream distortions of U.S. history, they have always held prominence in the histories, collective memories, oral traditions, and ceremonial spaces of their own tribal nations. This historical legacy of reciprocity, shared governance, and female spiritual empowerment fuels the belief among indigenous women that they do not need "liberation" since they have always been "liberated" within their own tribal structures (Bataille and Sands 1984).

In addition to the historically situated and shared presumption that they do not need feminism, indigenous women experience an inherent disjuncture between the contemporary feminist and indigenous political projects. Lorelei DeCora Means, a Minneconjou Lakota, AIM activist, and cofounder of the Women of All Red Nations (WARN), articulated the roots of this disjuncture in a speech delivered during International Women's Week at the University of Colorado at Boulder:

> We are American Indian women, in that order. We are oppressed first and foremost as American Indians, as peoples colonized by the United States of America, not as women. As Indians we can never forget that. Our survival, the survival of every one of us—man, woman, child—as Indians depends on it. Decolonization is the agenda, the whole agenda, and until it is accomplished, it is the only agenda that counts for American Indians. It will take every one of us—every single one of us—to get the job done. We haven't got the time,

energy or resources for anything else while our lands are being destroyed and our children are dying of avoidable diseases and malnutrition. So we tend to view those who come to us wanting to form alliances on the basis of new and different or broader or more important issues to be a little less than friends, especially since most of them come from the Euroamerican population which benefits most directly from our ongoing colonization. (cited in Jaimes 1992, 314)

Means's powerful words not only assert the primacy of the decolonization agenda but also allude to the ways other social agendas—whitestream feminism—depend upon and benefit from the continuation of the colonialist project.

Indigenous Hawaiian activist Haunani-Kay Trask (1996) similarly speaks of the inherent tensions between the feminist and indigenous political projects, recounting her foray in women's studies as a graduate student. After leaving academia and resuming her role as an Indian activist, Trask reports how the deep contradictions between indigenous struggles for land, language, self-determination, and the feminist political project compelled her to abandon feminism. She writes:

[A]s I decolonized my mind . . . feminism appeared as just another haole [Western] intrusion into a besieged Hawaiian world. . . . Their language revolved around First World "rights" talk, that Enlightenment individualism that takes for granted "individual" primacy. . . . It viewed the liberal state as the proper arbiter of rights and privileges. It accepted capitalism as the despised but inevitable economic force. And finally it insisted on the predicable racist assumption that all peoples are alike in their common "humanity"—a humanity imbued with Enlightenment values and best found in Euro-American states. . . . We are the colonized; they are the beneficiaries of colonialism. That some feminists are oblivious to this historical reality does not lessen their power in the colonial equation. (Trask 1996, 909, 911)

Trask positions the concerns of "haole" feminism as not only *different* from those of Native Hawaiian women but also as *contradictory*, noting (like Means) that haole feminists don't just benefit from the colonization of Native peoples, but depend on it.

American Indian scholar and activist Janet McCloud (cited in Jaimes 1992, 314) similarly calls attention to "progressive" feminist's failure to account for the benefits accrued by the continued occupation of indigenous lands. She writes:

[S]o let me toss out a different kind of progression to all you . . . feminists out there. You join us in liberating our land and lives. Lose the privilege you acquire at our expense by occupying our land. Make that your first priority for as long as it takes to make it happen . . . but if you're not willing to do that then don't presume to tell us how we should go about our own liberation, what priorities and values we should have. Since you're standing on our land, we've got to view you as another oppressor trying to hang onto what's ours.

McCloud goes on to suggest that calls for American Indian women to "join" the feminist movement are tantamount to asking them to participate as "equals" in their own colonization.

Indeed, to indigenous women who engage in peaceful and armed insurrections against global forces that aim to confiscate and deplete Indian lands and resources, feminist politics that aim to procure subsidized day care, equal pay for equal work, and access to power beyond the "glass ceiling" seem conspicuously tied to capitalist imperatives that necessitate those same lands and resources. As (Anishinabeg) Indian activist Winona LaDuke (1995) notes, women of First-World nations have fought for "women's" equal pay and equal status without stopping to consider how that pay and status continue to be based on a consumption model that not only deeply compromises the lives of indigenous women but also violates the rights, lands, and resources of their respective nations. Indigenous women, thus, remain highly suspicious of feminist discourses that merely assert the equality of female power and desire—sexual desire, consumerist desire, capitalist desire—viewing them first and foremost as accomplices to the projects of colonialism and global capitalism. As such, they continue to dismiss whitestream feminism as a "theory of property holders" and to view whitestream feminists as privileged subjects unwilling to examine their own complicity in the ongoing project of colonization.

Toward a Theory of *Indigenísta*

The historical analysis presented at the beginning of this chapter articulates the degree to which white women participated in the colonialist project, disrupting not only the social, political, economic, and cultural systems of indigenous peoples, but also the balance of gendered relations between American Indian men and women. Indeed, "family organization, child rearing, political and spiritual life, work and social activities were all disordered by a colonial system which positioned its own women as the property of men" (Smith 1999, 151). The lives of indigenous women continue to be impacted by this "disordering" that set in motion the "first wave" of deculturalization. Laguna Pueblo Paula Gunn Allen (1992, 189) writes:

American Indian women struggle on every front for the survival of our children, our people, our self-respect, our values systems, our way of life. . . . We survive

war and conquest, we survive colonization, acculturation, assimilation; we survive beating, rape, starvation, mutilation, sterilization, abandonment, neglect,
the death of our children, our loved ones, destruction of our land, our homes, our
past, our future. . . . Of course, some, many of us, just give up. Many are alcoholics, many are addicts. Many abandon the children, the old ones. Many commit suicide. Many become violent, go insane. Many go "white" and are never
seen or hard from again. But enough hold on to their traditions and their ways
so that even after almost five hundred brutal years, we endure.

Though the source of indigenous women's struggles may be differently located, their manifestations are similar to those of other poor and disenfranchised women. Thus, it isn't that traditional "women's issues" do not intersect with the concerns of American Indian women, as the issues of
reproductive rights, rape, domestic violence, self-hatred, and women's health
care all carry great import within indigenous communities. Rather, as Trask
(1996, 910) maintains, the difference is that "the answers to the specifics of
our own women's oppression reside in our people's collective achievement of
the larger goal"—indigenous sovereignty—and not in an exclusive feminist
agenda.

So, even when American Indian women endure similar struggles such as
rape, sexual abuse, and domestic violence, they may not construct them in
similar ways. Specifically, indigenous women do not view themselves as the
oppressed victims of a male patriarchy; rather, they perceive both men and
women as subjects of an imperialist order, choosing to confront their struggles as indigenous people and not only as indigenous women. As Trask notes:
"[O]ur sovereignty struggle requires working with our own people, including
our own men. This is preferable to working with white people, including feminists. Struggle with our men occurs laterally, across and within our movement. It does not occur vertically between white women and indigenous
women on one side and white men and [indigenous] men on the opposing
side" (1996, 914). In other words, for indigenous women, the central dominating force is colonization, not patriarchy; and the definitive political project is decolonization, not feminism.

Perhaps it is because indigenous women have retained decolonization as
their central struggle concept that they have managed to resist the gendered
divisions of colonialist rule. Indeed, indigenous women have consistently
shattered the gendered norms of white society, serving at the forefront of indigenous struggles. It was after all Marie Lego who provided the crucial leadership in the Pit River Nation's land claims; Janet McLoud (Tulalip) and Ra-
mona Bennett (Puyallup) who led their nation's struggles for fishing rights;
and Ellen Moves Camp and Gladys Bissonette who assumed the leadership in
establishing the Oglala Sioux Civil Rights Organization (OSCRO) (Jaimes

and Halsey 1992, 311). In addition, just as Tina Trudell and Anna Mae Pictou Aquash died defending their families and nations, countless numbers of indigenous women have served as warriors, leading their people in revolutionary struggles against government intervention and occupation. The Diné women engaged in the stand-off at Big Mountain, the Zapatista women who fight for sovereignty in Chiapas, and the Quechua women who helped bring the Shining Path and Peruvian government to their knees were not motivated by a feminist discourse, but rather mobilized by the indigenous desire for sovereignty.

As evidenced by the struggles listed above, the project of decolonization centers on issues of land, labor, resources, language, education, and culture as they relate to issues of sovereignty and self-determination. The main adversary in these struggles remains the U.S. government and other imperialist regimes intent on reaping capital gains from the control of indigenous lands, resources, and cultural and intellectual properties. The project, thus, becomes about keeping colonialist desire and capitalist greed at bay while also working for the increased recognition and extension of sovereign powers. LaDuke (1995) asserts that indigenous societies worldwide remain in a predatory/prey relationship with capitalism. She states, "we are the peoples with the land— land and natural resources required for someone else's development program and amassing of wealth," suggesting that the relationship between development and underdevelopment is what ultimately oppresses indigenous peoples and, consequently, indigenous women (LaDuke 1995, 2). In support of her claim, LaDuke provides the following snapshot of the state of Native America today:

> Over one million Indigenous peoples are slated for relocation because of dam projects in the next decade; almost all atomic weapons detonated in the world are detonated on Indigenous lands or waters; there are over one hundred separate proposals to dump toxic waste on reservation lands; the Brazilian rainforest is deforested at a rate of over one acre every nine seconds, Indigenous lands in Canada, at a rate of one acre every twelve seconds; and, in the Arctic, heavy metal and PCB contamination of Inuit women indicates that they have the highest levels of breast milk contamination in the world. It is also critical to point out that the only matrilineal societies that exist in the world today are those of Indigenous nations, and that these are the nations facing obliteration form the incessant desires of global capitalism. (LaDuke 1995)

The above realities indicate to LaDuke and other indigenous activists that the primary concern facing American Indian women (and men) is the "rapid industrialization of our bodies and nations" and the capitalist inevitabilities of colonialist rule (1995, 1).

Within this context, whitestream feminists' insistence on a universal patriarchy, obsession with the politics of identity, and retreat from the lived experiences of working-class women and women of color not only betrays the political project of indigenous women but also the feminist possibilities for all
women. Moreover, the current fascination with text, discourse, tropes, media,
and other symbolic modes as the major armaments in the struggle for liberation signifies a dangerous retreat from issues of labor and economics. In
short, it signifies an abandonment of feminist praxis in the trenches of front-
line struggle.

While there are feminisms that embrace radical critique—namely Marxist,
socialist, and transnational feminisms—such forms continue to be marginalized by the dominant modes of whitestream feminism, rendering their implication in the colonialist/capitalist project all the more suspect. Indeed,
whitestream feminists have, on many occasions, made their loyalties to colonization and capitalism known. For instance, in Hawaii, Trask (1996, 910) reports: "[H]aole feminists have] retreated to the defensive position that Hawaiian sovereignty is anti-haole, meaning racist, not merely anti-American.
Worse, they often contend that we Hawaiians are actually oppressing feminist
haole be asserting our claim to indigenous political and economic power."
Though whitestream feminists may feel compelled to dismiss such antipathy
as an aberration, indigenous women understand it as an extension of their
long-standing relationship to white imperialism and capitalist exploitation.
Indeed, Marxist-feminist scholar Teresa Ebert (1997, 20) questions, "why . . .
does socialism with its rigorous critique of and powerful explanation of the
destructive logic and injustices of capitalism seem so . . . irrelevant [to] . . .
feminists struggling to deal with the deteriorating global condition of
women?"

All things considered, indigenous women's dismissal of whitestream
feminism is warranted, but insofar as their disenchantment with this discourse has led to the dismissal of all forms of feminist critique it is unfortunate. Particularly as the lifeworlds of indigenous peoples continue to be
disrupted and transformed by the reckless and incessant forces of colonialist hegemony and its patriarchal structures, I believe that the insights of the
feminist critique as articulated by revolutionary feminisms (e.g., Marxist,
socialist, transnational, and antiracist feminisms) become increasingly relevant and informative. In contradistinction to whitestream feminism, such
feminisms center the importance of explanatory theory, proposing a historical–materialist critique that "enables us to *explain* how social differences—specifically gender, race, sexuality and class—have been systematically produced and continue to operate within regimes of exploitation"
(Ebert 1997, 811).

As such, revolutionary feminisms differ from whitestream feminism in its refusal to valorize "white middle-class female desire," revealing the quest for autonomy and achievement as just one more example of "bourgeois individualism" (Newton and Rosenfelt 1985, xxv). They also differ from whitestream feminism in their assumption that men as well as women are ideologically inscribed. Judith Newton and Deborah Rosenfelt (1985, xxvi) write, "where much feminist criticism refers to men and male domination as if men really were the free agents proposed by bourgeois and patriarchal ideology, materialist feminist criticism stresses men's relative imprisonment in ideology. In so doing it works against the notion that men are a monolithic." In the end, revolutionary feminist analysis offers a more complex and "less tragic" view of history than one "polarizing male and female, masculine and feminist; constructing gender relations as a simple and unified patriarchy; and constructing women as universally powerless and universally good" (Newton and Rosenfelt 1985, xxix). Such analytical frames would allow white women to theorize their subjectivity in a way that acknowledges the fact that at different moments in history "they have been both oppressed and oppressive, submissive and subversive, victim and agent, allies and enemies of both men and one another" (Newton and Rosenfelt 1985, xxix).

Though revolutionary feminisms have relevance for indigenous women, it remains critical for indigenous scholars to question how the experiences of indigenous peoples are reshaped and transformed when articulated through the epistemic frames of Western theory, whether it is postmodern, feminist, or Marxist theory. As Trask notes, all haole—whether revolutionary or conservative—benefit from the control of American Indian land and resources, and the self-determination of indigenous peoples has never been the goal of marxism, feminism, or any other First World ideology (Trask 1996, 912). For instance, in contradistinction to Marxist theory, indigenous scholars do not view participation in the colonialist project to be determined by class. As Trask notes: "[E]ven poor haole take for granted their freedom of travel, power of purchase, and the familiar intercourse of their language and institutions and customs in [indigenous] homeland[s]. *American citizenship* is the passport to [Indian] country; the American dollar is the economic and political currency; English is the official as well as everyday language" (Trask 1996, 912).

Thus, before current articulations of Marxist or any First-World theory can be considered as useful tools in the process of articulating a critical theory of *indigenísta*, important questions need to be examined. At the same time, in this moment of late capitalism and advanced colonialism, it is critically important for indigenous scholars to examine, articulate, and disrupt the global capitalistic forces that work to imperil tribal existence, making the work of revolutionary feminist scholars increasingly relevant.

Ultimately, however, indigenous scholars—both men and women—will need to construct their own theoretical systems relevant to their current struggles and conditions. The precipitating theory of *indigenísta* needs to remain rooted in the struggles of indigenous peoples and the quest for sovereignty and self-determination, as well as be elastic enough to incorporate the diversity of American Indian women's lives. As we work in recognition of this diversity, however, we must also struggle to find the common ground, to assert the primacy of the struggle for self-determination and to work in solidarity against the burgeoning effects of the colonialist project. With this goal in mind, I close with words of indigenous scholar, activist, and warrior-woman M. Annette Jaimes Guerrero:

> The only way to reverse the dominant colonialist mentality and pro-development agenda is for traditionally oriented Native peoples to reclaim their birthright, internally and outwardly. In such a liberation movement, Native women can be seen as proactive agents of change leading the way as "exemplars of Indigenism." This indigenous movement is about our decolonization; it is focused on the recovery of our health and respective cultures, the healing of our mind, body, and spirit, among our kinship relations of both genders of all ages. Such a movement exists in reciprocity with our natural environment and is part of the reclaiming of our respective homelands for our liberation through decolonization. This is the significance of ecocultural connection to the Earth, as the archetypal Feminine Principle, and as a living organic presence that we Native daughters, love, honor, and respect, the Mother of Us All. (James Guerrero 1997, 218)

NOTES

1. Though indigenous women share with other women a position of marginality and the experience of structural subordination, I believe their distinct subjectivity as colonized peoples and members of "domestic dependent nations" places the historical materiality of their lives more on a par with indigenous men than any other subcategory of "woman." I do, however, recognize the salience of gender as a category as well as the importance of a gendered, pro-woman, antisexist analysis.

2. Other characteristics of whitestream feminism include a heavy dependence on postmodern/post-structuralist theories, a privileging of "academic feminism" over the feminist political project, and an undertheorizing of patriarchy as the universal oppression of all women.

3. These are direct quotes from editors who rejected earlier versions of this chapter.

4. To be clear, the "early ethnographic studies" referenced by Shoemaker are those conducted by white women, namely, Ruth Landes, Eleanor Leacock, Michelle Rosaldo, and Louise Spindler.

5. Though often discussed as a repressive discourse, the Cult of True Womanhood also enabled white middle-class women to impose their social class interests and standards of morality on working-class women and women of color.

6. While contemporary researchers have not found an absolute correlation between matrilineal descent and women's status and power, it has been found to benefit women in particular areas such as land ownership.

7. It should be noted that while antimodernists may have championed the "rights" of full citizenship for Indians, American Indians did not desire "citizenship" but rather sovereignty and self-determination. As such, their participation in such campaigns may have done more to deteriorate Indian "rights" than further them.

8. It should be noted that (in theory) there has never been a feminist consensus on the efficacy of postmodern and post-structuralist theories and, moreover, that the current trend has been toward increased scrutiny of their supposedly unlimited possibilities.

9. It should be noted that while all of these scholars theorize whiteness, they do so through vastly different means of analysis. Also, very few employ Marxist–feminist analyses, leaving broader connections to historical-material forces unexamined. Though white feminists who work to theorize whiteness are also often marginalized, viewed implicitly as "race traitors" and "troublemakers."

10. Frances A. Maher and Janie Victoria Ward (2002), Amanda Coffey and Sara Delamont (2000), Kathleen Weiler (2001), and Frances A. Maher and Mary Kay Thompson Tetreault (2001).

11. Though they recognize the interplay of gender, race, class, and sexuality, Maher and Ward clearly foreground gender as the central lens through which difference is negotiated (see Maher and Ward 2002).

12. While it could be argued that this divide is the most significant in terms of the intellectual history of U.S. feminism, this argument is not made and the voices of Asian American, Latina, indigenous. and other marginalized women are excluded.

13. For a more extensive discussion of Marxist and Marxist-feminist responses to Lather's critique of historical-materialist analysis and marxism, see Hill et al. (2002).

14. John Upton and Donna Terrell (1974, 24) reports that many of the largest and most important Indian peoples were matrilineal, "[a]mong them were: in the east, the Iroquois, the Siouan [nations] of the Piedmont and Atlantic Coastal Plain, the Mohegan, the Delaware, various other nations of New England, and the divisions of the Powhatan Confederacy in Virginia; in the South the Creek, Choctaw, Chickasaw, Seminole, and the [nations] of the Caddoan linguistic family; inn the Great Plains, the Pawnee, Hidasta, Mandan, Oto, Missouri, Crow and other Siouan [nations]; in the Soutwest the Navajo, the numerous so-called Pueblo nations, including the Hopi, Acoma, and Zuni."

Chapter Six

Better Red than Dead: Toward a Nation-Peoples and a Peoples Nation

Wanuymi aswan allin, qonqorchaki kausaytaqa.[1]

Laqtakunag atipayninwan, teqrimuyuta kuyuchisunchis.[2]

I have lived and experienced the mythical reality of modern life: all the magical machines, the separation of self from the clan, the deification of Reason and measure, the illusion of the infiniteness of the finite, and the metamorphosis of nature as vital superordinate power to spiritless, subordinate commodity. Weaving its way throughout this experience, like a small but earnest mountain stream, is the memory and soul of my grandmother. All that she and her ancient culture represent are, lovingly but relentlessly, embodied within me. Inside I feel her dark weathered skin, her waist-long, horse-tail-thick, salt-and-pepper braid, the fresh combed feel of hand-woven fabric, and I think of how these textures resemble me. Through them I feel connected to the immense journey of all our souls as children of this earth. I remember and still sense her smell. I wonder, is it the collective scent of a lost time, a lost culture, a lost people, and, therefore, an aroma of death? Or is it a smell of becoming-ness, of the eternity of all beings and, therefore, the scent of life?

This dual consciousness of ancient and modern, tradition and innovation has both plagued and enriched my existence. School never discussed the "philosophy" of my ancestors—that discourse was either ignored or left for history class; and, in school, history never lived. It was all talk of dead, albeit grand, civilizations and peoples. We studied relics, archives, maps, bones, and other miscellaneous vestiges of the past. Occasionally these remnants carried that same scent of my grandmother, and again I would wonder (in silence) how was it possible for something to be extinct, relegated to history, and yet be so alive, especially in me?

159

I remember my first visit to Peru, where I was brought face-to-face with the presence of my past, and the oddity of returning to my parents' home and feeling like a stranger. We were never made to feel like outsiders; it was somehow just implicit, regardless of all the grand homecoming celebrations. The "stranger" seemed to come from within, like a shadow trapped beneath my skin. I could feel, I could sense, I could see—in all the dark eyes that examined me—the reflection of its presence. There was a little girl, Ilda, smaller but not much younger than I, whose eyes I remember the most. They were the only part of her that looked bolder than any part of me. I think often of the images that must have passed before those eyes and those that have passed before mine, and I marvel at the immensity of the human experience.

September 11, 2001, is a day that lives in infamy. The world mourns it as the day terrorists murdered over 3,000 citizens, unleashing fear upon a once-thought-of impenetrable empire. Native America remembers it as the day unimaginable disaster struck, but also, was miraculously averted. It is little known (and significantly underpublicized) that September 11, 2001, was also the day that tribal leaders from across the country met in Washington, D.C.—just miles from the Pentagon—to discuss the accelerating trend of U.S. Supreme Court decisions aimed at diminishing tribal sovereignty. Like everything else that day, the meeting came to an abrupt halt as the horrors of the morning unfolded. But after a time of grieving and prayers, the tribal leaders (then detained in their hotel) decided to continue the meeting. They determined that the need for tribal leadership to unify around the common cause of sovereignty was only "heightened by the sense of loss caused by the day's terrible events"(Tribal Sovereignty Protection Initiative 2001). The juxtaposition of events is riddled with irony: as the infamous seeds were being laid for America's latest adventures in empire building, the subjects of their last great "conquest" were busy strategizing against the ongoing and myriad effects of occupation.[3]

In the months following September 11, the nation prepared for war; and Indians, like other citizens, began to consider the implications. Under any circumstances, the threat of war irradiates questions of patriotism, citizenship, and nationalism, but under the Bush regime, such concerns have been reified to new levels. The Patriot Act, in particular, constitutes a new lowlight in the history of American democracy. As events have unfolded, the same buzz of the nation has echoed throughout Native America—discussions of retribution, reparations, invasion, and terrorism reverberated—only in Indian Country the discourse was saturated with double meaning.

Even so, as the threat of terrorism loomed, American Indians prepared to send their sons and daughters to serve the United States in numbers far exceeding their percentage of the general population. Indeed, Native peoples have an exceptionally long and strong history of military service. According to the Department of the Navy, during World War II more than 44,000 American Indians served out of a total population of less than 350,000. In Vietnam, 42,000 served, 90 percent of them as volunteers. Perhaps the most telling statistic, however, is the fact that one out of every four American Indian males is a military veteran.

As "weapons of mass destruction" grew increasingly elusive, however, and the war against terrorism morphed into Operation Iraqi Freedom, questions regarding the how's and why's of U.S. occupation began to rise above the din of statistics. For example, in a press conference two months before the war commenced, questions about how Iraq's oil fields would operate under a U.S.-led occupation were raised. In response, Secretary of State Colin Powell assured that all parties understood that the oil belonged to the Iraqi people and, while the United States would study "different models" to determine specific operations, the oil would be "held in trust" for their benefit (Snell 2003). In response to Powell's remarks, Native reporter Travis Snell of the *Cherokee Phoenix*, queried in a piercing commentary on U.S. colonialism, "When the United States takes control of Iraqi oil after the war, will it do a better job of holding 'in trust' that country's oil for its people than it did for Native Americans . . . and exactly who will handle the job, the BIA (Bureau of Iraqi Affairs)?" (Snell 2003).

Though Snell's voice was heard by the mainstream media, the idea of a "Bureau of Iraqi Affairs" actually first surfaced in the relatively decolonized spaces of the Internet. In one of the more famous postings ever to travel through Native chat lines, the following "letter" to the Iraqi people circulated among the networks:

BUREAU OF IRAQI AFFAIRS
Formed March 20, 2003

Dear People of Iraq,
Now that you have been liberated from your tyrannical oppressors, we at the BIA look forward to our relationship with you. Below you will find a list of what to expect from the services of our good offices.

1. Henceforth, English will be the spoken language of all government and associated offices. If you do not speak English, a translator fluent in German will be provided.
2. All Iraqi people will apply for a spot on a citizen roll. Citizenship will be open to those people who can prove that they are Iraqi back four generations with documents issued by the United States. Christian church records may also be given in support.

3. All hospitals will be issued with a standard emergency aid kit. The kit contains gauze, Band-aids, burn cream, iodine, tweezers, and duct tape.

4. Your oil is to be held in trust for you. We will appoint your new American-approved government lawyer with a background in the oil industry. Never mind that he works for the company that he will eventually cut a deal with. This close relationship will guarantee you more money for your oil.

5. Each citizen will be allotted one hundred acres of prime Iraqi desert. They will be issued plows, hoes, seed corn, and the King James Bible. All leftover land will be open to settlement by Israelis.

6. Each citizen is entitled to draw a ration of milk, sugar, flour, and lard. If you cannot use the rations for health or religious reasons you may file a complaint with your BIA appointed liaisons, Crisco. Those Iraqis showing signs of diabetes, heart disease, or glaucoma will be issued with double rations in place of adequate health care.

7. We will mismanage your trust monies, allowing any five-year-old with minimal computer skills to hack into the system and set up their own account. Records of your accounts will be kept but you must receive express written permission from the head of the BIA to examine them.

8. In keeping with the separation of church and state supported by the U.S. constitution, Christian missionaries will be sponsored through government funding. Only Iraqis who convert to Christianity will be allowed to hold jobs within the government.

9. For the purposes of treaty making, any single Iraqi will be found competent to sign on behalf of all other Iraqis.

10. Welcome to the Free World and have a nice day![4]

Though wrapped in humor, this clever commentary delivers an incisive message. It recounts the history of U.S. colonialism and the implications of "benign imperialism" posing as democracy.

The righteousness with which the Bush administration has re-centered "nation building" as the signature of U.S. foreign policy gives further credence to Robert Williams's (1986) claims that the organizing myths of the early Christian empire—unity and hierarchy—remain live and well. That is, the belief that it is our duty as occupants of "God's promised land," to export the good life to those living in darkness, liberating them from their own misfortune. In the war against terrorism, the United States and England have replaced the medieval papacy as the hierarchy in the new social order, and the notion of unity under democracy has replaced unity through Christianity. Indeed, in the twenty-first century, empire building remains the game, the enforcement of capital the objective, and democracy the medium by which *difference* is both displaced and eradicated.

Within this context, extending the relations of capital (i.e., creating new markets) remains the central political project. As Peter McLaren notes, "exporting democracy . . . really boils down to exporting neo-liberal free market ideology, policy, and practice"(McLaren, forthcoming). Indeed, in this latest effort to "export democracy," the occupying forces have been granted full political and economic power over Iraq by the United Nations. With power effectively secured, the first order of business was to guarantee U.S. corporations exclusive rights to the lucrative "reconstruction" contracts. Not surprisingly, standing in front of the corporate welfare line was the Halliburton Corporation, where Vice President Dick Cheney served as CEO for five years. The sordid relations between government and capital in the interest of "democracy" are recognized by American Indians as the relations of colonialism, reminiscent of everything from Dawes to the Indian Land Trust Fund.

In a special report for the *Navajo Times,* reporter Brenda Norell makes the connection between Iraq and Indian Country even more explicit. She writes, "What makes Big Mountain and Baghdad sister cities? The coal companies that contributed to President Bush's campaign" (Norell 2003). Norell reports that from the beginning, Cheney's task force on energy development privileged those who contributed to his political campaign and the Republican Party. She writes, "from Big Mountain to Baghdad, from the Artic National Wildlife Reserve to sacred sites throughout Indian Country, the Bush–Cheney national energy plan focuses on increasing oil, coal, and nuclear plants."

Among those in line to profit from "reconstruction" is Navajo nemesis Peabody Coal. According to Norell, Peabody and its affiliates contributed more than $900,000 to the Bush campaign. In recognition of their generosity the Bush administration took the unusual step of persuading the Supreme Court to rule in favor of Peabody even before Navajo lawyers were given a chance to argue their $600 million case against the coal company.[5] Not surprisingly, the Court ruled against the tribe arguing it was irrelevant that former interior secretary Donald Hodel met behind closed doors with Peabody officials before deciding the royalty rate for Navajo coal. Such duplicitous politics has led many in Indian Country to view "the real machinery" behind the war as oil, not human rights. For example, in an article appearing in the *Navajo Times,* a Nez Perce woman remarked, "the forces that started this war are the same forces that went against us, as a people. In some strange sense, this war is showing the world how evil those forces really are."

The politics of imperialism renders revolutionary theorists' analyses of the intersections among capital, free-market ideology, privatization, and education essential. They not only help theorize the exploitative relations of capitalism but also the wider implications of an imperialist system for indigenous and other colonized peoples. That is not to say that indigenous scholars have not similarly engaged such analyses, only that the work of revolutionary critical scholars deepens our current understanding of the complexities of imperialism, particularly as they intersect with education. Specifically, for indigenous and nonindigenous educators working in communities ravaged by the double punch of racism and poverty, revolutionary scholars' placement of conflicts over public education within the larger social struggles between labor and capital is highly relevant and informative.

Such analyses are particularly critical in times of war when poor black and brown communities experience a surge in school-to-service traffic. Specifically, critical analyses help reveal the racist forces behind the high levels of "participation" among American Indian students in the armed services. For example, in a report prepared by the United States Department of Navy entitled "20th Century Warriors: Native American Participation in the United States Military" the tradition of military service among American Indians is explained as an extension of the "great warrior spirit." The report reads:

> Native Americans have the highest record of service per capita when compared to other ethnic groups. The reasons behind this disproportionate contribution are complex and deeply rooted in traditional American Indian culture. [Native Americans] . . . have distinctive cultural values, which drive them to serve their country. One such value is their proud warrior tradition . . . best exemplified by the following qualities said to be inherent to most if not all Native American societies: strength, honor, pride, devotion, and wisdom. These qualities make a perfect fit with military tradition. . . . Military service affords an outlet for combat that fulfills a culturally determined role for the warrior. Therefore, the military is an opportunity for cultural self-fulfillment. By sending young tribal members off to be warriors, they return with experiences that make them valued members of their society. . . . With the 21st century on the horizon, the United States military can be expected to provide continuing opportunity for Native American men and women. For their part, Native Americans can be expected to carry on their centuries-old warrior tradition—serving with pride, courage, and distinction.[6]

While, indeed, many American Indian families have a very strong and proud tradition of military service, there are clearly multiple forces are at play in perpetuating the image of "Indians as warriors." Tim Johnson, executive editor of *Indian Country Today*, surmises there are two reasons American Indians are overrepresented in the military: the first is political (referring to the tradition of service to country), the second is economic (cited in Younge 2003). Given that Native Americans are the poorest among all racial and ethnic groups in the United States, Johnson states, "The military is one world where people can build lives and make something else of themselves"

(Younge 2003). In other words, while American Indians in the military may indeed be "pulled by patriotism," they are also "pushed by economics" (Younge 2003). Moreover, as the most undereducated segment of the population, the "choice" of American Indians to serve needs to be contextualized by their relative lack of options.

RED PEDAGOGY

As we raise yet another generation in a nation at war, it is even more imperative for schools to be reimagined as sites for social transformation and emancipation; as a place "where students are educated not only to be critical thinkers, but also to view the world as a place where their actions might make a difference" (McLaren 2003). More specifically, McLaren outlines the essential elements of a post–9/11 critical pedagogy: (1) to support the broader societal aim of freedom of speech; (2) to be willing to challenge the Bush administration's definition of "patriotism"; (3) to examine the linkages between government and transnational corporations; (4) to commit to critical self-reflexivity and dialogue in public conversations; (5) to enforce the separation between church and state; (6) to struggle for a media that does not serve corporate interests; and, above all, (7) to commit to understanding the fundamental basis of Marx's critique of capitalism (McLaren 2003) Indeed, in a time when the forces of free-market politics conspire not only to maintain the march of colonialism but also to dismantle (i.e., privatize) public education, such aims are essential.

In addition to these immediate concerns, the frameworks of revolutionary critical theory provide indigenous educators and scholars a way to think about the issues of sovereignty and self-determination that moves beyond simple cultural constructions and analyses. Specifically, their foregrounding of capitalist relations as the axis of exploitation helps to frame the history of indigenous peoples as one of dispossession and not simply oppression. Their trenchant critique of postmodernism helps to reveal the "problem" of identity (social representation) as a distraction from the need for social transformation. Similarly, the work of revolutionary critical feminists helps to explain how gendered differences have been systematically produced and continue to operate within regimes of exploitation. In all these ways, the analyses of revolutionary critical pedagogy prove invaluable.

As discussed in previous chapters, however, there are also ways in which the analysis of revolutionary theorists fails to consider their own enmeshment with the Western paradigm. Specifically, the notion of "democratization" remains rooted in Western concepts of property; the radical constructs of identity remain tied to Western notions of citizenship; the analyses of

Marxist-feminists retain Western notions of subjectivity and gender; and revolutionary conceptions of the "ecological crisis" presume the "finished project" of colonization.

Such aporias of revolutionary critical pedagogy, however, must not be viewed as deficiencies. Rather, they should be theorized as points of tension, helping to define the spaces in-between the Western and indigenous thought-worlds. Revolutionary scholars themselves acknowledge "no theory can fully anticipate or account for the consequences of its application but remains a living aperture through which specific histories are made visible and intelligible" (McLaren and Farahmandpur 2001, 301). In other words no theory can, or should be, everything to all peoples—difference in the material domain necessitates difference in discursive fields. Therefore, while revolutionary critical theory can serve as a vital tool for indigenous educators and scholars, the basis of Red pedagogy remains distinctive, rooted in indigenous knowledge and praxis.

Though a "tradition-based" revitalization project, Red pedagogy does not aim to reproduce an essentialist or romanticized view of "tradition." As several indigenous scholars have noted (e.g., Alfred, Deloria, Mihesuah, Warrior) the "return to tradition" is often a specious enterprise. In contradistinction to essentialist models of "tradition," Taiaiake Alfred suggests a model of "self-conscious traditionalism" for indigenous communities. He defines "self-conscious traditionalism" as an intellectual, social, and political movement to reinvigorate indigenous values, principles, and other cultural elements best suited to the larger contemporary political and economic reality (Alfred 1999, 81). In this context, tradition is not simply "predicated upon a set of uniform, unchanging beliefs" but rather is expressed as a *commitment* to the future sustainability of the group (Warrior 1995, xx). In other words, the struggle for freedom is not about "dressing up in the trappings of the past and making demands" but about being firmly rooted in "the ever changing experiences of the community." As such, the process of defining a Red pedagogy is necessarily ongoing and self-reflexive—a never-ending project that is continually informed by the work of critical and indigenous scholars and by the changing realities of indigenous peoples.

Though the process is continual, the overarching goal of Red pedagogy is stable. It is, and will always remain, decolonization. "Decolonization" (like democracy) is neither achievable nor definable, rendering it ephemeral as a goal, but perpetual as a process. That is not to say, however, that "progress" cannot be measured. Indeed, the degree to which indigenous peoples are able to define and exercise political, intellectual, and spiritual sovereignty is an accurate measure of colonialist relations. The dream of sovereignty in all of these realms, thus, forms the foundation of Red pedagogy. As such, indigenous responses to the international, transnational, postcolonial question are discussed in terms of Lyons's quest for a "nation-people," and Alfred's (1999) model for self-determined and self-directed communities.

Beyond the Inter-national and Postcolonial: Toward a Transnational, Fourth Space of Indigenism

Indigenous communities preceded the nation-state.[7] Indeed, the borders of empire were drawn around, through, and over their lands and peoples. Indigenous peoples were, thus, the first "border crossers." However, contrary to whitestream theories that construct "border crossing" as an insurgent "choice" of liberated subjectivities, indigenous peoples did not "choose" to ignore, resist, transcend, and/or transgress the borders of empire. They were, rather, forced into a struggle for their own survival. Thus, indigenous resistance to the grammar of empire—mixed-blood/full-blood, legal/illegal, alien/resident, immigrant/citizen, tribal/detribalized—must be examined in terms of the racist, nationalist, and colonialist frameworks from which it emerged. Nonetheless, indigenous peoples continue to be classified along nationalist lines, casting the shadow of "legitimacy" not on the imagined borders of the conqueror but on the indigenous bodies that "cross" them.

The forces of imperialism ensure that the current system of nation-states will remain the organizing framework by which capital is globally laundered. Thus, at the same time indigenous peoples resist its dictates, they must also ensure their own participation. Recognizing the power of the game, the indigenous diaspora[8] formally entered the international arena in 1940 with the founding of the Interamerican Institute. Among other purposes, the institute was created to assist coordination of all indigenous affairs and policies among the member states.[9] North American Indians more publicly entered the international arena when a delegation of Hopi peoples appeared before the United Nations in 1959, proclaiming their sovereignty and denouncing the legacy of colonialism. Both events galvanized indigenous peoples across national borders, igniting a burgeoning spirit of solidarity.

This spirit culminated in a gathering organized by the American Indian Movement (AIM) in Standing Rock, South Dakota, in 1974. Over 5000 representatives from approximately ninety-eight indigenous nations attended the meeting (IITC) [10] and the groundwork was laid for the formation of the International Indian Treaty Council (IITC). Three years later the IITC became the first organization of indigenous peoples to be recognized as a nongovernmental organization (NGO), convening later that same year at the International Nongovernmental Organizations Conference on the Indigenous Peoples of the Americas (Geneva, Switzerland, 1977). This key event established the presence of indigenous peoples in the international political context.

This engagement tendered several important milestones in the history of indigenous international relations. Specifically, between the years 1977–1987: the renowned "Declaration of Principles for the Defense of the Indigenous Nations and Peoples of the Western Hemisphere" was drafted; the first international conference on indigenous peoples and the land was held (Geneva, Switzerland, 1981); the International Indian Treaty Council (ITTC), the World Council of Indigenous Peoples (WCIP), and the Indian Law Resource Center (ILRC) all gained "consultative status" at the United Nations; the South American Indian Council (CISA) was formed; the Working Group on Indigenous Populations was established; and the Fourth Russell Tribunal of the Indians of the Americas was held in Rotterdam, Netherlands (November 1980).

All such activities served as a collective catalyst for more recent hallmarks in the realm of international indigenous relations. Specifically, within the past ten years: a "permanent forum" on indigenous issues was established by the United Nations; the years 1995–2004 were declared the International Decade of the World's Indigenous Peoples; and the Human Rights Commission appointed a "Special Rapporteur" on the situation of human rights and the fundamental freedoms of indigenous peoples. Such recognition firmly established indigenous peoples as integral players in the international scene of geopolitics.

Though indigenous involvement within formal political frameworks is essential, it is equally important to theorize the status of indigenous peoples outside Western political frameworks. To stay within such frames (classifying Native peoples as either pre- or postnational) ultimately serves to reify the hegemony of the state, the linearity of Western temporality, and the continued march of colonialism. In response, some critical indigenous scholars (e.g., Bryan Brayboy, Dolores Delgado-Bernal, Bernardo Gallegos, Enrique Murillo, Emma Pérez, Luis Urrieta, and Sofia Villenas) employ the liminal and interruptive spaces of postcolonialism to formulate a counterdiscourse of indigenous subjectivity. Such efforts provide a much-needed corrective to both Eurocentric and tribal-centric discourses that inadequately theorize indigenous identity.

Postcolonialism is, however, not without its critics. Some point to its "overhasty celebration of independence," arguing that it tends to gloss over the fact that colonialist relations persist as well as continue to be reformulated (i.e., globalization) (Bahri 1996). Marxist scholars question the rise of postcolonialism during a time when transnational movements of capital, labor, and culture are on the rise, arguing that the focus on the discursive occludes the material realities of exploitation. E. San Juan (Pozo 2003, 1) summarizes the Marxist critique of postcolonialism as follows:

First, post-colonialists obscure or erase historical determination in favor of rhetorical and linguistic idealization of the colonial experience; second, the post-colonialist mind refuses to be self-critical and assumes a self-righteous dogmatism that it is infallible and cannot be refuted; and third, the practical effect of post-colonialist prejudice is the unwitting justification or, if not apology for, the continued neocolonialist . . . depredation of non-Western peoples, in particular indigenous groups, women, and urban poor in Latin America, Asia and Africa.

Though it is an interesting and critical part of the discourse, this is not the appropriate space to rehearse the tensions between postcolonial and Marxist theories. For the purposes of a Red pedagogy, it is more important to recognize the ways in which each theoretical perspective can inform indigenous struggles for self-determination.

While it is profoundly inter- and cross-disciplinary, a Red pedagogy remains rooted in the fourth space of indigenism—a distinctive, alter-native space with its own history and discourse. As Alfred asserts, "returning the politics of Native communities to an indigenous basis means nothing less than reclaiming the inherent strength and power of indigenous governance systems, and freeing our collective souls from a divisive and destructive colonized politics" (Alfred 1999, 80). In other words, defining the shape of indigenism requires engagement in the processes of "self-conscious traditionalism," importing the language and visions of our ancestors to the concerns of the present. Lyons's model of a "nation people" moves us in this direction.

Toward a Nation-People

Lyons defines a "people" as "a group of human beings united together by history, language, culture or some combination therein—a community joined in union for a common purpose: the survival and flourishing of . . . itself" (Lyons 2000, 454). He maintains, "it has always been from an understanding of themselves as a people that Indian groups have constructed themselves as a nation" (Lyons 2000, 454). Similarly, Deloria notes that the concept of nationhood has been traditionally understood as "an exercise in decision making" engaged by Indians in the interest of their own survival and desire to thrive. Thus, from a historical perspective, the political life of indigenous peoples has not "been the work of a nation-state so much as that of a *nation-people*" (Lyons 2000, 455). Lyons maintains that in contrast to a nation-state—which is most concerned with the sovereignty of individuals and the privileging of procedure—a nation-people "takes as its supreme charge, the sovereignty of the group through a privileging of its traditions and culture and continuity" (Lyons 2002).

The idea of a nation-peoples seems a viable construct from which to (re)build the project of indigenous sovereignty. It disrupts the colonialist narrative of the nation-state at the same time it acknowledges its (self-replicating) legitimacy. In other words, it allows indigenous peoples to persist in their struggles for "sovereignty" and continued recognition as "domestic-dependent nations," at the same time it recognizes the distinctiveness of tribal peoples. The dual identity of Native peoples necessitates a dualistic political project—a nationalist struggle mediated by a postnationalist politics.

Pozo (2003) reminds us that "nationalist" struggles against imperialism are categorically different from those wedded to the neoliberal politics of the free market:

> The nationalism (if you can call the sovereignty struggle nationalist) of native Hawaiians . . . cannot be equated with the nationalism of the white and/or Japanese elite in Hawaii. Nor can the nationalism of the Moral Majority, of Pat Buchanan and Cheney, be similar to the nationalism of the East Timorese, or for that matter to the nationalism of the Zapatistas, the guerrillas of Colombia, the New People's Army in the Philippines. . . . All nationalisms are similar in that they try to arouse the sense of ethnic togetherness and solidarity. But the difference is: for whose benefit? What is at stake? Who is victimized? What goals of human liberation are promoted or damaged by nationalist activities?

As articulated by San Juan and myriad indigenous scholars, while the nationalist struggle of native peoples remains critical, it is also critical for this struggle to commence in and through a framework for sovereignty, that is, with the development of self-determined, self-directed communities. Drawing from the work of other indigenous scholars Alfred (1999, 82) identifies the following characteristics of "the contemporary ideal of a strong indigenous nation":

Wholeness with diversity: Expressed as strong commitment and solidarity to the group combined with tolerance for difference.

Shared culture: Clearly articulated values, norms, and traditions that are shared by the group.

Communication: Establishing an open and extensive network of communication within community. Establishing clear channels by which government institutions are to communicate with the group.

Respect and trust: "People care about and cooperate with each other and the government of the community, and they trust in one another's integrity."

Group maintenance: "People take great pride in their community and seek to remain part of it; they collectively establish clear cultural boundaries and membership criteria."

Participatory and consensus-based government: Community leaders are responsive and accountable to the rest of the community; all decisions are based on principle of consensus.

Youth empowerment: The community is committed to mentoring and educating its young people, involving them in decision-making processes.

Strong links to the outside world: "The community has extensive positive social, political, and economic relationships with people in other communities, and its leaders consistently seek to foster good relations and gain support among other indigenous peoples and in the international community."

As defined through the above framework, "sovereignty" becomes a project organized to defend and sustain the basic right of indigenous peoples to exist in "wholeness" and to thrive in their relations with other peoples. Local (tribal) and global aims come together in solidarity around the shared goal of decolonization.

Beyond Transnational and Postcolonial Subjectivities: *Indígena* as a Fourth Space of Being

Insofar as strong communities necessitate earnest and inspired leaders, the search for "comfortable modern identities" remains integral to the quest for sovereignty. The proposed construct of *indígena* is intended to guide the search for a theory of subjectivity in a direction that embraces the location of Native peoples in the "constitutive outside." Specifically, it claims a distinctively indigenous space shaped by and through a matrix of legacy, power, and ceremony. In so doing the fourth space of *indígena* stands outside the polarizing debates of essentialism and postmodernism, recognizing that both the timeless and temporal are essential for theorizing the complexity of indigenous realities (Dirlik 1999). Embodying *indígena* is about the choice to live differently, about standing in defiance of the vapid emptiness of the whitestream, and about resisting the kind of education where connections to Earth and the spirit world are looked upon with skepticism and derision. It is an assertion of the margin as more than a location defined by economic instability and political servitude. It is reimagined as a transgressive fourth space of both transience and permanence.

In its avoidance of the "death dance of dependence," the construct of *indígena* makes use of the postcolonial concept of the "decolonial imaginary" (Pérez 1999) as well as the revolutionary conception of "dialectics." Specifically, Pérez's notion of the "decolonial imaginary" helps theorize the physical and discursive "diasporic movements" of indigenous peoples across time, space, and tradition. Similarly, the notion of "dialectics" approximates the radical contingency of the past and present that is also inherent to *indígena*. In addition, the revolutionary constructs of historicity, capital, and struggle approximate and inform indigenous conceptions of legacy, power, and ceremony.

While the constructs of revolutionary and postcolonial theories provide for a common ground of understanding—allowing for cross-fertilization without the diminishment of difference—*indígena* remains grounded in the intellectual histories of indigenous peoples. As informed by this tradition, it is a subjectivity of shape more than temporality. Specifically, its spatial orientation derives from the deep connection among indigenous conceptions of land, identity, sovereignty, and self-determination. As Vine Deloria Jr. (1994, 76–77) notes, "most Americans raised in a society in which history is all encompassing . . . have very little idea of how radically their values would shift if they took the idea of place, both sacred and secular, seriously." The centrality of place in the indigenous thought-world is explicitly conveyed through tradition and language and implicitly through the relationship between human beings and the rest of nature.

In terms of tradition, while the historical–material realities of colonized peoples have always compelled "movement" throughout and among differing sets of cultural values and mental commitments, such "movement" has also always remained tied—through memory, ceremony, and place—to "traditional" ways of being. Consider, for example, the current conception of what it means to be a "traditional" Navajo (Diné). Among other things, a traditional Diné is recognized as one who speaks their language, participates in ceremonies, and practices traditional subsistence living (e.g., sheep herding). In addition, they nurture strong clan and kinship ties, serve as a vast repository of cultural and tribal history, and participate in tribal governance. Within the tribe, such individuals are held in high esteem and granted a great deal of respect and social power. While the Diné recognize this identity-type as only one among many accepted as "authentically" Diné, it is this traditional identity that composes the foundation of who they are as a people, that serves as the repository of their ancestral knowledge, and that roots them in space, time, and place.

What distinguishes the indigenous struggle for self-determination from others is, thus, their collective effort to protect the rights of their peoples to live in accordance with traditional ways. It is the struggle to effectively negotiate the line between fetishizing such identities and recognizing their importance to the continuance of Indians as tribal peoples. Thus, regardless of how any individual indigenous person chooses to live his or her life, they are responsible for protecting the right to live according to ancestral ways. As such, while indigenous peoples resist the kind of essentialism that recognizes only one way of being, they also work to retain a vast constellation of distinct traditions that serve as the defining characteristics of tribal life. As Deloria notes (1983) it is this allegiance to traditional knowledge that has protected American Indians from annihilation and absorption into the democratic mainstream.

This connection to "tradition" determines that while the project of decolonization requires the histories and experiences of nontribal, detribalized, and "mixed-blood" peoples to be theorized as an integral part of the indigenous diaspora, it must also operate to sustain and reinvigorate the life-ways of tribal peoples still among us. Particularly in this time when the dominant patterns of belief and practice are being widely recognized as integrally related to the cultural and ecological crises, the need for understanding and sustaining other cultural patterns is essential.

To this end, traditional tribal languages play a crucial role in maintaining the fabric of *indígena*. Indigenous languages are replete with metaphors of existence that implicitly convey notions of multiplicity, hybridity, dialectics, contingency, and a sense of the "imaginary." For example, in Quechua, the word for being, person, and Andean person is all the same—*runa*. As such, this root term has the potential to incorporate the many subcategories of beingness while retaining the same basic reference group as in the words *llaqtaruna* (inhabitants of the village) and *qualaruna* (foreigner, literally naked, peeled). In addition, the root can be used passively as in *yuyay runa* (one who is knowing or understanding), actively as in *runayachikk* (that which cultivates a person), or reflexively as in *runaman tukuy* (to complete oneself). In other words, *runa* is virtually a limitless category, one open to the sense of being as well as becoming. Thus, the "revolutionary" ideas of hybridity, relationality, and dialectics are neither new nor revolutionary to this indigenous community, but rather have been an integral part of the Quechua way of life for over five hundred years.

Another feature distinguishing indigenous matrices of identity is its disengagement from the "myth of male dominance," that is, the universal assumption that all societies have been defined by, and organized through, patriarchy. Indeed, for many indigenous peoples the constructs of legacy, power, and ceremony evoke ideas of "woman" and/or "Mother." Indeed, contrary to simplistic New Age commodifications of a passive, pastoral "mother earth," however, the traditions of tribal peoples conceive a more complex, proactive, and powerful entity.

Consider, for example, the traditional constructions of the Earth Mother by the Pueblo Indians. Paula Allen Gunn (Laguna Pueblo) states that the Laguna do not set up some "primitive" equation between fertility and womanhood; rather, they associate "the essential nature of femininity with the creative power of thought" (cited in Bierhorst 1994). This association emanates from the Laguna earth spirit herself, *Tse che nako*, or Thought Woman—a creator who inhabits the earth yet also stands apart from it (Bierhorst 1994). For the Laguna and other Pueblo groups of New Mexico, Thought Woman prepares for the creation of life on Earth while entrusting the task itself to a pair of sisters (Bierhorst 1994). Creation, thus, is both profoundly relational and essentially female.

For the Kuna people, the Earth Mother is said to have exerted her intellect in conjunction with a male companion and, together, they conceive the future "from the very beginning." Creation for the Kuna, thus, is also relational but equally shared by men and women. Similarly, in one of the Navajo creation stories, "the one called Earth mother" is said to have given humans the gift of intellect. Specifically, the mother is believed to have placed her hands on both sides of the human head, declaring "this will be your thinking, this you will think by" and from that time forward the Earth was in charge of human consciousness (Bierhorst 1994).[11]

Indigenous understandings of the (feminine) Earth are, thus, far from passive. On the contrary, she is constructed as a powerful and intellectual life force that has served as a guiding and directive entity since "the very beginning." Though the significance of these narratives varies from nation to nation and woman to woman, collectively they serve to ground the formation of indigenous subjectivity in a woman-centered sense of the universe. This grounding lays the foundation for strong conceptions of self in which the notion of woman is: (1) conceived in a deep and abiding relationship to a powerful and "enchanted universe" (Berman 1981); (2) positioned in dialectical relationship with man and all other beings; and (3) viewed as an extension of the Earth Mother herself, the life force and symbol of women's continuing strategies for creativity, intelligence, and empowerment.

None of this is to say that American Indian women (or men) are immune to the patriarchal system that surrounds them, only that such traditions enable indigenous peoples to draw upon a reserve of ancestral knowledge that inherits what whitestream feminism has been unable to instill—a pervasive understanding of woman as power. Therefore, as indigenous men and women increasingly suffer the ills of patriarchy, it becomes even more necessary to build a sense of *indígena* that conjures a decolonized sense of being in the world, one that sustains different ways of inhabiting the space of beingness, community, and family. Moreover, in times when fierce xenophobia is disguised as patriotic nationalism, it is incumbent upon all of us to conceptualize ways of being that operate beyond the dispirited, displaced, and patriarchal notions of nationhood and citizenship.

Implications for Schooling

In the words of Peter McLaren, "one of the first casualties of war is truth." History, in other words, belongs to the victors (McLaren 2003, 289). Perhaps no one understands this better than indigenous peoples who, in addition to suffering the depredations of genocide, colonization, and cultural annihilation, have been revictimized at the hands of whitestream history. The lesson here is pedagogical.

The imperative before us, as educators, is to ensure that we engage a thorough examination of the causes and effects of all wars, conflicts, and inter/intracultural encounters. We must engage the best of our creative and critical capacities to discern the path of social justice and then follow it. The ongoing injustices of the world call educators-as-students-as-activists to work together—to be in solidarity as we work to change the history of empire and struggle in the common project of decolonization. To do so requires courage, humility, and love (*muna*).

Moreover, revolutionary scholars remind us that "our struggle must not stop at calling for better wages and living conditions for teachers and other workers but must anticipate an alternative to capitalism that will bring about a better chance for democracy to live up to its promise" (McLaren 2003, 290). Though the promise of democracy has always been specious for American Indians, the notion of an anticapitalist society has not. Indigenous peoples continue to present such an alter-native vision, persisting in their lived experience of collectivity and connection to land, both of which vehemently defy capitalist desire.

Red pedagogy is the manifestation of sovereignty, engaging the development of "community-based power" in the interest of "a responsible political, economic, and spiritual society"[12] (Richardson and Villenas 2000, 272). Power in this context refers to the practice of "living out active presences and *survivances* rather than an illusionary democracy"(Richardson and Villenas 2000, 273). As articulated by Vizenor, the notion of *survivance* signifies a state of being beyond "survival, endurance, or a mere response to colonization," toward "an active presence . . . and active repudiation of dominance, tragedy and victimry"(Vizenor 1998, 15). The *survivance* narratives of indigenous peoples are those that articulate the active recovery, reimagination, and reinvestment of indigenous ways of being. These narratives assert the struggles of indigenous peoples and the lived reality of colonization as a complexity that extends far beyond the parameters of economic capitalist oppression.

Survivance narratives form the basis of a Red pedagogy. They compel it to move beyond romantic calls to an imagined past toward the development of a viable, competing moral vision. Specifically, a Red pedagogy implores our conversations about power to include an examination of responsibility, to consider our collective need "to live poorer and waste less." It implores struggles for human rights to move beyond the anthropocentric discourse of humans-only and to fetter battles for "voice" with an appreciation for silence.

In the end a Red pedagogy embraces an educative process that works to reenchant the universe, to reconnect peoples to the land, and is as much about belief and acquiescence as it is about questioning and empowerment. In so doing, it defines a viable space for tradition, rather than working to "rupture" our connections to it.

The hope is that such a pedagogy will help shape schools and processes of learning around the "decolonial imaginary." Within this fourth space of being, the dream is that indigenous and nonindigenous peoples will work in solidarity to envision a way of life free of exploitation and replete with spirit. The invitation is for scholars, educators, and students to exercise critical consciousness at the same time they recognize that the world of knowledge far exceeds our ability to know. It beckons all of us to acknowledge that only the mountain commands reverence, the bird freedom of thought, and the land comprehension of time. With this spirit in mind, I proceed on my own journey to learn, to teach, and to be.

NOTES

1. "It's better to die while standing than to live on your knees" (Quechua).

2. "When the villages work together, we will turn this world around" (Quechua).

3. Specifically, on that day tribal leaders came to consensus on the need to launch a comprehensive national campaign aimed at protecting tribal sovereignty from the "threats posed by the Supreme Court." At the meeting tribal leaders developed an overall strategy that included plans to: (1) develop a federal legislation to reaffirm tribal jurisdiction; (2) form a Supreme Court project to support and coordinate tribal advocacy before the Supreme Court; (3) promote strategies for tribal governance that will protect tribal jurisdiction; (4) increase tribal participation in the selection of the federal judiciary; (5) develop a media and advocacy strategy; and (6) implement a fund-raising campaign to support and promote the initiative. Updates of the progress of this initiative are posted on the National Council of American Indian web site.

4. The source for this posting is intermittently listed as anonymous and also as attributed to Dr. George Wasson, an adjunct professor of anthropology at the University of Oregon.

5. In their suit, the Navajo Nation alleged that a conspiracy between energy companies (including Peabody) and the Interior Department led to the Navajo Nation being denied a fair royalty rate for its coal.

6. The report goes on to discuss some of the specific characteristics of Native Americans that make them natural "warriors" and suited for military service. It reads: "Many traditional cultures recognize that war disrupts the natural order of life and causes a spiritual disharmony. To survive the chaos of war is to gain a more intimate knowledge of life. Therefore, military service is a unique way to develop an inner strength that is valued in Native American society. . . . Many Native Amer-

icans are raised on rural or remote reservations, an environment that fosters self-reliance, introspection, and a meditative way of thinking. These character traits can be very beneficial when adapting to the occasional isolation of military life in times of both peace and war. . . . Native American warriors are devoted to the survival of their people and their homeland. If necessary, warriors will lay down their lives for the preservation of their culture, for death to the American Indian warrior is but another step in the advancement of life. It is understood that the warrior's spirit lives on eternally. So, warriors do not fear death, but rather regard it as the ultimate sacrifice for their own and their people's continued survival. . . . In wartime, those Native Americans seeing heavy combat had to learn how to survive, often using skills that many unit commanders thought were inherent to the American Indian's cultural background. A Sac and Fox/Creek Korean veteran remarked: "My platoon commander always sent me out on patrols. He . . . probably thought that I could track down the enemy. I don't know for sure, but I guess he figured that Indians were warriors and hunters by nature."

7. Contrary to how they are perceived through the Eurocentric frames of Marx, indigenous communities are not simply "pre-state" societies but, rather, differently structured societies.

8. The term "diaspora" is not used here in its Western context, that is, one that presumes a sense of origin, but in an indigenous context that presumes a unity through relation and not origin.

9. The original member sates were Argentina, Bolivia, Brazil, Chile, Colombia, Costa Rica, Ecuador, El Salvador, Guatemala, Honduras, Mexico, Nicaragua, Panama, Paraguay, Peru, the United States, and Venezuela. The institute was also charged with promoting research and the training of individuals engaged in the development of indigenous communities. The institute has its headquarters in Mexico City.

10. IITC web site. The IITC is an organization of indigenous peoples from North, Central, and South America and the Pacific working for the sovereignty and self-determination of indigenous peoples for the recognition and protection of indigenous rights, traditional cultures, and sacred lands.

11. Other examples include the Haudenosaunnee who believe that the world rests on the back of a giant turtle and that the first person to dwell on it was woman, specifically, Sky Woman (Billson 1995, 13). The Shawnee honor a spiritual holy woman named Our Grandmother who received assistance from the Great Spirit in creating humankind; she gave the Shawnee life, as well as their code of ethics and most of their religious ceremonies (Allen 1992, 7). The Quechua recognize Pachamama (Mother Earth) and Mamaquila (Grandmother moon) as central figures in the Quechua belief system.

Bibliography

Albers, Patricia, and Medicine, Beatrice, eds. 1983. *The Hidden Half: Studies of Plains Indian Women*. Lanham, Md.: University Press of America.

Alexander, M. Jacqui, and Chandra Mohanty, eds. 1997. *Feminist Genealogies, Colonial Legacies, Democratic Futures*. New York: Routledge.

Alfred, Taiaiake. 1999. *Peace, Power, Righteousness: An Indigenous Manifesto*. Oxford: Oxford University Press.

Alice, L. 1995. "What Is Postfeminism? Or, Having It Both Ways." In L. Alice ed. *Feminism, Postmodernism, Postfeminism: Conference Proceedings*. New Zealand: Massey University, 7–35.

Allen, Paul Gunn. 1992. *The Sacred Hoop*. Boston: Beacon Press.

Allman, Paula. 2001. *Critical Education Against Global Capital: Karl Marx and Revolutionary Critical Education*. Westport, Conn.: Bergin & Garvey.

Almeida, D. 1997. "The Hidden Half: A History of Native American Women's Education." *Harvard Educational Review* 67, no. 4 (Winter): 757–71.

American Council on Education. 2002. *Nineteenth Annual Report on the Status of Minorities in Higher Education*. Washington, D.C.: American Council on Education.

American Indian Policy Review Commission: Final Report. 1976. Washington, D.C.: U.S. Government Printing Office.

Ang, Ien. 1995. "I'm a Feminist But. . . . 'Other' Women and Postnational Feminism." In *Transitions: New Australian Feminisms*. New York: St. Martin's Press.

Anzaldúa, G. 1987. *Borderlands, la Frontera: The New Mestiza*. San Francisco: Aunt Lutte Books.

Bahri, Deepika. 1996. "Emory University Postcolonial Studies." Online: www.emory .edu/ENGLISH/Bahri/index.html.

Banuri, Tariq. 1990. "Modernization and Its Discontents: A Cultural Perspective on the Theories of Development." In *Dominating Knowledge: Development, Culture, and Resistance*, ed. Frederique A. Marglin and Steven A. Marglin. Oxford: Oxford University Press.

Barrett, Michele. 1992. "Words and Things: Materialism and Method in Contemporary Feminist Analysis." In *Destabilizing Theory: Contemporary Feminist Debates*, ed. M. Barrett and A. Phillips. Cambridge: Polity Press.

Barriero, José. 1995. "Indigenous Peoples and Development in the Americas: Lessons From A Consultation." http://www.brocku.ca/epi/casid/barriero.html. July 29, 2003.

Bataille, Gretchen, and Kathleen Sands. 1984. *American Indian Women: Telling Their Lives*. Lincoln: University of Nebraska Press.

Battiste, Marie, ed. 2002. *Reclaiming Indigenous Voice and Vision*. Vancouver: University of British Colombia Press.

Beaulieu, David. 2000. "Comprehensive Reform and American Indian Education. *Journal of American Indian Education* 39 no. 2: 29–38.

Bee, Robert L. 1981. *Crosscurrents along the Colorado: The Impact of Government Policy on the Quechan Indians.* Tucson: University of Arizona Press.

Berkhofer, R. F. Jr. 1978. *The White Man's Indian: Images of the American Indian from Columbus to the Present.* New York: Random House.

Berman, Morris. 1981. *The Reenchantment of the World.* New York: Bantam Books.

Bierhorst, John. 1994. *The Way of the Earth: Native American and the Environment.* New York: William Morrow.

Billson, Janet M. 1995. *Keepers of the Culture: The Power of Tradition in Women's Lives*. New York: Lexington Books.

Bowers, C. A. 1993. *Critical Essays on Education, Modernity and the Recovery of the Ecological Imperative.* New York: Teachers College Press.

———. 2003. "Can Critical Pedagogy be Greened?" *Educational Studies* 34, no. 1 (Spring): 11–21.

Boydston, J., ed. 1987. *John Dewey, the Later Works.* Carbondale: Southern Illinois University Press.

Brandt, Deborah. 1991. *To Change This House: Popular Education Under the Sandanistas.* Toronto: Between the Lines.

Brinkley, Joel. 2003. "American Indians Say Documents Show Government Has Cheated Them Out of Billions." *New York Times,* January 6.

Brooks, Ann. 1997. *Postfeminisms: Feminism, Cultural Theory and Cultural Forms.* New York: Routledge.

Brown, Brian E. 1999. *Religion, Law and the Land: Native Americans and the Judicial Interpretation of Sacred Land.* Westport, Conn.: Greenwood Press.

Brugge, David. 1999. *The Navajo–Hopi Land Dispute: An American Tragedy.* Albuquerque: University of New Mexico Press.

Buege, Douglas J. 1996. "The Ecologically Noble Savage Revisited." *Environmental Ethics* 18: 76.

Burrows, Beth. 1994. "Life Liberty and the Pursuit of Patents." *The Boycott Quarterly* 2:1: 33.

Butterfield, Robin. 1994. *Blueprints for Indian Education: Improving Mainstream Schooling* (ERIC Documents reproduction Service No. ED 372 898).

Cajete, Greg. 1994. *Look to the Mountain: An Ecology of Indigenous Education.* Durango, Colo.: Kivakí Press.

Carter, Patricia. 1995. "Completely Discouraged: Women Teachers' Resistance in the Bureau of Indian Affairs Schools 1900-1910." *Frontiers* XV, no. 3: 53–86.

Castillo, Anna. 1995. *Massacre of the Dreamers: Essays On Xicanisma.* New York: Penguin Books.

Charleston, G. M. 1994. "Toward True Native Education: A Treaty of 1992. Final Report of the Indian at Nations Risk Task Force." Draft 3. *Journal of American Indian Education* 33 no. 2: 756.

Cherokee. 2003. "Bureau of Iraqi Affairs? A Native American Perspective." Online: portland.indymedia.org/en/2003/06/267229.shtml.

Cheyfitz, E. 2003. "The Colonial Double Bind: Sovereignty and Civil Rights in Indian Country." *Journal of Constitutional Law* 5, no. 2 (January): 223–40.

Churchill, W. 1999. "The Tragedy and the Travesty: The Subversion of Indigenous Sovereignty in North America." In *Contemporary Native American Political Issues*, ed. Troy Johnson. Walnut Creek, Calif.: AltaMira Press, 1999.

Churchill, Ward, and Glenn T. Morris. 1992. "Table: Key Indian Cases." In *State of Native America: Genocide, Colonization and Resistance*, ed. M. Annette Jaimes. Boston: South End Press.

Clarke, Ardy Sixkiller. 2002. "Social and Emotional Distress Among American Indian and Alaska Native Students: Research Findings." ERIC Digest January 2002 EDO RC 01-11 (January).

Clow, Richmond, and Irme Sutton. 2001. *Trusteeship in Charge: Toward Tribal Autonomy in Resource Management.* Boulder: University of Colorado Press.

Coates, Gary J. 1981. *Resettling America: Energy, Ecology, and Community.* Andover, Mass: Brick House.

Coffey, Amanda, and Sara Delamont. 2000. *Feminism and the Classroom Teacher: Research, Praxis and Pedagogy.* London: Routledge.

Cohen, Betsy. 2001. "Trying to Right a Wrong." *The Missoulian.* February 15, 2001. Associated Press.

College Board and American Indian Science and Engineering Society. 1989. "Our Voices, Our Vision: American Indians Speak Out for Educational Excellence." New York: College Entrance Examination Board.

Cook-Lynn, Elizabeth. 1998. American Indian Intellectualism and the New Indian Story. In *Natives and Academics: Researching and Writing about American Indians*, ed. D. A. Mihesuah, 111–38. Lincoln: University of Nebraska Press.

Cornell, S., and J. P. Kalt. 1998. "Sovereignty and Nation-Building: The Development Challenge in Indian Country Today." *American Indian Culture and Research Journal* 22, no. 3: 187–214.

Cronin, John, and Robert F. Kennedy. 1997. *The Riverkeepers: The Activists Fight to Keep Our Environment a Basic Human Right.* New York: Simon & Schuster.

Darder, A. 1991. *Culture and Power in the Classroom: A Critical Foundation for Bicultural Education.* Westport, Conn.: Bergin & Garvey.

———. 1995. *Culture and Difference: Critical Perspectives on the Bicultural Experience in the United States.* Westport, Conn.: Bergin & Garvey.

Darder, A., R. Torres, and H. Gutiérrez, eds. 1997. *Latinos and Education: A Critical Reader.* New York: Routledge.

Delgado-Bernal, Dolores. 1998. "Using a Chicana Feminist Epistemology in Educational Research." *Harvard Educational Review* 68, no. 4: 555–82.

Deloria, Philip. 1999. *Playing Indian*. New Haven, Conn.: Yale University Press.

Deloria, Vine Jr. 1970. *We Talk, You Listen: New Tribes, New Turf*. New York: Macmillan.

———. 1983. *American Indians, American Justice*. Austin: University of Texas Press.

———. 1983. *Of Utmost Good Faith*. New York: Simon and Schuster.

———. 1985. *Behind the Trail of Broken Treaties: An Indian Declaration of Independence*. Austin: University of Texas Press.

———. 1991. *Indian Education in America*. Boulder, Colo.: American Indian Science and Engineering Society.

———. 1992. "The Application of the Constitution to American Indians." In *Exiled in the Land of the Free: Democracy, Indian Nations, and the U.S. Constitution*. eds. Chief Oren Lyons and John Mohawk. Santa Fe, N. M.: Clear Light, 292–315.

———. 1994. *God Is Red: A Native View of Religion*. Golden, Colo.: Fulcrum Publishing.

———. 1998. "Comfortable Fictions and the Struggles for Turf: An Essay Review of the Invented Indian: Cultural Fictions and Government Policies." In *Natives and Academics: Researching and Writing about American Indians*, ed. D. A. Mihesuah, 65–83. Lincoln: University of Nebraska Press.

———. 1999. *For This Land: Writings On Religion in America*. New York: Routledge.

Deloria, Vine Jr., and Clifford M. Lytle. 1983. *American Indians, American Justice*. Austin: University of Texas Press.

———. 1984. *The Nations Within: The Past and Future of American Indian Sovereignty*. Austin: University of Texas Press.

de Lauretis, Teresa. 1989. "The Essence of the Triangle; or Taking the Risk of Essnetialism Seriously: Feminist Theory in Italy, the U.S. and Britain." *Differences* 1, no. 2: 3–37.

Denis, Claude. 1997. *We Are Not You*. Toronto: Broadview.

d'Errico, P. 1997. "American Indian Sovereignty: Now You See It, Now You Don't." Lecture presented at the American Civics Project at Humboldt State University, Arcata, California.

Deyhle, Donna. 1995. Navajo Youth and Anglo Racism: Cultural Integrity and Resistance. *Harvard Educational Review* 65, no. 3: 403–44.

Deyhle, Donna, and Karen Swisher. 1997. "Research in American Indian and Alaska Native Education: From Assimilation to Self-Determination." In *Review of Research in Education*, ed. Michael Apple, 113–94. Washington, D.C.: American Educational Research Association.

Dillard, C. B. 1997. "The Substance of Things Hoped for, the Evidence of Things Not Seen: Toward an Endarkened Feminist Ideology in Research." Paper presented at the annual meeting of the American Educational Research Association, Chicago.

di Leornardo, Micaela. 1998. *Exotics at Home: Anthropologies, Others, and American Modernity*. Chicago: University of Chicago Press.

Dirlik, Arif. 1999. "The Past as Legacy and Project: Postcolonial Criticism in the Perspective of Indigenous Historicism." In *Contemporary Native American Political Issues*, ed. Troy Johnson, 73–97. Walnut Creek, Calif.: AltaMira Press.

Dreeben, Robert. 1968. *On What Is Learned in Schools.* Reading, Mass.: Addison Wesley, 1968.

Durning, Alan. 1992. "Guardians of the Land: Indigenous Peoples and the Health of the Earth." Worldwatch Institute Paper no. 112.

Ebert, Teresa. 1991. "Writing In the Political: Resistance (Post)modernism." Legal Studies Forum 15, no. 4: 291–304.

———. 1991. "Writing in the Political: Resistance (Post) modernism." Legal Studies Forum, vol. Xv, 4: 291–303.

———. 1996a. "For a Red Pedagogy: Feminism, Desire, and Need." *College English* 58, no. 7 (November): 795–819.

———. 1996b. *Ludic Feminism and After: Postmodernism, Desire, and Labor in Late Capitalism.* Ann Arbor: University of Michigan Press.

———. 1997. "Toward a Red Feminism." *New Socialist.* 2, no. 1: 20–21.

Edgerton, Robert B. 1992. *Sick Societies: Challenging the Myth of Primitive Harmony.* New York: The Free Press.

Ellsworth, Elizabeth. 1989. "Why Doesn't This Feel empowering? Working Through the Repressive Myths of Critical Pedagogy." *Harvard Educational Review* 59, no. 3: 297–24.

Engels, Friedrich. 1972. *The Origin of the Family, Private Property, and the State.* New York: International Publishers.

Everden, Neil. 1992. *The Social Creation of Nature.* Baltimore, Md.: The Johns Hopkins University Press.

Faludi, Susan. 1992. Backlash. London: Vintage.

Fine, Michelle. 1989. "Silencing and Nurturing Voice in an Improbable Context: Urban Adolescents in Public School." In *Critical Pedagogy, the State and Cultural Struggle*, eds. Henry Giroux and Peter McLaren. New York: State University of New York Press.

Fishman, Gustavo, and Peter McLaren. 2000. "Schooling for Democracy: Toward a Critical Utopianism." *Contemporary Sociology* 29, no. 1: 168–79.

Fiske, J. 2000. "By, For, or About?: Shifting Directions in the Representations of Aboriginal Women." *Atlantis* 25, no. 1 (Fall/Winter): 11–26.

Fixico, Donald. 1998. *The Invasion of Indian Country in the Twentieth Century: American Capitalism and Tribal Natural Resources.* Boulder: The University of Colorado Press.

Forbes, Jack. 1965. *Warriors of the Colorado: The Yumas and the Quechan Nation and Their Neighbors.* Norman: University of Oklahoma Press.

Friere, Paulo. 1998. *Pedagogy of Freedom: Ethics, Democracy, and Civic Courage.* Lanham, Md.: Rowman & Littlefield.

Fuchs, E., and R. Havighurst. 1972. *To Live On This Earth: American Indian Education*, 1st ed. Garden City, N.Y.: Doubleday.

Fusco, Coco. 1995. *English Is Broken Here: Notes on the Cultural Fusion in the Americas.* New York: New Press, 1995.

Gallagher, Brian Thomas. 2000. "Tribes Face an Uphill Battle to Blend Culture with Traditional Coursework: Teaching (Native) America." *The Nation*, June 5, 36.

Gallegos, Bernardo, Sofia Villenas, and Brian Brayboy, eds. 2003. "Indigenous Education in the Americas: Diasporic Identities, Epistemologies and Postcolonial

Spaces." Special issue, *Educational Studies: A Journal of the American Educational Studies Association* 34, no. 2 (Summer).

Galtung, Joan. 1986. "The Green Movement: A Socio-Historical Explanation." *International Sociology* 1: 75–90.

Giddens, Anthony. 1990. *The Consequences of Modernity*. Stanford, Calif.: Stanford University Press.

Gill, Sam. 1987. *Mother Earth*. Chicago: University of Chicago Press.

Giroux, Henry. 1990. "Perspectives and Imperatives: Curriculum Theory, Textual Authority, and the Role of Teachers as Public Intellectuals." *Journal of Curriculum and Supervision* 5, no. 4 (Summer): 361–83.

———. 1992. *Border Crossings: Cultural Workers and the Politics of Education*. New York: Routledge.

———. 1997. "Crossing the Boundaries of Educational Discourse: Modernism, Postmodernism, and Feminism." In *Education: Culture, Economy, Society*, ed. A. H. Halsey, Hugh Lauder, Phillip Brown, and Amy Stuart Wells. Oxford: Oxford University Press, 113–31.

———. 2001. "Pedagogy of the Depressed: Beyond the New Politics of Cynicism." *College Literature* 28, no. 3 (Fall): 1–32.

Gordon, Suzanne. 1973. *Black Mesa: The Angel of Death*. New York: The John Day Company.

Grande, S. 1997. "Critical Multicultural Education and the Modern Project: An Exploratory Analysis." Doctoral dissertation, Kent State University.

———. (forthcoming). "American Indian Identity and Intellectualism: The Quest for a New Red Pedagogy." *Journal of Qualitative Studies in Education*.

Green, Rayna. 1983. *Native American Women: A Contextual Bibliography*. Bloomington: Indiana University Press.

Guerrero, James. 1997. "Examplars of Indigenism: Native North American Women for De/Colonization and Liberation." In *Women Transforming Politics: An Alternative Reader*, ed. Cathy J. Cohen, Kathleen Jones, and Joan C. Tronto. New York: NYU Press.

Guerrero, M. Annette Jaimes. 1996. "Academic Apartheid: American Indian Studies and 'Multiculturalism.'" In *Mapping Multiculturalism*, ed. A. Gordon and C. Newfield. Minneapolis: University of Minnesota Press.

Guthrie, Daniel A. 1971. "A Primitive Man's Relationship to Nature," *Bioscience* 21, no. 13: 721–23.

Haines, R. 1997. "U.S. Citizenship and Tribal Membership: A Contest for Political Identity and Rights of Tribal Self-Determination in Southern California." *American Indian Culture and Research Journal* 21, no. 3: 211–30.

Hamme, Linda Van. 1996. "American Indian Cultures and the Classroom." *Journal of American Indian Education*, 35, no. 2: 21–36.

Harraway, D. J. 1991. *Simians, Cyborgs, and Women*. New York: Routledge.

Hauptman, Laurence M. 1992. "Congress, Plenary Power, and the American Indian, 1870-1992." In *Exiled in the Land of the Free: Democracy, Indian Nations and the U.S. Constitution* eds. Chief Oren Lyons, and John Mohawk. Santa Fe, N. M.: Clear Light Publishers 318–36.

Havighurst, Robert J. 1970. National Study of American Indian Education. Washington, D.C.: Office of Education.

Hendrix, Janey B. 1983. "Redbird Smith and the Nighthawk Keetowahs." *Journal of Cherokee Studies* 8, no. 1 (Spring): 32.

Hester, Thurman Lee. 2001. *Political Principles and Indian Sovereignty.* New York: Routledge.

Heywood, L., and J. Drake, eds. 1997. *Third Wave Agenda: Being Feminist, Doing Feminism.* Minneapolis: University of Minnesota Press.

Hill, Dave, Peter McLaren, Mike Cole, and Glen Rikowski, eds. 2002. *Marxism Versus Postmodernism in Educational Theory.* Lanham, Md.: Lexington Books.

hooks, bell. 1981. *Ain't I a Woman: Black Women and Feminism.* Boston: South End Press.

———. 1989. *Talking Back: Thinking Feminist, Thinking Black.* Boston: South End Press.

Hughes, Donald. 1983, *American Indian Ecology.* El Paso: Texas Western Press.

Ignatieff, Michael. 1984. *The Needs of Strangers: An Essay on Privacy, Solidarity, and the Politics of Being Human.* New York: Penguin.

Indian Arts and Crafts Board. *Rules and Regulations for the Enforcement of the Indian Arts and Crafts Act.* Washington, D.C.: Indian Arts and Crafts Board, 1996.

Jacobs, Margaret. 1991. *Engendered Encounters: Feminism and Pueblo Cultures 1879–1934.* Lincoln: University of Nebraska Press.

Jaimes, Annette M., ed. 1992. *State of Native America: Genocide, Colonization and Resistance.* Boston: South End Press.

Jaimes, Annette, and Theresa Halsey. 1992. "American Indian Women: At the Center of Indigenous Resistance in North America. In Jaimes, Annette M., ed. *State of Native America: Genocide, Colonization and resistance.* Boston: South End Press. 311–44.

Joe, J. R., and D. L. Miller. 1997. "Cultural Survival and Contemporary American Indian Women in the City." In *Indigenous Women Transforming Politics: An Alternative Reader*, ed. Cathy J. Cohen, 137–50. New York: New York University Press.

Johnson, Troy R., ed. 1999. *Contemporary Native American Political Issues.* Walnut Creek, Calif.: AltaMira Press.

Kaestle, Carl. 1983. *Pillars of the Republic: Common Schools and American Society 1780-1860.* New York: Hill and Wang.

Katz, Jane, ed. 1995. *Messengers of the Wind: Native American Women Tell Their Life Stories.* New York: Ballatine Books.

Katz, Michael. 1968. *The Irony of School Reform.* Cambridge, Mass: Harvard University Press.

Kenway, Jane. 2001. "Remembering and Regenerating Gramsci." In *Feminist Engagements: Reading, Resisting, and Revisioning Male Theorists in Education and Cultural Studies*, ed. Kathleen Weiler. New York: Routledge.

Kincheloe, J., and S. Steinberg. 1997. *Changing Multiculturalism.* Bristol, Pa.: Open University Press.

King, Gaye Leia. 1994. "Forward." *Journal of American Indian Education* 33, no. 2.

King, Joyce. 1991. "Dysconcious Racism: Ideology, Identity and the Miseducation of Teachers." *Journal of New Education* 60: 133–46.

Klein, L. F., and L. Ackerman, eds. 1995. *Women and Power in Native North America.* Norman: University of Oklahoma Press.

Krech, Shepard III. 1999. *The Ecological Indian: Myth and History.* New York: W.W. Norton & Co.

Kumar, Amitava. 1997. *Class Issues: Pedagogy, Cultural Studies and the Public Sphere.* New York: New York University Press.

LaDuke, W. 1995. "The Indigenous Women's Network: Our Future, Our Responsibility." Speech presented at the Seventh Generation Fund at the United Nations Fourth World Conference on Women, Beijing, China.

Lankshear, Colin, and Peter McLaren, eds. 1993. *Critical Literacy: Politics, Praxis, and the Postmodern.* New York: SUNY Press.

Lather, Patty. 1998. "Critical Pedagogy and Its Complicities: A Praxis of Stuck Places." *Educational Theory* 48, no. 4: 431–62.

———. 2001. "Ten Years Later, Yet Again: Critical Pedagogy and Its Complicities." In *Feminist Engagements: Reading, Resisting, and Revisioning Male Theorists in Education and Cultural Studies*, ed. Kathleen Weiler. New York: Routledge.

Layman, Martha Elizabeth. 1942. "A History of Indian Education in the United States." Ph.D. diss., University of Minnesota.

Lomawaima, K. T. 2000. "Tribal Sovereigns: Reframing Research in American Indian Education." *Harvard Educational Review* 70, no. 1 (Spring): 1–21.

———. 1994. *They Called It Prairie Light: The Story of the Chilocco Indian School.* Lincoln: University of Nebraska Press.

Lomawaima, K. T., and T. L. McCarty. 2002. "When Tribal Sovereignty Challenges Democracy: American Indian Education and the Democratic Ideal." *American Educational Research Journal* 39, no. 2 (Summer): 279–305.

Luke, C., and J. Gore. 1992. *Feminism and Critical Pedagogy.* New York: Routledge.

Lyons, Chief Oren, and John Mohawk, eds. 1992. *Exiled in the Land of the Free: Democracy, Indian Nations, and the U.S. Constitution.* Santa Fe, N. M.: Clear Light.

Lyons, S. R. 2000. "Rhetorical Sovereignty: What Do American Indians Want from Writing?" *College, Composition and Communication* 51, no. 3 (February): 447–68.

Lyotard, Jean Francois. 1984. *The Postmodern Condition: A Report on Knowledge.* Minneapolis: University of Minnesota Press.

Machamer, A. M. 1997. "Ethnic Fraud in the University: Serious Implications for American Indian Education." *Native Bruin* 2: 1–2.

Maher, Frances A., and Janie Victoria Ward. 2002. *Gender and Teaching.* Mahwah, N. J.: Lawrence Erlbaum Associates.

Maher, Frances A., and Mary Kay Thompson Tetreault. 2001. *The Feminist Classroom: Dynamics of Gender, Race, and Privilege.* Lanham, Md.: Rowman & Littlefield.

Malcomson, Scott. 2000. *One Drop of Blood: The American Misadventure of Race.* New York: Farrar, Straus, and Giroux.

Maltz, Daniel, and JoAllyn Archambault. 1995. "Gender and Power in Native North America." In *Women and Power in Native North America*, L. F. Klein and L. Ackerman, eds.. Norman: University of Oklahoma Press, 1995.

Mandle, Joan. "How Political Is the Personal?: Identity Politics, Feminism and Social Change." Online: research.umbc.edu (September 9, 2003).

Martin, Calvin. 1981. "The American Indian as Miscast Ecologist." In *Ecological Consciousness*, ed. Robert C. Schultz and J. Donald Hughes. Lanham, Md.: University Press of America.

Marx, Karl. 1977. *Capital: A Critique of Political Economy*. Vol. 1. Trans. B. Fowkes. New York: Vintage Books.

McCarthy, C. 1995. "The Problem with Origins: Race and the Contrapuntal Nature of the Educational Experience." *Multicultural Education, Critical Pedagogy and the Politics of Difference*, ed. Peter McLaren and C. Sleeter, 245–68. Albany, N.Y.: SUNY Press.

McCarthy, C., and W. Crichlow. 1993. *Race and Identity and Representation in Education*. New York: Routledge.

McCarthy, C., and Michael Apple. 1988. "Race, Class Gender in American Educational Research: Toward a Nonsynchronous Parraellist Position." In *Class, Race and gender in American Education,* Lois Weis ed. Albany, N.Y.: State University of New York Press.

McCombs, B. 1991. *Metacognition and Motivation in Higher Level Thinking*. Paper presented at the annual meeting of the American Educational Research Association, Chicago, Illinois.

McLaren, Peter. 1991. "The Emptiness of Nothingness: Criticism as Imperial Anti-Politics." *Curriculum Inquiry* 21.

——. 1995. Critical Pedagogy and Predatory Culture: Oppositional Politics in a Postmodern Culture. New York: Routledge.

——. 1997. *Revolutionary Multiculturalism: Pedagogies of Dissent for the New Millennium*. Boulder, Colo.: Westview Press.

——. 1998. "Revolutionary Pedagogy in Post-Revolutionary Times: Rethinking the Political Economy of Critical Education." *Educational Theory* 48, no. 4: 431–62.

——. 1999. *Che Guevara, Paulo Freire and the Pedagogy of Revolution*. Lanham, Md.: Rowman & Littlefield.

——. 2003. *Life in Schools: An Introduction to Critical Pedagogy in the Foundations of Education*. 4th ed. Boston: Allyn & Bacon.

——. 2003b. "Critical Pedagogy in the Age of Neoliberal Globalization: Notes from History's Underside." *Democracy and Nature* 9, no. 1: 65–90.

——. (forthcoming) "Traveling the Path of Most Resistance: Peter McLaren's Pedagogy of Dissent." *Professing Education*.

McLaren, Peter, and Ramin Farahmandpur. 2001. "The Globalization of Capitalism and the New Imperialism: Notes Toward a Revolutionary Pedagogy." *Review of Education, Pedagogy, Cultural Studies* 23: 271–315

McLaren, Peter, and Henry Giroux. 1997. "Writing from the Margins: Geographies of Identity, Pedagogy, and Power." In *Revolutionary Multiculturalism: Pedagogies of Dissent for the New Millennium*, 16–41. Boulder, Colo.: Westview Press.

McLaren, Peter, and C. Sleeter, eds. 1995. *Multicultural Education, Critical Pedagogy and the Politics of Difference.* Albany, N.Y.: SUNY Press.

McQuaig, Linda. 2001. *All You Can Eat: Greed Lust and the New Capitalism*. Toronto: Penguin Books.

Mihesuah, Devon, ed. 1998. *Native Americans and Academics: Researching and Writing about American Indians.* Lincoln: University of Nebraska Press.

——. 1996. *American Indians: Stereotypes and Realities.* Atlanta, Ga.: Clarity Press, Inc.

——. 1994. *Cultivating the Rosebuds: The Education of Women at the Cherokee Female Seminary (1851-1909).* Urbana: University of Illinois Press.

Miller, Brad. 2002. "Draining Life from the Land: Mining Indigenous People." *Earth Island Journal*, 17.

Mitchell, Katharyne. 2001. "Education for Democratic Citizenship: Transnationalism, Multiculturalism, and the Limits of Liberalism." *Harvard Educational Review* 71, no. 1 (Spring): 51–78.

Mohawk, J. C. 1992."Indians and Democracy: No One Ever Told Us." In *Exiled in the Land of the Free: Democracy, Indian Nations and the U.S. Constitution*, ed. Oren Lyons and John Mohawk. Santa Fe, N. M.: Clear Light Publishers.

Moss, Glenda. 2001. "Critical Translation for Education." *Multicultural Education* (Winter).

Murrillo, E. G. 1997. "Research under Cultural Assault: Mojado Ethnography." Paper presented at the annual meeting of the American Educational Studies Association, San Diego, California.

Nagel, Joane. 1995. "American Indian Ethnic Renewal: Politics and the Resurgence of Identity." *American Sociological Review* 60: 947–965.

National Indian Education Association and National Congress of American Indians. 1996. "Comprehensive Federal Indian Education Policy Statement." Washington, D.C.: Government Printing Office.

Native American Consultants, Inc. 1980. "Indian Definition Study." Submitted to the Office of the Assistant Secretary of Education, U. S. Department of Education, Washington, D.C.

New York Times, "U.N.: Gap Between Rich, Poor Grows," September 9, 1998.

Newton, Judith, and Deborah Rosenfelt. 1985. "Introduction: Toward a Materialist-Feminist Criticism." In *Feminist Criticism and Social Change: Sex, Class and Race in Literature and Culture,* Judith Newton and Deborah Rosenfelt (eds.). xv–xxxix. New York: Methuen.

Nieto, Sonia. 1995. *Affirming Diversity: The Sociopolitical Context of Multicultural Education* 2d ed. New York: Longman Press.

Norell, B. 2000. *Indian Country Today*, August 30.

——. 2003. "Big Mountain to Baghdad, Bush's Coal and Oil Contributors Pave the Way." *Navajo Times*, April 11.

Noriega, J. 1992. "American Indian Education in the United States: Indoctrination for Subordination to Colonialism." In *The State of Native America*, ed. M. Annette Jaimes. Boston: South End Press.

Ogbu, John. 1986. "Class Stratification, Racial Stratification, and Schooling," In L. Weis ed. *Race, Class and Schooling* 17, no. 22. Special Studies in Comparative Education, Comparative Eduction Center, Faculty of Educational Studies, State University of New York at Buffalo.

Oliver, Donald, and Kathleen Gershman. 1989. *Education, Modernity, and Fractured Meaning: Toward a Theory of Process Education*. Albany: SUNY Press.

Ortiz, Roxanne Dunbar. 1984. *Indians of the Americas: Human Rights and Self-Determination*. Westport, Conn.: Greenwood Press.

PBS Online Newshour. 2002. "Broken Trust?" Online: *www.pbs.org/newshour/bb/ fedagencies/july-dec02/indiantrusts_12-18.html*.

Piacentini, P. (Ed.). (1993). *Story Earth: Native Voices on the Environment*. San Francisco, Mercury House.

Pearson, Ryan. "Indians Aim to Form Plan to Protect Sacred Lands." Associated Press, January 4, 2003.

Pérez, Emma. 1999. *The Decolonial Imaginary, Writing Chicanas into History*. Bloomington: Indiana University Press.

Pozo, Mike. 2003. "An Interview with E. San Juan Jr.: Reflections on Postcolonial Theory, the Filipino Diaspora, and Contemporary Cultural Studies." *St. John's University Humanities Review* 1, no. 3 (April). http://www.geocities.com/icasocot/sanjuan_interview.html (access date August 19, 2003).

Prygoski, Phillip. 1998. From Marshall to Marshall: The Supreme Court's Chnaging Stance on Tribal Sovereignty." http://www.yvwiiusdinvnohii.net/govlaw/sovereignty.htm (access date July 12, 2003)

Reyhner, Jon, ed. 1992. *Teaching American Indian Students*. Norman: University of Oklahoma Press.

Reyhner, Jon and Jeanne Eder. 1992. "A History of Indian Education." In Reyhner, Jon, ed. *Teaching American Indian Students*. Norman: University of Oklahoma Press.

———. 1989. "Changes in American Indian Education: A Historical Retrospective for Education in the United States." *ERIC Digest* no. 314228.

Richardson, T., and Sofia Villenas. 2000. "'Other' Encounters: Dances with Whiteness in Multicultural Education." *Educational Theory* 50, no. 2 (Spring): 255–73.

Ritchie, M. 1995. "Whose Voice Is It Anyway?: Vocalizing Multicultural Analysis." In *Multicultural Education, Critical Pedagogy and the Politics of Difference*, ed. Peter McLaren and C. Sleeter, 309–16. Albany, N.Y.: SUNY Press.

Rizvi, Mashhood. 2002. "Educating for Social Justice and Liberation: An Interview with Peter McLaren." *Znet: A Community of People Committed to Social Change* (August).

Rosaldo, Renato. "Imperialist Nostalgia." *Culture and Truth: The Remaking of Social Analysis*. 2nd. ed. Boston: Beacon, 1993. 68–87.

Said, E. 1985. "Orientalism Reconsidered." *Race and Class* 26, no. 1: 1–15.

———. 1993. *Culture and Imperialism*. London: Vintage.

Sampson, Edward. 1993. *Celebrating the Other: A Dialogic Account of Human Nature*. Boulder, Colo.: Westview Press.

Sandoval, C. 1998. "Mestizaje as Method: Feminists of Color Challenge the Canon." In *Living Chicana Theory*, ed. C. Trujillo, 352–70. Berkeley, Calif.: Third Woman Press.

Scatamburlo-D'Annibale, V., and P. McLaren. "The Strategic Centrality of Class in the Politics of 'Race' and 'Difference.'" *Cultural Studies/Critical Methodologies* 3, no. 2 (May): 148–75.

Schwartz, Douglas O. 1987. "Changing Perspectives and a Modest Proposal" *Environmental Ethics* 9:291–302.

Seligman, Martin. 1990. *Learned Optimism.* New York: Knopf.

Shapiro, Svi. 1995. "Educational Change and the Crisis of the Left: Toward a Postmodern educational Discourse." In *Critical Multiculturalism: Uncommon Voices in a Common Struggle*, eds. Barry Kanpol and Peter McLaren. Westport, Conn.: Bergin and Garvey 19–38.

Sherry, John. 2002. *Land, Wind and Hard Words: A Story of Navajo Activism.* Albuquerque: University of New Mexico Press.

Shoemaker, Nancy, ed. 1995. *Negotiators of Change: Historical Perspectives on Native American Women.* New York: Routledge Press.

Spring, Joel. 2001. *The American School: 1642–2000.* 5th ed. Boston: McGraw-Hill, 2001.

Skar, S. L. 1994. *Lives Together, Worlds Apart: Quechua Colonization in Jungle and City.* New York: Scandinavian University Press.

Smith, Gregory. 1992. *Education and the Environment: Learning to Live with Limits.* Albany, N.Y.: SUNY Press.

Smith, Linda Tuhiwai. 1999. *Decolonizing Methodologies: Research and Indigenous Peoples.* London: Zed Books, 1999.

Snell, Travis. 2003. "Bureau of Iraqi Affairs? A Native American Perspective." *Cherokee Phoenix*, June 28.

St. Germaine, Richard. 1995 (a). "Bureau Schools Adopt Goals 2000." *Journal of American Indian Education,* 35 no. 1: 39–43.

St. Germaine, Richard. 1995 (b). "Drop Out rates Among American Indian and Alaska Native Students: Beyond Cultural Discontinuity." ERIC Clearinghouse on Rural Education and Small Schools, no 388492: West Virginia, Charleston.

Stavenhagen, R. 1992. "Challenging the Nation-State in Latin America." *Journal of International Affairs* 34, no. 2: 423.

Stevens, Scott Manning. 2003. "New World Contacts and the Trope of the 'Naked Savage.'" In *Sensible Flesh: On Touch in Early Modern Culture*, ed. Elizabeth Harvey. Philadelphia: University of Pennsylvania Press.

Stiffarm, Lenore, and Phil Lane Jr. 1992. "The Demography of Native North America: A Question of American Indian Survival." In *The State of Native America*, ed. M. Annette Jaimes. Boston: South End Press.

Strauss, A., and J. Corbin. 1990. *Basics of Qualitative Research: Grounded Theory Procedures and Techniques.* Newbury Park, Calif.: Sage.

Swisher, Karen. 1998. "Why Indian People Should Write about Indian Education." In *Natives and Academics: Researching and Writing about American Indians*, ed. D. A. Mihesuah, 190–99. Omaha: University of Nebraska Press.

Szasz, Margaret Connell. 1999. *Education and the American Indian: The Road to Self-Determination since 1928.* 3rd ed. Albuquerque: University of New Mexico Press.

Tarnas, Richard. 1991. *The Passion of the Western Mind: Understanding the Ideas that Have Shaped Our Worldview.* New York: Harmony Books.

Tauli-Corpus, Victoria. 1993. "We Are Part of Biodiversity, Respect Our Rights." *Third World Resurgence* 36: 25.

Thompson, Thomas. 1978. *The Schooling of Native America.* Washington, D.C.: American Association of Colleges for Teacher Education (AACTE) with the Teacher Corps, U.S. Office of Education.

Torres, Carlos Alberto. 1998. *Democracy, Education and Multiculturalism: Dilemmas of Citizenship in a Global World.* Lanham, Md.: Rowman & Littlefield.

Trask, Hunani Kay. 1996. "Feminism and Indigenous Hawaiian Nationalism." *Signs: Journal of Women in Culture and Society* 21, no. 4 (Summer): 906–916.

——. 1993. *From a Native Daughter: Colonialism and Sovereignty in Hawaii.* 1st ed. Monroe, ME: Common Courage Press.

Tribal Sovereignty Protection Initiative."Summary of September 11th Tribal Leaders Forum: A Strategic Plan to Stop the Supreme Court's Erosion of Tribal Sovereignty September 17, 2001." Online: www.ncai.org.

Trujillo, Octavia V. 2000. "Preface." *Journal of American Indian Education* 39, no. 2: 2.

Upton, John, and Donna M. Terrell. 1974. *Indian Women of the Western Morning: Their Life in Early America.* New York: Anchor Books.

U.S. Congress. 1953. House Concurrent Resolution (HCR) No. 108. Washington, D.C.: Government Printing Office.

U.S. Congress, Senate. 1969. Indian Education: A National Tragedy—A National Challenge. Washington, D.C.: Government Printing Office.

U.S.D., Bureau Of Indian Affairs, 209 manual 8, 83.7. mandatory Criteria fir Federal Recognition. 44 U.S.C. 3501 (et seq.) n.d.

Valle, V., and R. Torres. 1995. "The Idea of Mestizaje and the 'Race' Problematic: Racialized Media Discourse in a Post-Fordist Landscape." In *Culture and Difference: Critical Perspectives on the Bi-Cultural Experience in the United States,* ed. A. Darder. Westport, Conn.: Bergin and Garvey.

Van Cott, D. L. 1994. *Indigenous Peoples and Democracy in Latin America.* New York: St. Martin's Press.

Villenas, Sofia. 1996. "The Colonizer/Colonized Chicana Ethnographer: Identity, Marginalization, and Co-optation in the Field." *Harvard Educational Review* 66: 711–731.

Vizenor, Gerald. 1993. The Ruins of Representation. *American Indian Quarterly* 17: 1–7.

——. 1998. *Fugitive Poses: Native American Indian Scenes of Absence and Presence.* Lincoln: University of Nebraska Press.

Warrior, Robert Allen. 1995. *Tribal Secrets: Recovering American Indian Intellectual Traditions.* Minneapolis: University of Minnesota.

Wax, M., R. Wax,, and R. Dumont Jr. 1989. *Formal Education in an American Indian Community.* Prospect Heights, Ill.: Waveland Press.

Weiler, Kathleen, ed. 2001. *Feminist Engagements: Reading, Resisting, and Revisioning Male Theorists in Education and Cultural Studies.* New York: Routledge.

Weis, Lois. *Between Two Worlds: Black Students in an Urban Community College.* Boston: Routledge and Kegan Paul, 1985.

Welter, Barbara. "The Cult of True Womanhood, 1820-1860," *American Quarterly,* 18 (Summer 1966): 150–74.

White, Hayden. 1976. "The Noble Savage: Theme as Fetish." In *First Images of America,* ed. F. Chiapelli. Berkeley: University of California Press.

White House, The. President William J. Clinton. 1998. Executive Order on American Indian and Alaska Native Education. Washington, D.C.: Government Printing Office.

Whitt, Laurie Ann. 1998. "Cultural Imperialism and the Marketing of Native America." In *Natives and Academics: Researching and Writing about American Indians*, ed. D. A. Mihesuah, 139–71. Omaha: University of Nebraska Press.

Wilkins, David E., and K. Tsianina Lomawaima. 2001. *Uneven Ground: American Indian Sovereignty and Federal Law*. Norman: University of Oklahoma Press.

Williams, Robert A. Jr. 1986. "The Algebra of Federal Indian Law: The Hard Trail of Decolonizing and Americanizing the White Man's Indian Jurisprudence." *Wisconsin Law Review* 219 (March/April).

———. 1990. *The American Indian in Western Legal Thought*. Cambridge: Oxford University Press.

———. 2000. "Documents of Barbarism: The Contemporary Legacy of European Racism and Colonialism in the Narrative Traditions of Federal Indian Law." In *Critical Race Theory: The Cutting Edge*, 2nd ed., ed. Richard Delgado and Jean Stefanic, 98–109. Philadelphia: Temple University Press.

Willis, Paul. 1977. *Learning to Labor*. Lexington, England: D.C. Heath.

Witkin, A. 1995. "To Silence a Drum: The Imposition of United States Citizenship on Native Peoples." *Historical Reflections* 21, no. 2: 353–83.

Wolcott, H. F. (1967). *A Kwakiutl Village and School*. Prospect Heights, Ill.: L Waveland.

Wullenjohn, Chuck. Chief Public Affairs Office. http://www.yuma.army.mil/public-affairs/quechan.html (access date: November 2003).

Wunder, John R., ed. 1996. *Native American Sovereignty*. New York: Garland.

Wunder, John R., and Cynthia Willis Esqueda, eds. 1997. *Native Americans: Interdisciplinary Perspectives*. New York: Garland.

Yashar, Deborah J. (forthcoming). *Contesting Citizenship: Indigenous Movements and the Postliberal Challenge in Latin America*. Cambridge: Cambridge University Press.

Younge, Gary. 2003. "What about Private Lori?" Online: www.guardian.co.uk/Iraq/Story/0,2763,933586,00.html

About the Author

Sandy Grande is an Associate Professor in the Education Department at Connecticut College. Her research is profoundly inter- and cross-disciplinary, and has included the integration of critical, feminist and Marxist theories with the concerns of Native American education. Through her research, she hopes to draw connections between the political project of forming a new critical democracy and the Indigenous struggle for self-determination and tribal sovereignty. Professor Grande has written several articles including "Beyond the Ecologically Noble Savage: Deconstructing the White Man's Indian," *Journal of Environmental Ethics*; "Critical Theory and American Indian Identity and Intellectualism," *The International Journal of Qualitative Studies in Education,* and "American Indian Geographies of Identity and Power: At the Crossroads of Indigena and Mestizaje," *Harvard Educational Review.*